u. 3

£3
HIS
RM

Leachman: 'OC Desert'

Leachman: 'OC Desert'

The Life of Lieutenant-Colonel Gerard Leachman D.S.O.

H.V.F. Winstone

Quartet Books
London Melbourne New York

For Ruth

First Published by Quartet Books Limited 1982
A member of the Namara Group
27/29 Goodge Street, London W1P 1FD

British Library Cataloguing in Publication Data

Winstone, H.V.F.
    Leachman.
    1. Leachman, Gerard   2. Soldiers—
    England—Biography
    I. Title
    940.4'15'0924   D568.5

    ISBN 0-7043-2330-3

Phototypeset by MC Typeset, Rochester, Kent
Printed and bound in Great Britain by
Mackays of Chatham Limited, Kent

Contents

Illustrations

The family crest and motto.
Dr A. W. and Mrs Leachman.
Leachman's sister Mildred.
'Fairley', Petersfield, the Leachman family home, c. 1880.
Leachman the cadet, 1898.
War Office service telegram, January 1900.
Subaltern in South Africa, 1900.
Letter from Military Secretary, August 1900.
In charge of regimental football team, India, 1903.
At home.
India. 1904.
In dress uniform of Royal Sussex Regiment, 1905.
At home.
In Arab dress.
Fahed Bey ibn Hadhal with grandchild. (Photograph by Gertrude Bell, *University of Newcastle upon Tyne.*)
Tent of Sadun Pasha, 1910.
With the Muntafiq, 1910.
Princes and retainers of the Sauds, Riyadh 1912. (*Royal Geographical Society.*)
The Hasa Gate, Riyadh, 1910. (*Royal Geographical Society.*)
Watering the camels, Damascus–Baghdad journey, 1910.
Leachman's house at Karbala and Majid Husain.
With Turkish prisoners-of-war.
Stealing aircraft from Turkish aerodrome. (Photo by Lance-Corporal Jack Summers).
Leading Turk envoys to armistice meeting, November 1918.
Light Armoured Motor Brigade vehicle 'Avenger', and Rolls Royce 'Silver Dart', with Jack Summers. (Photo by Captain Kermit Roosevelt.)
Caravanserai at Khan Nuqta where Leachman was killed.
The re-interment, 1 March 1921, Baghdad.

Maps

Maps drawn by Dean Hilborne ARIBA.

Preface

Leachman's life story has a chequered history. When he died in
1920 on the tribal battlefield of the Euphrates, Lt-Col. Gerard
Leachman of the Royal Sussex Regiment was among the most
famed and respected of British Officers – the soldier's soldier
whose wartime exploits were the stuff of regimental magazines
and heroic schoolboy adventures. But already another legend
had begun to overtake his, as the press tirelessly reproduced
pictures of T. E. Lawrence in his princely white garb and gold-
embroidered head-dress; as men and women flocked in their
hundreds of thousands to the Royal Opera House and the Albert
Hall in London and to the most capacious theatres in America
to hear President Wilson's propagandist, Professor Lowell
Thomas, tell with the aid of lantern slides of the fantastic and
often fabulous adventures of 'Lawrence of Arabia'. By the mid
twenties the myth of 'Aurens' had so gripped the imagination of
the English-speaking peoples that there was hardly room for
another account of wartime adventure or achievement in the
eastern theatre, whether based on fact or imagination.

Yet there remained a determined lobby of military men – and a
few prominent politicians – who were anxious that Leachman's
exploits in the Arab lands should be placed on record. They
turned to the bright new star in the Arabian firmament, Harry St
John Philby. Already distinguished as traveller and explorer, a
first-rate Arabist, and the author of two highly praised books on
the Kingdom of the Sauds, he was the obvious choice, the more
so as he had worked in Mesopotamia alongside Leachman, knew

vii

at first hand of his work and fighting qualities, and had travelled the lands which Leachman made his own.

In 1926 Philby agreed to write Leachman's biography and approached the family for the loan of documents. These were handed over by Col. A.A.H. Beaman, a friend of the subject's sisters and in-laws, the Parhams, subject to a sight of the manuscript before publication. In 1927 Philby went off to Jiddah on the Red Sea coast to write *The Legend of Lijman*. As the work progressed he became increasingly excited about its prospects and even sent a synopsis to the *Atlantic Monthly* magazine which was offering a prize of £1,000 for the 'biography of the year'.

On 8 April 1928 the author wrote to Beaman, 'At last it is finished, the great work!' Beaman replied: 'If you were to win the prize (*Atlantic Monthly*), it would, I fear, put me in a very embarrassing position.' The family did not approve of the book. Worse, the prospective publishers, Allen and Unwin, did not like it either. Mr Philip Unwin wrote: 'It requires a certain amount of overhaul.' In fact his editors insisted that it would have to be re-written, preferably by another author, if it was to have any chance of publication. There the matter rested for four years. Philby put away his draft and forgot about it until an article by a wartime colleague of Leachman, Capt. Chalmers, appeared in *Blackwood's* entitled 'OC Desert'. There was a renewed call for a biography of the subject. This time Sir Arnold Wilson was asked to write it. Historian of the Persian Gulf, Leachman's chief in Mesopotamia in post-war years as Civil Commissioner of the conquered territory, he too was an ideal candidate.

The *Letters of Gertrude Bell* had been published by this time and were proving best sellers in Britain and America. Before admitting defeat, Philby had written, 'Leachman will restore the equilibrium of the reading public which has been thrown off its balance by Gertrude Bell and Lawrence.' He handed over to Wilson his own manuscript and the documents he had been loaned with 'great cordiality'. But Wilson was busy in other fields at this time and decided that he could not undertake the work.

In 1934 one of Leachman's closest and most admiring disciples, Maj. N.N.E. Bray, a staff officer who had worked in the Hijaz with Lawrence, of whom he had the poorest opinion, and in Mesopotamia with Leachman for whom he had nothing but admiration, took on the task. *A Paladin of Arabia* was published by Unicorn Press of London in 1936. It carried a foreword by Sir

Samuel Hoare who had admired Leachman from afar in wartime and who had himself considered writing a biography. Bray had already told something of his hero's adventures in his book *Shifting Sands* which had been modestly successful, and he had been pressed by Austen Chamberlain, the wartime Secretary of State at the India Office, to write a full life story. Bray's work was a testament of admiration, but it lacked objectivity and care. It even got the subject's first name wrong. It is not, however, for the present writer to attempt a criticism of either Philby's unpublished treatise (which now lies in the archives of the Middle East Centre at St Antony's College, Oxford), or Bray's published words.

Philby wrote well of his own journeys and adventures, but he was magniloquent when writing of others. There was little empathy between the biographer and his subject during the three years they spent together in wartime Mesopotamia, from 1915 to 1918 – one a civilian administrator who embraced the cause of the Amir Ibn Saud of central Arabia and rejected his own country in the Second World War, the other a soldier of unquestioning loyalty to King and Empire. In life Leachman accused Philby of 'megalomania', and the accusation was to be made by others in the course of time. The maverick intellectual of the British administration in Mesopotamia, or Iraq as it became, was not the ideal choice as it turned out to write an expected panegyric of the patriotic soldier to whom duty and service were almost sacred words.

When my own biography appeared of Leachman's great rival in the desert, *Captain Shakespear*, a number of army men and civilians who had served in Mesopotamia during and after the Great War, especially retired officers of the Royal Sussex Regiment, suggested that I should turn my hand to the other hero-figure of the army. When my subsequent life of *Gertrude Bell* appeared I was approached by Iraqi film-makers who told me that they were about to resurrect on the screen the sorry story of the tribal rebellion of 1920 and of Leachman's part in the struggle which brought about his death. The film would also feature Gertrude Bell, one of the 'Politicals' with whom Leachman was at daggers-drawn. And so I put my hand to a much-used plough, and shamelessly adopted Capt. Chalmers's title, used in *Blackwood's* magazine in 1932.

H.V.F.W.   January 1982

Acknowledgements

The only direct survivors of the Leachman family are the Parhams, descendants of my subject's sister who married Mr Bernard Parham of Norrington in Wiltshire. Without their unstinting and generous help I could not have written this story. I thank them all most warmly: Mrs H.J. Parham the widow of Gen. Hetman Jack, Brig. John Parham, and Miss Belinda Parham. All photographs and documents, unless otherwise acknowledged, are also reproduced by their kind permission.

I would also like to thank Mr Frank Stafford CMG, CBE, a distinguished servant of British administrations in Iraq and elsewhere who knew Leachman and many of his comrades and passed his knowledge on to me with the utmost helpfulness. Others to whom I would like to express my gratitude are Mrs Rosemary Carruthers, Mr Colin Imray, the late Maj. George Horne, Mr John Locke, Mr J. Bodem, Ms Rosemary Meynell, Mr Robert Lacey, Ms Jacqueline Williams, Sameerah Amani, Saleh Niazi, Suad Attar and by no means least my daughter Ruth and her husband Maj. Peter Mallas who went over the paths of my subject in northern India and Kashmir, correcting some of my wilder geographical assumptions as they went.

My grateful thanks, too, to Mr Brian Rees, Headmaster of Charterhouse School, and the school archivist and librarian; the directors and staff of the India Office Library, the Royal Geographical Society, the Public Records Office, the Ministry of Defence Library, the Middle East Centre, St Antony's College, Oxford, and the Royal Sussex Regimental Museum (and the Chichester Museum with which it is now merged).

1

Tribute

Tuesday, 18 January 1921: A bright, cool morning in Baghdad. People who had obeyed the call to jihad and taken up arms against the British army of occupation but a few months before went about their tasks amiably. And then, later in the day, they began to gather in excited groups. The writing was on the wall once more; mostly illiterate, but it served the purpose of the mullahs and *mujtahids*, the fighters for the cause.

'Woe betide you O Ministers – rotten prisoners of the British.'

'Does your conscience not blame you?'

'Death to the infidel invader!'

As the crowds gathered, anonymous men moved among them with hurriedly printed leaflets which bore simple, provocative messages.

'Christians and Jews are not satisfied until you follow their religion,' said one message, written boldly in Arabic.

But the appeal of the holy men was not only to Arabs. They had appealed before to the divided loyalties of Muslim troops in the British army; and they did so again.

'O thou Muhammadan Indian Military Brethren who are ignorant of the events of the world.' The script was Urdu.

'O countrymen, Muhammadan and Hindu warrior brethren. You know that all the pomp and power of the British is due to India. They feed their people by taking to England millions of maunds of corn and rupees; while in India millions are harassed and die by hunger and famine . . . They have treated you like beasts in Transvaal, Egypt, Persia, Afghanistan and China,' read the message underneath.

By midday the British police chief Col. Prescott had sent out working-parties to obliterate the graffiti and arrest the ring-leaders. By evening Baghdad had returned to a noisy normality, the mullahs went back to peaceful pursuits and the Pan-Islamites went to ground.

On Saturday, 26 February 1921 an august party boarded the Tigris river steamer by the steps of the British High Commission. They were bound for Basra where they would join RIMS *Hardinge* for the journey to Cairo, whence they had been summoned by the new Colonial Secretary, Winston Churchill.

The Baghdad team was led by Maj.-Gen. Sir Percy Cox, recently appointed High Commissioner in place of Sir Arnold Wilson. Among its members were the GOC Mesopotamia, Gen. Sir Aylmer Haldane; Sasun Effendi Haskail the Minister of Finance in the provisional Government that had been established three months before in the aftermath of the rebellion; Gen. Jafar Pasha al Askari, who had fought with the Turks and with Faisal, the son of the Sharif of Mecca, in war, and was now Minister of Defence in the reborn Iraq; Maj.-Gen. Atkinson, adviser to the Ministry of Works; Lt-Col. Slater, financial adviser; Maj.-Gen. Ironside, commander of British troops in Persia who had lately fought with the White Russian army of the Caucasus against Lenin's 'Reds'; and Miss Gertrude Bell, Oriental Secretary to the High Commission.

They set out to create a new nation in the ancient land of the two rivers, the Tigris and Euphrates, a constitutional monarchy on the pattern of Britain. The Iraq. On the day of their departure the nationalist newspaper *Istiqlal* carried rumours emanating from the Peace Conference in Paris that Faisal, the son of the Sharif Husain of Mecca, was about to be made King of Iraq, though his supporters had named him King of Syria, and had proclaimed his elder brother, Abdullah, the rightful occupant of the promised throne of Baghdad. But Churchill would find another throne for Abdullah.

Sunday, 27 February 1921. A bright warm day. Lieut Goring had driven to Fallujah on the Euphrates, where the body of

2

Leachman had been disinterred from its unmarked grave, to take it back to Baghdad for a decent burial in the British cemetery. He drove the 6th Light Armoured Motor Battery's 'Harvester', the vehicle in which he had picked up Leachman on the day of his death when he lay in a pool of blood at the caravan park of Khan Nuqta, half-way between Baghdad and the river. The tribal revolt was in full flood then and Goring had buried his former chief and comrade hurriedly among the dozens of young men who fell at the rail terminus of Fallujah in the war and its aftermath.

Now the 'Harvester' made a slow watchful journey into the capital protected by a convoy of LAMBs, for danger still hid in the towns and deserts of Mesopotamia and death was still the penalty of carelessness. Its charge, a bright new coffin, was guarded by an armed NCO. Its polished brass plate gleamed in the sunlight.

Lieutenant-Colonel G. E. Leachman
Royal Sussex Regiment
died 12 August 1920
age 40

The convoy crossed the Tigris by the Maude bridge to the garrison church of the British army in the serai of the palace once used by the Turkish Wali of Baghdad. The coffin was placed on a catafalque and an armed guard kept watch as Arabs and compatriots who had known him in war and in the belligerent peace came in their hundreds to pay homage.

Tuesday, 1 March 1921. The service began at two o'clock. Of the notables of Baghdad only Sir Edgar Bonham Carter, the Judicial Adviser, remained behind to take temporary charge of the administration. He took his place in the front row. Otherwise it was the army's day of mourning.

The world's press reported the event. Leachman had become an heroic figure to millions of English-speaking people when his wartime exploits were told at the time of his murder by the son of a tribal shaikh in August, when the rebellion was at its height and he became its most famous victim. The church was filled to overflowing and hundreds of mourners crowded outside the open doors to hear the words of the Revd J. T. Hales, principal chaplain of the army.

The *Baghdad Times* reported that the service was 'impressive in its simplicity'. Then the reburial.

> The coffin was borne from the church to a waiting gun-carriage. Two double companies of Rifles, and a detachment of Arab Levies, and a brass bugle band formed the military escort, and the military personnel present stood respectfully at the salute while the civil community bared their heads as the procession filed its way out of the Serai. A very large number of people followed the coffin to its last resting-place at the North Gate Cemetery, and the spectacle presented as the long line of mourners wound their way to the burial place to the solemn strains of a slow march was moving in the extreme.

Leachman's closest friends and companions in the desert war were the pall-bearers: Capt. Williams, the Euphrates police chief who had been the unsuspecting guest of the murderer's family the night before Leachman was killed; the Political Officers Capts. Carver and Flaxman of the LAMBs; the reckless young Lieut Pitcairn; and the older officers, Leachman's contemporaries with crowns on their shoulders, Bruce Hay, Jeffcoat, Wilson, Dent. But rank meant little to Leachman or his companions. There was unspoken equality among the men who accompanied Leachman on his dangerous exploits in the deserts and the holy cities of the Shi'a Moslems, among the Kurds and the Euphrates tribes; men who now bore him to the grave.

The *Baghdad Times* ended its report:

> The graveside reached, the last rites were solemnly performed and the body lowered into the ground. A volley was discharged by the firing party, after which the *General Salute* was sounded followed by the *Last Post* and *Reveille*. This concluded the moving ceremony; one which will live in the minds of all present for many years to come as a fitting last tribute of respect, admiration and appreciation of the great work of a very gallant gentleman.

4

2

Man of Empire

That England which embraced the infant Gerard Evelyn
Leachman on 27 July 1880 had set out on the last phase of its long
imperial adventure. There were discernible cracks in the edifice,
divisions at home and stirring abroad which would grow as the
century neared its end until the tranquillity of an Empire born of
horse-power, sailing ships and elephant muscle was shattered by
the screeching whistle of the Orient Express and the crackle of a
myriad telegraph wires.

The Congress of Berlin was but two years old. The Queen had
assumed the title 'Empress of India' but four years earlier. And
in little more than a decade past Bismarck had crushed Austria
and France, created a German Empire and humbled Britain. As
he departed from the great ones of Berlin in July 1878 Disraeli
is said to have 'enquired discreetly' about the defence of
Mesopotamia should a Russian incursion materialize and so
threaten India. By 1880 Disraeli's last Ministry had given way to
Liberal rule and Gladstone was master for the second time. The
eternal problem of Ireland once more monopolized Britain's
domestic politics and began to sap its vitality abroad. Home Rule
became the issue of the day.

It is to be doubted whether the Leachmans shared Gladstone's
view of the world. They were conservative people in the literal
and political senses of the word; not of the Primrose League but
not of the National Liberal 'Caucus' either. If they doubted the

soundness of some of Dizzy's more jingoistic flights of rhetoric, and of his long flirtation with the 'Terrible Turk', it may be supposed that they found the brash commercialism of Joseph Chamberlain and the free-trade philosophy of Gladstone's earlier Ministry even less congenial.

As a family the Leachmans boasted no Empire builders or hell-raisers. They were quiet, popular people. Father, Albert Warren, Doctor of Medicine, was a man of considerable scientific and musical ability, but ill health had dogged much of his adult life and he had settled amiably for the modest rewards of the country physician, held as he was in the deepest respect by his patients and little known beyond his rural backwater. Mother, Louise Caroline Blandford, who came of the Singers of Hertfordshire, was likewise a woman of charm with no overweening ambition for herself or her children. Gerard was their sixth child but only three daughters – Mabel, Mildred and Janet – survived to the time of his birth. Two brothers died in infancy.

If the fates sometimes give subtle pointers to the future, they were generous, perhaps over generous in the case of the infant Leachman. On the day of his birth at the home they named 'Fairley', Gladstone's new Cabinet met to hear Foreign Secretary Earl Granville's report on the withdrawal of 'Little Bob's' army from Afghanistan after the occupation which followed the massacre of Britons in Kabul in 1879. In the same year Charles Doughty had arrived home from his soul-searing journey in the central Arabian deserts, his mind full to overflowing with the asperities of his wanderings in the 'illimitable empty wastes', prepared to devote himself for the next eight years to recording his experiences in the strange, part-biblical, part-Spenserian language of his unique book, *Arabia Deserta*. And the Blunts who followed him in those deserts came home too, charmed by the East and its 'absence of intellectual life', to establish the Arab thoroughbred in England and sing the praises of that 'only true democracy' which they found among the wild men of the inner deserts.

He was a withdrawn child. The only son brought up among older sisters in a conventional home, Gerard was protected from danger and discouraged from making any show of independence more vigorous than a sojourn in the New Forest – though even then he was usually accompanied by his sister Janet – or entertaining guests with a rendering of a family favourite in the high-pitched tones of a choirboy.

As the years went by he became secretive in manner, with an unbecoming touch of cynicism in his make-up. His mother, devoted and outgoing in manner, felt increasingly estranged from her undemonstrative son. His father, occupied with his medical practice and rural politics, found refuge from work and the effects of indifferent health in the company of fellow doctors and a fraternity of keen amateur musicians. He was scarcely aware of the bursts of temper and the recourse to sarcastic onslaughts on mother and sisters which marked the veiled cry of his son for identity and escape from the cosseting embrace of the family. By the age of seven he showed a fussiness about his dress, an interest in good food and a certain natural ability to act his way out of embarrassing situations which augured anything but an imposing progress to manhood.

In this same year, Gerard was sent to a private boarding-school, at Ovingdean, near Brighton. He approved of the food, which was plentiful, but of nothing else. 'A dreadful place', he wrote towards the end of his four-year stint, 'the boys use awful words, fool and ass, all the time.' He showed enthusiasm neither for games nor lessons; nor for the companionship of his fellows. Too much emphasis should not be placed on the letters of a schoolboy away from home and family, trying to come to terms with a hostile world. All the same, it would be hard to disguise a note of priggishness in the schoolboy voice.

When Gerard was two years old a young officer on leave in England was called to the War Office where he was briefed by Lord Northbrook, the ex-Viceroy who headed the secret service. That officer was Lieut W.J. Gill, Kipling's man through and through, strong, fearless and intensely patriotic, and wealthy. He had crossed trans-Caspia with Valentine Baker in 1874, and four years later went alone on the dangerous land route to China following the Mogul armies of earlier centuries, mapping and note-making as he went. The journey won him the gold medal of the Royal Geographical Society and on his return to England he was asked to join the Quartermaster-General's intelligence department at the War Office. Now, in 1882, came his most dangerous task. Britain, provided with an opportunity by disturbances in Alexandria incited by the nationalist leader 'Arabi', decided to occupy Egypt, which it did with a decent display of reluctance. But Egypt belonged by title to Britain's oldest ally in the East, to the Ottoman Empire of the Sultan Abdal Hamid in Constantinople. Abdal Hamid's Turkish army occupied Sinai, the buffer between Egypt and Syria, and Sinai was thick with the Sultan's spies, its recalcitrant tribes in sympathy with Arabi's nationalist schemes.

Whitehall decided to send the ageing Professor Palmer, a great expert on Sinai and the finest Arabic scholar of his day, into the wilderness. Lieut Gill of the Royal Engineers and Lieut Charrington RN were sent to protect the professor and to cut the telegraph wires which kept the Egyptian trouble-makers in touch with Ottoman agents in Sinai and with Constantinople. In August 1882 they went into the desert carrying £30,000 in gold coin. They were never seen again.

There was panic in London and Cairo as the search for the missing agents brought the illegal mission to light. Capt. Richard Burton, the Consul at Trieste, was summoned to join with another sapper, Maj. Maitland, to go in search of the missing men. Col. Warren, an intelligence officer with a penchant for the high life, who was to become the Commissioner of Metropolitan Police was also sent to seek the missing men. The Sultan was secretly amused by the plight of British intelligence but he affected mock horror and threatened retaliation. The War Office in London was forced to withdraw all its intelligence officers and agents from Constantinople and a wholesale reorganization of the military intelligence service followed.

Col. Warren's men discovered the essential facts of the brutal murder of the Britishers by Sinai tribesmen and some of the culprits were arrested and punished. They discovered that Gill was the last of them to die; that he fought alone against a horde of armed men incited by the sight of gold, until eventually he was overpowered, shot and thrown over a cliff. The Royal Geographical Society in London struck a medal in his memory. Gerard Leachman would one day wear the Gill memorial medal with pride though it was perhaps the least of the awards which came his way for desert exploration and for bravery and enterprise in battle. Some of the officers who sent Palmer, Gill and Charrington on their luckless mission, and some of those who went in search of the victims, would become Leachman's superiors in the course of time.

In September 1893 Gerard went to Charterhouse School which twenty years before had moved from its ancient site in London to Godalming, in Surrey, not far from the Leachman home in Hampshire. A famous school with a liberal tradition, Charterhouse could boast many famous sons. Thackeray was educated there along with a relative from India, Dowdeswell Shakespear, who became the novelist's model for Col. Newcome in his portrayal of Greyfriars, a barely concealed rendering of life at Charterhouse in his own day. The school was not an academic hot-house in the late nineteenth century; its record of academic achievement was high but by no means paramount. Cricket and other sports were important ingredients of the all-round education it offered. Indeed, England in Leachman's school years was a place of many-sided activity and mighty achievement for those who could afford leisure and a good education. In an age of great men, of artistic, scientific and political debate and disputation which saw the publication of Dickens's and Thackeray's novels, of the *Origin of Species* and *Das Kapital*, witnessed the noisy emergence of the pre-Raphaelites in art and the Utopian idealism of the craft movement led by William Morris, the gladiatorial confrontations of Disraeli and Bismarck, and the idolization of Gladstone, it was a man of sport, the massive bearded figure of Dr William Gilbert Grace that was the most instantly recognized in all England. It is said that a public schoolmaster of the day, though perhaps not of Charterhouse, grew a beard exactly like WG's so that with a comparable frame he was taken for the 'Champion' and was ever after signalled on to railway trains without paying his fare, received with ceremony wherever he went and accorded a fame and respect which would otherwise have been denied him. Men and boys, the complements of the great schools of England, would rather have succeeded by and large to the title of 'The Doctor' than to that of Gladstone and Disraeli.

The young Leachman was unmoved by the calls of fame and ambition. He shone in neither academic nor sporting endeavour. Yet he did have a hero, one god in an otherwise empty firmament: Sir Charles James Napier, the quarrelsome, hasty-tempered Commander-in-Chief East Indies from 1842 to 1847 who destroyed the Baluchi and Afghan amirs of Sind and who arrived home in England in 1847 to a tumultuous welcome, having assailed every authority in India, including the entire

Board of the East India Company, with his sharp tongue, and threatened several of them with his fists. At some stage in his life Leachman was to acquire a collection of seals of office, signed by Napier 'General, Commander-in-Chief, East Indies'. At the end of his life they remained the only possession which he valued. He had chosen an apposite hero.

The desire of the youngster to prosper in uncongenial regions is apparent from the only letter to survive from his school years. Written in his second year and dated 12 July 1894, it reads:

Dear Father,
The examination was not so hard as I expected except the algebra and of course the II/III book of Euclid. Another thing that was rather hard was this. A master read out a long piece of very uninteresting history twice and then we had to write what we remembered down word for word. I could not do the verses very well but I did two of them. We have just lost the Ashburton shield it is horrid. There were about 60 fellows going in for the scholarship, young Bennion went in for it.

Do have that collie dog Janet wants and it will be nice having that magpie. I did my best to do a good paper, but I daresay I did not get anything.

Love to all, Gerard

Many a father, whatever kind of school his pride and joy went to, carries fond memories of such a jumble of unconnected thoughts and unrealizable ambitions.

Gerard Leachman ventured in and out of Charterhouse between the years 1893 and 1897 without causing a ripple on the calm surface of that school. He was a Saunderite and thus belonged to the House traditionally presided over by the headmaster. In his day Dr William Haig Brown, the famous headmaster who transferred the school from London to Godalming, occupied the position. He and Leachman did not, it seems, have a great deal to do with each other. In his penultimate year one of the masters, Mr Evans, wrote pessimistically to Dr Leachman:

My dear Sir,
I wish I could say that I think your boy would succeed in getting into Sandhurst from Charterhouse, for I find him a

nice boy to have to do with and I should be very glad to see him achieve any object upon which he had set his heart. But I have little hesitation in saying that he would scarcely be likely to get into Sandhurst without working hard and doing it under greater pressure than could be applied here. I should say that his abilities are not very good, not above the average, and something more than this is wanted in these days of severe competition – but I believe him to be a willing boy and perhaps with a fixed object before him he might cultivate sufficient industry to reach his goal.

He did gain entrance to Sandhurst in his final term, with the help of a 'crammer', despite his master's gloomy view and his father's despair.

Several of Leachman's Charterhouse contemporaries were to rub shoulders with him on battlefields and in army camps, and on the highways and byways of Empire. One of them, a year younger and a world apart, was a precociously bright scholar by the name of Ronald Storrs. He left the school with an abiding recollection: a sixpenny sweep on the election of a new Pope in 1903. He drew Rampolla, 'a likely starter' he thought, but was cheated at the last moment by the unexpected resort of the Emperor of Austria to his historic right of veto over the College of Cardinals, a power which was never to be exercised again. Storrs went on to Cambridge and to the Residency at Cairo; and to the Governorship of Jerusalem in succession, as he liked to point out, to Pontius Pilate. But that was a long way off as Leachman packed his school bags and donned cadet's uniform.

Like a cadet who went from Harrow to the Royal Military College a year or two before him, Winston Churchill, he endured rather than enjoyed an advantaged education. And like that other cadet he emerged into the world with no recorded aptitude and no noticeable interest, save a profound veneration of his country, a deep involvement in its imperial past, and a resolve to serve it in the present.

3

What Ho!

Leachman's time at Sandhurst, from the beginning of 1898 to the autumn of 1899, came to an end while he was still in his nineteenth year. He had worked with steady application, forming few friendships and exciting neither devotion nor enmity on the part of fellow cadets or masters. He was, as he had been throughout his school years, a solitary youngster; often to be found brooding in isolation; avoiding the heap in which young men at military college and elsewhere usually prefer to live, and deeply suspicious of the smart-Alick. Above all he had learnt to live with himself, to endure his own company, and find sustenance in his own thoughts and imaginings. He left Sandhurst with an inner strength which would serve him well in years to come. Just as importantly for the testing work that was in store for him he had developed immense physical strength in his lithe, lanky frame. Occasionally the dark countenance, the sombre brown eyes, would connive at a smile; or respond in a brief flash to injury or insult and his pent-up strength would be released, cat-like, as if a tightly wound coil had been set free. Woe betide the man who stood in his way when his temper was roused!

If his own life at the Royal Military College had been largely uneventful, however, his country's fortunes took a dramatic turn as the century neared its end. The sirdar of the Egyptian army, Maj.-Gen. Sir Herbert Horatio Kitchener, had avenged the insolent siege of Khartoum and the murder of Gordon.

Omdurman, the new capital of the Sudanese insurgents, had been taken and the Mahdi's black flag sent home to the Queen in token of a famous victory. The army's prestige stood high. It was a good time to don officer's uniform and the subaltern's single pip. But if national pride had been restored, Omdurman could not in a moment revive the flagging strength of an army that had become little more than a social institution since the Crimea. There had, admittedly, been border skirmishes and one or two genuine battles in the intervening thirty years. Hazara, Chitral, the Nile Expedition and several other distant battlegrounds were inscribed on regimental rolls of honour. Yet in the main Britain's military arm had become moribund.

Kitchener had come home to receive the adulation of the Queen and her people, and to express his contempt for the War Office with its lack of purpose and staff organization. Intelligence, woefully lacking despite the efforts of a few officers working under Sir John Ardagh in a private house in Queen Anne's Gate behind Whitehall, had been Kitchener's trump card in the Sudan. He had shown himself to be a master in the 'dirty tricks' department, and he saw the need for a much more penetrative force of agents in the world at large, for far readier access to information on the strengths and purposes of other armies, and for less division of counsel and authority within Britain's military administration. As Kitchener made his dour appearance and received a hero's welcome, Wilhelm II, King of Prussia and Emperor of Germany, stood before a gathering of Turkish officials, Arabs and Jews in Damascus and proclaimed himself the friend and protector of Islam. And in South Africa the long-festering antagonism between Cape colonists and the Boers was about to burst into a vicious war.

By the summer of 1899 Leachman and many of the young men who passed out with him were destined to find their baptism in a genuine conflict; and those who survived would find challenges enough in the emergence of Germany as the supreme threat to Britain's imperial position in the world.

From Sandhurst Leachman was gazetted to the 1st Battalion of the Royal Sussex Regiment, under orders to embark for Cape Town. With eight other officers and 534 men he left Southampton on 10 February 1900 aboard SS *Pavonia*. The Bay of Biscay was rough and most of the officers above deck were laid low with seasickness. Below decks, where the troops were crammed into the hold, conditions were grim. They would become worse as the voyage proceeded, for more men were to be picked up *en route* and packed with their worldly belongings into already over-crowded compartments.

News of the war came to them on the voyage. Joubert was trying to cut off Buller's forces. 'We don't seem to be getting on very fast,' he wrote in his diary. It was the black abyss of the war, the fourth month of the siege of Ladysmith.

They reached Malta, where the main body of the regiment embarked, on 19 February. 'A lovely place, just as if it were built of cardboard.' The news was still bad. Another thousand men seethed and fought for precious space in the sweaty regions below. On the upper decks officers shared out their cabin space and formed their first impressions of each other. Leachman was assigned to 'C' Company and met the Colonel, 'a very nice chap', and the company commander, Capt. Robinson. Both men had seen service in the Sudan. So had his cabin mate, the fellow subaltern Nelson who had been with the Seaforth Highlanders in Kitchener's successful, yet so nearly disastrous, campaign. Leachman was the untried junior of the mess, greatly impressed by the tales of fellow officers and anxious to gain a little war service, a few battle scars even, to put him on a par with the seasoned campaigners around him.

On 24 February they passed Gibraltar for the second time to Leachman's dismay, and were told to 'heave to'. He was terrified that the order to proceed to the Cape might have been changed, that he might after all miss the war. But it was only to take ashore stowaways who had secreted themselves aboard at Malta in the hope of reaching South Africa and sharing in the adventure of battle. The tug that came to take off the stowaways brought telegrams containing the casualty lists from the fronts. Their frightening extent can be gauged from Leachman's laconic comment: 'What a lot of men from around Petersfield.'

Teneriffe: 'The peak is wonderful.' A glimpse of another liner rushing home to pick up more troops, or perhaps nurses, war correspondents, politicians; and carrying the wounded to recuperation centres so that they could return and fight again in the vicious, fanatical war that raged over veldt and mountain, river and homestead, six thousand miles from the British Isles at the tip of the African continent.

14

The language of the young officer at the dawn of the new century was the lingo of the emergent boys' magazine; public school jargon transformed into the dashing and often trite bravado of young heroes who defended the Empire at its most distant reaches beyond the northern borders of India and in the central Asian regions where the Czar's ambitions had encroached closer and closer to the heart of imperial Britain.

The letters of Leachman and his companions read much like pages from the *Boy's Own Paper*. Those of the men below spoke the language of Kipling's rankers, thrown in at the deep end, forgotten easily, expected always to bear the worst discomforts, suffer the worst torments, and to die with good grace if the need arose. Theirs was an existence that few of the officers knew or cared about: 'An' you might 'ave called us dirty, an' you might ha' called us dry, An' you might 'ave 'eard us talkin'. . .' There was no peace for them to write letters home; no deck space for exercise; no room to sleep. Leachman would go below to the troop decks, to chat with the men, endure the stench. Some of them had chased Arabi's men in the desert twenty years before. Some had been at Omdurman. He, Leachman, was a beginner. It was a privilege to talk to them. But it wasn't done to get too close, to be too friendly. He thought about their privations when he was basking on the upper deck or languishing in a hot bath, and he mentioned them a good deal in his letters. 'The worst thing we do on board is to go into the troop decks,' he wrote indignantly. 'If there's a sight on board that would prevent a man enlisting it's the sight beneath the decks . . .'

He crossed the equator for the first time on Tuesday, 8 March. They had left St Vincent six days earlier, 'I never saw a more barren beastly place in my life.' But they had learnt while there that Ladysmith had been relieved and Cronje captured. Spirits were high when they anchored at the Cape on 20 March.

In the early chaos of the Boer War the right hand seldom knew what the left hand proposed. The first staff officer to board the *Pavonia* at Cape Town told the CO that his men would disembark and proceed to Bloemfontein which Lord Roberts had entered seven days before. Six days later a pilot came out to the ship to take it into dock. The men went ashore with unconcealed joy after their six cramped weeks aboard, hardly able to believe their good fortune. A fine clean city with women and girls,

15

entertainment and shops; but nobody had time to sample the pleasures in store. Staff officer number two informed the CO that his men would rejoin the ship and disembark at East London, and so the men were rounded up on their first day ashore and marched back to the *Pavonia*. They went ashore again on 1 April 1900.

During his first and only day in Cape Town Leachman had met several people he knew in England during his school-days and at Sandhurst, and one of his fellow officers was asked by a stranger on a brief train journey if Lieut Leachman was aboard. He had known the doctor of Petersfield before emigrating from the district to South Africa, and someone had written to him to say that the doctor's son was on his way to the war. It was a propitious start. But there were to be few such days of quiet reflection and renewed friendship. The Royal Sussex were to join Lord Roberts's force at Bloemfontein after all.

On 6 April Leachman wrote to his parents:

> We got through safely and reached Bloemfontein at 10.30 on Thursday . . . we leave in a terrific thunderstorm for camp . . . I had nothing to eat from breakfast Wednesday till 7.0 p.m. Thursday (nearly 36 hours – What ho!). However I am enjoying myself really well. There are 60,000 troops in the camp round us and it is very hard to get anything to eat . . . I wasn't able to get a wash from Monday till Thursday.

The greenstick officer was not altogether accurate in his reports to the family. There were 45,000 men in camp. Conditions were even worse than his letters indicated however. He had begun a life of hardship and deprivation from which he would find only the briefest escape in the rest of his years; and perhaps the severest sacrifice of the life which began for him on the plain of Bloemfontein was food. His thin gangling frame, 6 ft 1 in. with not an ounce of fat to fall back on, needed fodder to keep up flagging energy and spirit on long marches and, later, in the chosen isolation and sparseness of desert and wilderness. In South Africa he learnt to endure the pangs of hunger; to keep going when illness or tiredness, or both, combined with an empty stomach to make every step a supreme act of will, an almost instinctive act of survival.

'Last night Lord Roberts came up here and I was introduced to him; he does look a fine old man. He did us a great honour by naming our kopje "Fort Sussex".' So he wrote on 11 April. A week later they were still at Fort Sussex, encamped in slush and mud amid never-ending thunderstorms and forked lightning which was attracted, it was said, by the rich iron deposits of the region.

Rimington's Guides were posted near by and Leachman spent a good deal of time with the 'Tigers' and their famous leader. Rimington saw courage and strength of purpose under the melancholy look of the young subaltern who sought his friendship and the men became close in the few days before the push on Pretoria began.

Preparations had been in hand for six weeks. On 3 May the great march began. It was no easy advance: the Boers defended every inch of ground with fanatical devotion, and when the odds became too great they retired stealthily leaving behind them an eerie desolation and silence. On the second day of the march Leachman had his first experience of artillery fire.

They reached Bloemplaats on 9 May and enjoyed a brief respite from battle. Deer meat for dinner, a rare treat; and in the terrible indifference to life in the front line of war a Tommy was shot in the excited hunt for antelope.

On the journey by foot and truck to Bloemfontein his diary recorded 'Awful night' and 'fearfully cold, without even a rug'. Kitchener had turned up at Klein Ospruit as the men bivouacked in the cold of night, without bedding or a warm drink at night. Leachman would have complained to the victor of Omdurman, the imperious Lysander of the British army, if he could have come within earshot. But he had to save his protest. Next day, 29 April, he wrote to the King, giving his sovereign chapter and verse of the shortcomings of the army organization. Whether the field censor allowed the letter to be sent is not known. It was certainly posted however, if not acknowledged. The King did not customarily reply to letters of complaint from newly commissioned first lieutenants. Leachman had no fear of authority. He was soon to show also that he feared neither danger nor death. A man of changeable mood, capable of extreme responses, of intense compassion and at times of hard insensitivity.

The Sussex were grouped with the Derbyshire Regiment, the CIVs and Camerons in Gen. Bruce-Hamilton's Brigade for the advance on Pretoria. The Boers had taken up a strong position on the opposite bank of the Zand river, their defended line stretching for twenty miles under the command of the two Bothas.

'We started at 3 in the morning and marched to the Zand river,' wrote Leachman.

> We waded across up to our waists and then lay down for two hours, oh! it was cold. This day we were the second company of the leading regiment, so we were in the thick of it the whole time . . . all manner of projectiles coming at us including pom-poms (one pounder automatic guns) which are really awful . . . I don't understand all that talk about men not taking cover. I can tell you we took cover soon enough . . . Those pom-poms make one wish one were home again. Our casualties were 3 killed and 8 wounded. We don't get much to eat except biscuits, 4 a day . . . We managed to loot a good deal coming along.

It was much like any other young soldier's letters home. Matter-of-fact and a little prosaic. The war had been bitter and nasty from the outset. Now, Leachman noted, the Boers were using 'split' cartridges, exploding on impact and causing ghastly wounds which with few medical resources and only horse-drawn ambulances to care for the victims became gangrenous as often as not.

Kitchener had already begun to set up the infamous 'concentration' camps. The 'scorched earth' strategy was in full swing. Two embittered peoples, each believing that it had a prior title to the wasteland over which they fought, faced each other in a fight to the death. Leachman and his comrades did not stop to ask *Why*? They knew only that they had a simple choice: to kill or be killed.

Lord Roberts of Kandahar – 'little Bobs' as the troops called the commander they idolized – had hoped to catch the Boer high command at Kroonstadt, headquarters of the mobile Free State Government, but all escaped including President Steyn, the Bothas and the quicksilver de Wet. The army halted there for eight days to replenish. Then it was on the march again. Linley, Heilbron, the Boers on the flanks of the advancing army making tactical withdrawals to conserve their outnumbered force. On 24 May Leachman's unit crossed the main army on the road to the Vaal river. On the 26th they waded across the river without meeting opposition.

We seem to have done pretty well; at least Lord Roberts sent us a note to say that he was pleased. We marched until 1 p.m. without hearing a shot fired and then proceeded to march up a valley which the enemy was holding on the front and right. I can tell you the bullets did whizz about. There was no cover as the Boers had burnt all the grass . . . After a bit I didn't mind the bullets . . . We advanced for about an hour by rushes and at 4.45 we charged the position. We found several dead Boers on the top mostly about 18 years old!

Next day, 27 May, they were at Florida, a suburb of Johannesburg.

It was certainly a case of the beggars coming to town. I never saw such a lot of ruffians. Few have proper soles to their boots, none hardly have seats to their breeches, many are wearing civilian trousers; we hadn't washed for two days . . . Oh! we were a lot! . . . We marched for eleven days without a rest at an average of twelve miles a day. Your beloved son is such a pretty boy at present . . . I'm very fit, fitter than I ever remember being.

So far Leachman's battalion had marched 330 miles in thirty-four days, including rest periods.

On 4 June the advance column camped outside Pretoria. Next day the army entered the Boer capital, Roberts taking the salute, and hope of an armistice ran high. But the Boers were in no mood to surrender or even to discuss the future of the land they regarded as theirs. On 9 June Leachman told his family that a big fight was promised the next day. The enemy was said to be six thousand strong with twenty big guns. 'What ho!'

The battle of Diamond Hill began as Leachman had predicted on the 11th. Botha could not be left in control of the fortifications to which he had retreated only fifteen miles from Pretoria; the Boers were determined that they would not be dislodged from their rocky bastion. The battle was won in two days of fierce fighting in which the Sussex, Derbyshires and CIVs under Hamilton distinguished themselves. But Leachman said nothing of the battle itself in his letters. 'I expect you will read about it in the papers,' he told his family.

After the battle of Diamond Hill the brigade marched back to Heidelberg, a five-day stint at fifteen miles a day. Strangely, in that devastated land, trains still ran more or less to time, and stations kept up a peacetime standard of service. Leachman was able to enjoy a meal served on a 'nice clean tablecloth'; and to write home on an Afrikaans railway traffic form. Draught beer made a welcome change from the putrid water they had been drinking on the way from streams contaminated by the rotting carcasses of mules and horses.

More marching. Another hundred miles of veldt in eleven days; but Leachman was fit and strong and in good spirits. His first real bed since arriving in South Africa, in a Boer home lent to the troops by a widow in the hope that she would thus save it from being looted, put him in even better heart.

In mid July the Royal Sussex joined up with Gen. Hunter's column – Hunter having taken over from Bruce-Hamilton who had broken a collar-bone – and they marched through the hills around Bethlehem and Sevastapol to join Ridley's mounted infantry. The main Boer army was gradually surrounded. De Wet broke through. But other leaders were cornered. The Sussex and Seaforths suffered severe casualties as they inched forward at Retief's Neck while the Highland Brigade commanded the heights above them.

On 23 July Leachman received his first severe injury.

Well [he wrote with light-hearted regret], we were going up quite merrily, and when we had got within 1,400 yards of the head of the pass the Boers opened fire . . . Up one side of the pass there was a certain amount of cover and we advanced under this till within 400 yards of the position. I fired 56 rounds and ran out of ammunition. This was about 4 p.m. [23 July]. An officer came up to me behind a rock and gave me a note to take forward to the leading company with orders to retire at dusk. I ran forward about 40 yards and just as I got into cover again a bullet hit me on the thigh. I managed to get behind a stone. Luckily there was a man behind it and between us we managed to bandage up the wound . . . I precious nearly fainted. At dark four men carried me back about half a mile and then a stretcher came up and I proceeded on that to camp about two miles.

Three men and four officers of the Sussex regiment were killed in the same engagement. Thirty-one men were wounded.

20

Leachman was taken by ox-wagon to the field hospital at Bethlehem, a converted girls' school, and then on to Winberg, a painful journey with no food and only an occasional sip of water to comfort him and the other wounded. The bullet had entered his thigh just above the knee and skirted the bone, spiralling through flesh until it came out of his buttock, damaging the sciatic nerve on its path.

The Boers surrendered on 29 July, but Leachman was on his way to hospital when his comrades collected up the arms of a brave and formidable enemy. In August he was sent on to the hospital at Deelfontein. Champagne and cigars were there for the asking. 'But the great attraction is the nurses,' he wrote. His twentieth birthday had passed without notice while he was a patient at the temporary hospital in Bethlehem.

In the meantime his parents had been worried by lack of news and by reports of the savage maulings which the Boers continued to inflict on the British army. Dr Leachman wrote to the War Office to ask if they had any knowledge of his son's whereabouts and the Military Secretary, accustomed to assuming the worst in connection with anxious enquiries, replied on black-bordered official notepaper:

> War Office, 28th August 1900
> The Military Secretary presents his compliments to Mr Leachman, and begs to acquaint him in reply to his letter of the 26th instant that it is regretted that there is no information available as to the whereabouts of 2nd Lieut Leachman, Sussex Regiment. It is indeed, possible that this officer never went into hospital with his wound, and in any case, all communications telegraphic or otherwise . . . will be forwarded to wherever this officer may be.

The family was reassured a few days after receiving this somewhat perfunctory War Office communication. Gerard sent them a telegram. Never one to spend money unnecessarily his message was to the point, reading simply 'Well'. On 15 September he boarded the *Kildonian Castle* at Cape Town, bound for sick leave in England.

Respite was offered sparingly in the Boer War. Casualties were heavy. Young life was given freely while talk of peace vied with an ever more bitter escalation of war. Guerrilla war such as the Boers were commanded to wage is always vicious. On the last day of the year 1900 Leachman was on his way back to the battlefields of South Africa. He disembarked at the Cape on 18 January 1901, fit and well again and anxious to resume his part in the imperial adventure.

While home in England he had read in the newspapers accounts of de Wet's attempt to break through to the Cape Colony; of de la Rey's exploits in the north against a British force which never knew where the next blow would be struck, trudging back and forth in endless marches in pursuit of an elusive foe.

His regiment was now with the Derbyshires and Camerons, back under Bruce-Hamilton's command. He joined them at Kroonstad as they entrained for the southward journey to the Ventersburg road in pursuit once more of de Wet:

[1 February:] We have had a time since I last wrote [Saturday 25 January] . . . we left Ventersburg Road station at 5 a.m. and marched about 12 miles to Ventersburg where de Wet was supposed to be. At 5 p.m. we found he had left so we stopped for two hours and then started for the Zand river at 7.30 at night. It started raining and we all got drenched and at midnight we found we had lost our way.

Five days later they were back at the scene of earlier encounters, Bethulie. 'The heat is dreadful . . . the country seems in a very unsettled state and we get sniped at wherever we go.'

They were trying to get ahead of de Wet by a series of short train journeys and marches. Now it was decided to give horses to the Sussex infantrymen to make them more mobile, and Leachman, whose home in Hampshire boasted a riding-stable of which he had made indifferent use in his boyhood (his sisters were keener riders), volunteered to help train the men in the equestrian arts. In a few days a hundred or so infantrymen had become apprentice and perhaps over-ambitious horsemen.

On 19 February he left Bethulie at the head of a mounted convoy making for Hamilton's main force. The pursuit of de Wet, who was now about twenty-four hours ahead of them and again liable to break through a thinly stretched British line of defence, was exhilarating. 'Next day we went 21 miles to Prier's

Siding, next day 27 miles to Philippolis and the next 20 miles to Zand Drift on the Orange River . . . we are taking a long time to get across the river as the water is up to the horses' shoulders.'

27 February: 'We are still on the track, you see; my goodness, we have been marching!'

There was more contaminated water on the route and Leachman had a second bout of fever and had to be conveyed by horse-drawn ambulance for the next four days. They reached Strydenburg after a march of 200 miles in four days and reached Paun Pan on 26 February. The men had little knowledge of horses and Leachman had to see that they were unbridled, watered and fed after the day's work: 'Oh, I can tell you, mounted infantry is not all jam.'

De Wet's latest attempt at breakthrough had failed. But the elusive Boer had got away again and returned to his hide-out in the north.

The campaign had taken another turn in its evil course. The recalcitrant Boers had shown themselves unwilling to compromise with men they believed to be intruders in their lands. Britain responded with insensitive rigour. The policy of clearing entire districts began in earnest. Cattle and sheep were driven from the farms. Whole populations were removed to Kitchener's concentration camps far from their homes. Leachman and his fellow officers and the happy band of horse-mounted warriors he had formed were about to take part in the last and perhaps the grimmest stage of the old-style war in which men and animals unprotected by armour of any kind fought to the death and devastated the lands they fought over.

We left Edenburg on Wednesday 13th [March] with a convoy of 180 wagons for de Wetsdorf. We had quite a nice little skirmish one day. I was the advanced guard and had a great gallop after the Boers who held a ridge against us for a bit . . . we laid waste all the country round de Wetsdorf as it is a great stronghold of the Boers. We have burnt all the farms and taken all the cattle and everything we could lay hands on. We left . . . with a hundred empty ox-wagons, three hundred refugees, 80,000 sheep, 7,000 horses and 17,000 cattle, you can imagine the length of the column. We had a skirmish every day except the day we got into Bloemfontein.

The Boers, dressing now in khaki and often taken for British patrols, harassed the vast column of men and creatures as it made its slow trek to Bloemfontein. On one occasion two troopers were snatched as they wandered a few hundred yards from the main force. Bennet Burleigh, the correspondent of the London *Daily Telegraph*, took breakfast with Leachman and other officers on 23 March: '. . . so we can expect a lot of trumpeting in the *Daily Telegraph*'.

The ferocity of the war became more and more apparent from the regular letters Leachman wrote to his parents at this time. Simple, honest, matter-of-fact portrayals of the daily occurrences in a fight in which stubborn patriotism became zealous chauvinism, and in the end honour and decency and the rules of war were thrown to the wind as murder, rape and malevolence assumed a frightful normality.

4 April from Bethulie: 'We left next day and marched to Bethulie which we reached yesterday. We came under very heavy fire one day; I was burning a house full of wheat and had a picket out, when the Boers opened fire at long range and killed eleven horses, but luckily hit no men.'

So it went on. Back to Bloemfontein, to Smithfield and Edenburg; reminders of places familiar to Englishman and Dutchman half-way round the world, names given to the dorps and scrubland settlements that had been established painfully in a far-off land and were being destroyed with meticulous thoroughness.

By late April Leachman had raised another company of mounted infantry at Edenburg and had been made adjutant and quartermaster of a detachment of five companies. They moved off to de Wetsdorf yet again, leaving a trail of destruction behind. Thousands of new recruits were arriving at the battlefronts from Britain, untrained, unprepared for the tasks that awaited them. Green yeomanry joined up with Leachman's detachment. 'A shocking lot.'

Smithfield was cleared of every inhabitant. 'We passed through Rouxville yesterday which is a little town – there was not a living thing in it of any sort.'

It was hard now to distinguish compassion and concern from bravado in the letters home. 'It was very queer to see a fair-sized town without anybody in it.'

Commendation came with hard work and reports of bravery

and reliability at the battlefront. And winter came with its crop of colds and more serious illnesses. 'The weather is too awful for anything, with cold and terrible blizzards, there seems no chance of getting away from this beastly country.'

The work of herding the Afrikaner prisoners between the long cordons of barbed-wire stretched from village to village across the country, hand-to-hand fighting with Boer groups which broke through the closing net, and the cold of winter took a toll of the British force. But the Boers were now on the defensive and had lost the initiative everywhere.

Leachman was made acting staff officer to Col. du Moulin, 'a ripping chap' who had ridden The Roarer to victory as an amateur rider in the Grand National at 66–1. Almost as soon as he took on his new task he was struck down with jaundice. Rest, the mandatory treatment for that condition, was impossible and Leachman dragged himself to duty despite constant nausea and weakness. He became thinner than ever and may have done his health irreparable harm at this time for he never regained the weight he lost. In June 1901 he wrote to Bernard Parham, husband of his sister Mabel and a keen field sportsman: 'Our last trek has been great fun and we did jolly well too, getting fifty-three prisoners. It was just like a big pheasant drive . . .'

He was in charge of a column pursuing straggling bands of Afrikaners to the Basutoland border. He had been awarded an extra five shillings a day in his more senior role and he thought the increase worthy of 'a good bit of extra work'. In July he was sent up to Norval's Port to arrange for the enlistment of native children as intelligence 'news-agents' – his introduction, meagre though it was, to a service that would become central to his life's work. He was back in Philippolis for his twenty-first birthday, an event that went almost unnoticed in the final phases of the war. Indeed, his official entry into manhood was marked by nothing more memorable than a carbuncle on the cheek which the company doctor said was due to drinking too much beer, and a badly sprained ankle sustained in jumping over a wall. For Leachman the war seemed to be dragging to a tedious conclusion. But he was wrong. It was to burst into yet another spiteful, bloody episode.

Christmas week 1901 was spent on the veldt, marching from Edenburg to Jagersfontein, taking prisoners on the way and, after a field court martial, shooting one of them who wore the khaki uniform of a British Tommy. On to Fauresmith for Christmas Day, a 'ripping little town' full of fruits and good things, 'the only place I have come across where there is any loot'. Leachman helped himself to a set of pictures which adorned many a Victorian home: 'The Day of Reckoning', 'A Gambler's Wife', and so on.

He was at Vlakfontein when 1902 dawned under grey skies to the accompaniment of a new upsurge of Boer belligerence.

> I suppose you saw in the papers of the death of Colonel du Moulin. It was a dreadful thing. The Boers got right into our camp and we had a close shave of all being scuppered . . . We were woken up by the bullets coming all around us, firing at about thirty yards' range, and during the whole fight I was dressed in a pair of pyjamas and had no shoes on.

Eleven men of the Sussex regiment were killed and six wounded, figures which give some indication of the hand-to-hand nature of the night-time fight which took place at Abrahamskraal on 28 January. Leachman's brief description of the encounter was written at Vlakfontein, to which town the unit returned next day, a march of forty-five miles.

> My dearest mother,
> Oh we have done some trekking lately [he wrote on 13 January 1902]. We left our centre at Vlakfontein . . . on the 4th and we have been marching every night. We start at about 8 p.m. and march till midnight, have a couple of hours sleep and arrive at our destination at dawn. We then rest all day and go on again at night. It is mighty tiring, but I think it is the only way to do any good . . . We have come into the land of thunderstorms again; we have one regularly every night now, and as we have no tents it is a bit trying . . . Bye the bye I don't think I ever thanked father for the two boxes of cigars, and Mil and Jan [his unmarried sisters] for 'Lysbeth'. It is a ripping book. Also 'Kim'.

By now the British army had adopted the mobile guerrilla tactics of the Boers, forced into a pursuit of small bands of men who knew every inch of the country and were prepared to fight for possession of it, if necessary with their last drop of blood. Artillery was abandoned. It was too heavy to move quickly. And the strategic plan was scrapped along with the heavy gun. The horse and the ox-cart became, as they had been all along for the Boers, the chief instruments of the British army's last campaigns. The morality of the guerrilla-fighter drawn into necessary intimacy with a few like-minded companions, prepared to scrounge, loot and kill indiscriminately to survive, became the morality of bands of Britishers as they withdrew from the disciplines imposed by a high command on a conventional army. They found comfort in the companionship of men of their own kind and background. Snobbery, cruelty and contempt for life flourish easily when the constraints of military discipline are absent.

> Of course we never carry tents, as the only chance we have of catching Boers is by concealing our camps and making raids from them . . . we have a very weak column now. We have just sent away a draft of a hundred and forty men to India and a like number are being sent from India to join us. I think it is an excellent thing as a little new blood is wanted badly in the regiment . . . I see we have just had four gentlemen cadets appointed to us, we are all very pleased as they are generally a much better class of fellow than the militiamen. We have been having awfully good buck-shooting lately, there are hundreds of them about here and they are fairly tame and give us good shots.

He was made staff officer to Maj. Gilbert following the death of du Moulin and by late February his rough-and-ready column was attached to Driscoll's Scouts on a march north that was to provide ample scope for Leachman's fiery temperament and insatiable need for action.

From their camp at Boshof they made for the township of Hoopstad; a rag-tag army of vagabonds now, bereft of stores and supplies, living off the land, shooting first and asking questions after, tired, dirty and exhilarated. The country they passed through was swarming with Boers, usually organized into parties of some 200 men, elusive and willing to fight to the last ditch when forced into an engagement. Usually they preferred to scout the edges of the British columns which passed through their territory, picking off the Brits by sniper fire.

On 6 March Leachman's column rode all night and at dawn they bivouacked for a brief rest. Within minutes they were surrounded by the enemy. The Boers had followed them in the night and had taken up vantage points all round them. They occupied a ridge overlooking the British position. About 120 of Driscoll's Scouts and eighty Sussex men were detailed to attack the Boer vantage point. The ridge was nearly two miles long, with 200 men at one end, half that number at the other; the centre was unmanned.

The British force had about 800 yards to ride over open country. The Boers held their fire until the enemy was some 300 yards from the ridge. Then they let go, and Driscoll's men and the Sussex men, with Leachman very much to the fore and enjoying every moment, rode hell for leather through the fusilade to take the weaker force. But the hundred Boers on the right extremity melted away and the larger force on the left took the British in the rear. Strangely, the Boer tactic seems to have been to kill the horses rather than the men. At the end of a fierce battle in which the 'Dutchmen' were eventually driven off, the ridge was littered with dead animals. Only one of the British force was killed and six seriously wounded. Boer casualties were heavy. But the ridge was occupied and Leachman was able to report that at the end of the day his men and the Scouts had taken up 'a strong position'. Losses were 'marvellously small' considering the intensity of the fire.

Other excitements lay in wait as the force made its way north. It rained incessantly. 'I don't mind if I am wet or dry, as one never feels any ill effects,' he wrote. He was back to full fitness and having the time of his life. Unshaven, unbathed, their uniforms in tatters, some of the men wearing stolen civilian clothes, stealing chickens and pigs as they went, the force was united in the adversity of terrain and weather and the elation of battle.

His detachment decided to raid the deserted township of Fauresmith on their way to the river Vaal where de la Rey with a big force of infantry and guns was trying to cross to join up with the indomitable de Wet. They entered the silent, empty town at 2 a.m., hoping to find a few of the enemy taking temporary refuge in its deserted houses. A small band with Leachman at its head was sent in to search. The first house provided expectation of a good bag. A trooper came out to report breathlessly that a man was asleep in one of the bedrooms. Leachman and three of the men crept into the house and sure enough found a body wrapped in a blanket on the floor.

'Hands up.' At the peremptory demand the figure jumped up and knocked one of the Englishmen to the floor. Leachman and his companions dived at the massive 'Boer' and tried to overpower him but he was too strong for them. They had disturbed a baboon which had decided to take a nap in the unexpected shelter it had found at Fauresmith.

By 19 March they were at camp on the bank of the Vaal. For the moment the high jinks of guerrilla war were over and Leachman's detachment and the Scouts were merged into a force of 20,000 men whose task was to encircle the great Boer leader de la Rey who was making a last desperate bid to break out of the northern Transvaal, cross the river and join de Wet. Leachman's column was now under Col. Rochefort's command and they moved north with the main army on 23 March. Another long, relentless march; more prisoners taken; more excesses on both sides; men and horses tested to the last dregs of courage and resourcefulness. But the British in months of indiscriminate and undisciplined warfare had learnt the lessons of mobility. The Boers no longer enjoyed their early advantage of hit-and-run strategy. They escaped the British trap but were unable to break through in sufficient force to join de Wet's army.

Leachman's column returned to its base at Commando Drift. He was sent to join another column under the command of Gen. Western and offered a staff job as Provost-Marshal. 'I jumped at it.' The thousand-strong force was about to cross the Vaal – thirty-six hours hard work taking wagons and men across on rafts – and to march into the Transvaal.

On 20 April Leachman gave his family an account of his whereabouts: he was at Bloemhof. 'If you want to find it on the map, you should follow the Vaal west from Bothaville and you will find it about thirty miles west of Hoopstad.'

Another, more attractive side of his belligerent nature became apparent in his letters at this time. Lessons learnt in the hardest school of all, the front line, were beginning to erase some of the thoughtless assumptions of youth. The imperious character of the man was softened by a respect for a brave and courageous enemy, and an amiable regard for the men around him.

I have just handed over my prisoners . . . They were a very

decent lot of fellows and, as many of them spoke English, I heard a lot of good yarns. The most interesting of them was an adjutant of de Wet, who had been through the whole show. He told me a lot of good stories about how de Wet used to get out when we had cornered him.

There was evidence, too, of his taste for the fight in which he had accumulated wounds and mentions in despatches over two hard years in the field. 'There seems to be a lot of talk about peace now. I hope they go on to the bitter end instead of stopping. It will look much better, because in years to come people will say that we had to make peace.'

There were a few more 'spirited little engagements'. But the young Leachman's plea for total victory was not to be answered. 'It seems quite strange to see the Boers riding in with white flags,' he wrote, and added: 'I can tell you that after their games with white flags we don't trust them further than we can see them.'

The final drive against de la Rey began on 7 May. By the 11th Leachman was at Vryburg in Bechuanaland.

We left Bloemhof on the night of the 7th, and the southern columns were in position at dawn on the 8th. We then moved forward westward and got into touch with the northern columns on the night of the 9th. Then the whole line of about seventy miles moved toward the Kimberley–Mafeking railway line . . . Up here they are betting ten to one on peace by May 15. It will be odd if they do arrange it.

Peace came, in fact, on Sunday 1 June: a divisive peace in which two nationalities which laid claim to the rich lands at the southern tip of Africa were left to go their separate ways.

Many a soldier had found his baptism in a bitter and inconclusive struggle, not the least of them Lieut Gerard Evelyn Leachman. He had learnt to live with other men of many nationalities and to know that magnanimity in victory was as attractive a quality as valour in the battle. 'I expect I shall have tons of work in a few days, as when the Boers begin to come in they will all be shoved under my charge and I am sure it will be hard work preventing them from being robbed.'

He had been awarded the Queen's medal and four clasps and recommended for the DSO, but he was deemed too young for the latter award.

In the peace he had dreaded because of the humdrum life it would take him back to, he discovered some of the sports and team activities that had escaped him in school and cadet years. He began to play polo and found that he was 'quite good' at it. He played football on the veldt and golf on an improvised course. But he still sought the irresistible balm of military action. He decided not to return home on leave after nearly two-and-a-half years of war, but to proceed with his regiment to India. His Colonel ordered him home, however, and he left Cape Town aboard *SS Bavaria* bound for England on 18 August 1902. He was yet too close to the events of the fight to endorse the verdict of the high-priest of Empire, Rudyard Kipling: 'Let us admit it fairly, as business people should, We have had no end of a lesson; it will do us no end of good.'

It is doubtful whether Leachman would ever have it in his make-up to share such an epitaph. Neither for himself nor for his country could he conceive anything short of victory.

In the friendships he had made among both junior and senior officers who had come to know and respect his hard, combative spirit, he had become *Gerald* Leachman. Henceforth his correct first name was seldom used except by his family.[1]

4

The Raj

Home leave was but a lull in the new tempo of life. Leachman had changed beyond recognition in the two years of war in South Africa. The brooding countenance, the withdrawn manner, had become infused with vitality. Sudden bursts of temper, long silences, the impulsive response to injury, real and often imagined, were part of the man still, as they had been characteristic of the boy. But conversational wit, a new-found ability to make friendships and a capacity to enjoy the simple pleasures and frolics of youth had intervened. It was a very different son whom the family at Petersfield welcomed home in the autumn of 1902.

Riding, shooting and hunting were his favourite pastimes – his brother-in-law Bernard Parham was a comfortable yeoman farmer and he spent much of his time with him and his sister Mabel at their home in Wiltshire. He was even said to have become an accomplished ballroom dancer. At home music was still the dominant activity of father and friends, and they found an unwelcome accompanist in sister Janet's collie dog which Gerard had mentioned in his letter from Charterhouse in 1894. She had proved a musical bitch and whenever piano or ensemble struck up she would hide under a convenient piece of furniture and howl in chorus, always off-key, to the annoyance of Albert Leachman.

In the sudden burst of social life which came with his first real leave, the house in the Hampshire countryside was filled with young couples, and with friends encountered in the South African wild and in the turmoil of camp life. But there is no evidence of girlfriends. People who came close to Leachman in later years sometimes thought he was awkward with women. The opposite was the truth. Like many sons brought up as the younger child among a regiment of sisters, he was perfectly at ease with them; nonchalant perhaps. Women held little mystery for him.

It was not easy for young men of ambition and modest means to settle down after the Boer War, to embrace the comforts and quiescence of English middle-class life after the years of conflict. For the army officer at the start of his career it was India that beckoned, the empire within an Empire, its own army and administration governing huge chunks of Asia, offering almost limitless opportunities to men who were willing to sacrifice home and family life for service of King and country; and to pay their own way.

Leachman joined the 1st Battalion of his regiment at Sitapur in Bengal in January 1903. Christmas Day 1902 had been spent aboard ship with plenty to drink and 'quite a nice dance'. Bombay he thought 'a wonderful place', and the 'ghary wallahs beat a London cabby hollow'.

On 15 January he wrote from Sitapur:

I have had a week of it . . . I have started a *moonshi* to teach me Hindustani. I have him for an hour every day and I hope to go up for my lower standard Hindustani in April . . . Nearly all the other subalterns are going up to the hills next week for two months, for a course of instruction in military subjects, but as I was at Sandhurst I don't have to go, thank goodness.

Sport, learning, the social life of the mess; activities and precepts which had so far escaped him came flooding in and he began to embrace them with typical zest. 'I played golf today for the first time . . . there are quite good tennis courts here and I have played several times! . . . tomorrow we are going shooting', a pastime of which he knew a great deal. 'The new Colonel is a ripping chap . . . always laughing and joking . . . send me books which are hard to get here . . . I played hockey the other day and had a tremendously fast game.'

The discomforts as well as the new-found joys of life came to the surface in Sitapur. 'I am having a row with my landlord, and have refused to pay him any rent until he makes certain repairs . . . the jackals sit under one's window at night and make a most fiendish noise and the rats eat the candles off the table by the side of one's bed.' And rumblings of financial unease: 'One can get nothing in this country without paying for it.'

The young officer in India was perpetually hard up unless his parents were singularly well-off. 'I wish they would be quick and make me a lieutenant; I can't think why they are taking so long. Several officers have joined us lately and they all have to pay their own passages out.'

He was preceded to the sub-continent by his Commander-in-Chief from the South African War. Kitchener, who had taken the place of the kindly 'Bobs' and substituted fear on both sides for the cautious methods which Lord Roberts practised, had returned home to a hero's welcome. It was the second such welcome in three years, for the echoing praises for the victor of Omdurman had hardly died away before he was called to South Africa to bring ruthless method and iron resolve to a command which had become weakened by Roberts's illness. Yet when the fighting eventually came to an end Kitchener brought goodwill to the peace talks, while Milner remained, as he had been from the outset, tough and obdurate with the Boers. And it was Kitchener who returned to a land decorated with flags, to banquets and street parties, to the adulation of the people and the rewards of a grateful King and Parliament: the Order of Merit, rank of full General, a viscountcy and a pension. He was just fifty years old. If the young Liberal politician Lloyd George had compared the nation's hero with Herod, his was a lonely voice. To most men, Kitchener had yet again struck an imperial note when all seemed to be going against Britain. With such men in charge the sun would surely not set on the British Empire. With Cromer in Egypt, Curzon in India and Kitchener ever ready when danger threatened, would any nation be foolish enough to challenge the place and power of Britain in the world?

Curzon had been Viceroy of India for three years when the Boer War ended. That most urbane of politicians and pro-consuls, the high intellectual of a party which instinctively mistrusted intellectuals, had become the youngest of Viceroys under Salisbury's stewardship. By 1902 Balfour was Prime Minister and the Liberal threat which Gladstone's Home Rule for Ireland policy had posed by implication to the rest of the Empire was held temporarily at bay.

Kitchener was the man Curzon wanted to organize the Indian army which was then under the benign command of Gen. Sir Arthur Power Palmer. The victor of Omdurman and the Transvaal, the sirdar who had transformed the Egyptian army, would surely make the Indian army into an instrument worthy of the eastern empire it protected. But military reputations are seldom reliable. The senior officers who knew Kitchener at close quarters, in Egypt and South Africa, loathed him. The public, the junior officers of the army and other ranks who knew nothing of the private man, of his secretiveness (which was probably due to a natural shyness), of his slow, plodding, taciturn style of leadership and his dislike of socializing, saw only the public image, dynamic and unyielding. Curzon made a mistake which was to be his own undoing. The two men fought from the outset over the matter of the Viceroy's right to a say in the conduct of military affairs through the military member of his Council. As Commander-in-Chief of the Indian army Kitchener would brook no interference, and used his friend Lady Cranbourne, Balfour's cousin who had married into the Cecils, as his sounding-board.

The private war of the giants may seem remote from the life of a young subaltern about to make his first contact with India, but it was very relevant to the future of Leachman and the hundreds of men like him who sought an outlet for their patriotism in the beckoning spaces of the Viceroy's diocese. By early 1903 when Leachman stepped ashore at Bombay, the row between the Viceroy and the C-in-C was the favourite subject of club gossip. Leachman, like the rest of the army except the most senior officers who worked with the chief at Fort William in Calcutta and at summer HQ in Simla, sided with Kitchener.

The passage to India had been ill timed. Leachman not only missed the Christmas festivities with his family, but the great event of the new century in India itself, the Delhi Durbar at which Curzon represented King Edward VII in his role as Emperor, took place while he was at sea. But tales of the vast assembly on the Delhi Plain awaited him and he was soon in the thick of the rumour and back-biting which came in the wake of that event, where the troops had refused to cheer the Viceroy though they gave their applause to the C-in-C. One of his first letters from the hill station of Ranikhet near the Tibetan border to which his regiment moved, gave the army view of the dispute: 'Kitchener is very quiet and subdued here at present, I think George Nathaniel, as everyone calls Curzon, sits on him in the same way as he does all the army. Every one is praying for the time when he will give up being Viceroy; he is very unpopular.'

Politics were of no more than passing interest to subalterns in India in the first years of the twentieth century. Polo was now Leachman's passion and he quickly became a passable player of that difficult game. He decided to approach his father for an advance on his next half-yearly allowance in order to buy a pony. By March he was on his way to Lucknow for a transport course, complete with polo pony, where his skill as a horseman ensured his instant acceptance into the officers' mess of the Gloucester Regiment.

Several Sandhurst and South African acquaintanceships blossomed into friendship in Lucknow. And he began to come to close quarters with the native Indian, viewing the ordinary people around him with that odd mixture of admiration and patronizing scorn which reflected his age and class: 'I am getting into the ways of the natives by degrees, and I can't say that I like them any better. At least the ordinary run of natives: of course the native regiments are awfully fine, especially the infantry. What I object to is the way they are always trying to get the better of one.'

He had completed his course by May and returned to his regiment in the foothills of the Himalayas, where he and most of the British were afflicted with strange stomach disorders. 'This place is very unhealthy,' he wrote in June, 'there are such a lot of smells everywhere.' There was an outbreak of cholera higher up at Naini Tal. Everyone was 'dashing down to the plains'. It was a fortunate pestilence as far as Leachman was concerned, for it brought to his remote station a young woman who was to be the first and only love of his life; the one girl who could turn his mind from military ambition and from distant visions of adventure, to thoughts of marriage and a settled existence in India, or perhaps even at home in England. Their meeting at this time was casual and promised nothing more than a pleasant friendship.

Other personal matters occupied him at the time of her appearance. While home on leave he had begun his inititation

36

into Freemasonry and there was a lodge at the remote outpost of Ranikhet where he was able to complete his 'degree'. Being 'on the square' was not essential to the progress of an officer of the army in India, but it helped to form useful friendships and high-level contacts. Kitchener was the luminary of the masonic fraternity of India from the moment of his arrival; District Grand Master of all the Punjab lodges, and a name to conjure with even among the grandiloquent figures of Indian Freemasonry: the Duke of Connaught and his successor as Governor of Bombay, Lord Northcote; Lord Ampthill, Governor of Madras and District Grand Master; Lord Sandhurst, a Governor of Bombay too and Grand Master of all Scottish Freemasonry in India; and the Maharajah of Cooch Behar. Almost alone among the dignitaries of British India at that time, the Viceroy was not of the brotherhood.

Even the countryside, something which Leachman like most people with a rural upbringing took for granted in the ordinary course of events, acquired a purple glow. 'I can't describe the hills, but all I can say is that they're simply perfect,' he told his mother in May. And he reassured her on a matter about which she had made discreet enquiry: 'Bye the bye, in case you are frightened about me, I will let you know at once if I get engaged to anyone!'

He was due to leave for a musketry course at Pachmari in August. And already he was planning a journey that was strictly forbidden by the powers of the day, as soon as he could get away on leave – a journey into Tibet. Even the glacier peaks which framed the skyline of his regimental camp north-west of Nepal had begun to infect him with the wanderlust, the urge to seek adventure and danger that was to determine the rest of his life. Only the girl in Naini Tal a few miles to the south stopped him in his tracks.

Just before he was due to leave for Pachmari he was struck down by a mysterious illness. 'I found that I could not move my left leg at all but I thought it had only gone to sleep; however, it got worse and worse and finally the left leg was numb up to the hip and the right leg as far as the knee.'

After three weeks the strange malady was no better. He was unable to move either leg. The regimental MO thought it was probably 'neuritis'. Perhaps it was something to do with the girl at Naini Tal, in quarantine while the cholera still raged in the towns and villages around.

It was a worrying time to be sick in India. The great plague epidemic which broke out at the turn of the old century had hardly died out when Leachman arrived. Cholera was rife and 'cholera-camp' the common chore of the army unit. Fevers, from which Leachman like most of his colleagues suffered frequently, and sudden attacks of paralysis were perplexing to his physician father who received from his son alarmingly graphic accounts and very little accurate detail. Dr Leachman had problems of his own, however, and in July his son had written a note of sympathetic appreciation and somewhat ingratiating loyalty.

> I was sorry to see that you did not get in for the Urban District Council, but I think you did very well considering that you did not canvass at all. Of course it is a sign of what modern Petersfield is when they elect a man like B——. The one thing I do object to is when he says that 'Dr Leachman is a man of honour'; no one asked him to give his opinion on the state of your honour. Beastly cheek I call it.

The rather clumsy attempt to placate his father was not as naïve as a casual reading suggests. He expected at the time to be moving down to Pachmari and the expense of his stable and his polo pony had left him short, so that he needed to touch the doctor for yet another advance. Praise, even by oblique condemnation of the opponent, might soften the ground.

In September he was still hobbling. His Hindustani examination, compulsory among officers of the British regiments, was coming up and he worked for it, much against his will, while the other officers went on a hunting expedition.

Leachman and those like him who went to India without a colonial background were at a disadvantage compared with the majority of officers in the Indian army itself, most of whom came from families of long standing in India and had grown up with native servants. They could usually speak Hindi, Pushtu or Urdu as infants, mastering alien sounds with the ease of childhood, and usually other Oriental languges came with facility. For the adult Englishman with no experience of such languages, learning was a hard slog. Leachman passed his exam all the same, with indifferent marks, and he began to make himself understood with the few peremptory words he needed.

In October the regiment was due to leave the high, cold station of Ranikhet. He still found it hard to stand up, but he prepared to move with his men on horseback. He made the best of his last few days at the camp. 'We always sit at night in front of a big fire and drink hot grog.' He complained only of Curzon who arrived in the district on a viceregal hunting expedition and had all roads closed for his magisterial passage. But the mighty Curzon was nothing like as unapproachable or dog-in-the-manger as Leachman imagined. Probably because of his still frail health he was given the soft option of commanding the guard at the Viceroy's hunting lodge, and he was invited to dinner by George Nathaniel: 'He was most affable and talked away a lot; he does nothing but ask questions . . . After dinner, which lasted about two and a half hours, he went straight back to work with his secretary and was up at six the next morning, so he can't get much sleep.'

The last night at Ranikhet was celebrated by a fancy-dress ball at the English Club which he saw through to the end though he had to leave at four in the morning, in charge of transport. It was a five-day march through the hills of the northern part of the United Provinces to Kathgodam, where the regiment entrained for the journey south to Sitapur and the cosmopolitan pleasures of Lucknow. He had been nearly a year in the cold and strangely beautiful hill country of the north and though he had spent much of his time in the agony of strange, undiagnosed illness, he soon longed to be back. Gen. Barrow, an important officer of the Indian army who was to become military secretary to the India Office in London, had left for home leave as the Sussex Regiment made its way southward. And Barrow's family were old friends of Leachman's mother and her family. He wrote home urgently to ask his mother to pull a few wires. 'You just see him, and see if you can't get something out of him for me, because he's a bit of a power in the land out here.' But there was no need of wire-pulling. The enterprising Col. Skinner, 'the best shot in India', had taken over command of the regiment. And the post of station officer at Naini Tal became vacant. Meanwhile polo and a little golf, and a good tip at the Lucknow races, kept him occupied and contented.

A signalling course at Kasauli came up in the new year. The Colonel had turned out to be 'a perfect ripper'. He was, wrote

Leachman in early January 1904, 'as keen as mustard on every-thing, and doesn't care a bit about the people who play up to him'. It was a fair assessment of Skinner and showed something of Leachman's dislike of men who toadied to superiors. It showed too the artless judgements of the time. Everyone was either a 'ripper' or a 'rotter' in the days when the last Conservative Government to rule in Britain for nearly two dec-ades came to the end of its tether in London, and the last of the great men of Empire saw out their reigns in India and Egypt. In-between men, ordinarily good or indifferent men did not seem to exist in the annals of that in-between time.

Kasauli was four months off when Leachman greeted the year 1904 by falling off a bicycle in a rainstorm at night time and injuring one of his still partly lame legs. A few days later he fell off his pony over the jumps and nearly broke his neck, but in fact sustaining nothing worse than a bruised spine, a black eye and lacerated nose. Made for the life of the open spaces, for adventure where neither doctor nor law-maker would interrupt the course of natural hazard, he had undergone a formidable training by the time he reached his mid twenties. One of the young men of the Indian army who met him at Ambala, Lieut Arnold Wilson of the 32nd Sikh Pioneers, formed an impression of unusual powers of leadership and predicted great things.

Wilson spoke in passing of the need for gentlemanly behaviour on the part of officers, and Leachman told him in words that he was to remember in times of adversity: 'Gentlemen know how to behave, but they must sometimes be taught how to misbehave.'

Wilson, who was destined for high office in the East and was to become the historian of the Persian Gulf, found in Gibbon an apt description of the impulsive Leachman, 'a lion in battle, a lamb in society, and an angel in council'. And in later years he wrote:

> He took to soldiering very seriously (South Africa had left its mark on him in more ways than one); he was seldom seen in the Club, social events left him cold; but wherever he was – in mess or in the field – he was a leader who would not always have been on the side of the angels but for his very strong sense of discipline. He was a martinet on parade, and all his life had very clear-cut ideas of what was and was not right and proper for young officers to do and say in the presence of their elders.

The regiment went back to the hills beyond Delhi, passing through Naini Tal, but Leachman had to remain behind to nurse his wounds and get on with signalling practice. When he eventually arrived at Kasauli in April he did well in his exams, coming first among the trainee signallers. Here was something he could bite on; no abstract theory, but method and technique. For the first time in his life he was top of the class. At the end of the course there was the usual social whirl – wild parties, dances and picnics. But he was not in the mood for fun without the partner who waited for him at Naini Tal. 'The natives always think the sahibs have gone mad on these occasions, and I don't wonder.'

The hill station appointment had been kept open while he attended his signalling course. The regiment went off to Rawalpindi and a three-month stint on the North-West Frontier. He went off in June, joyously, to Naini Tal where he was to spend the last truly happy year of his life.

5

Playing the Game

Gen. Gaselee was in command of the important hill station to which Leachman was posted. The garrison was small and social life was pleasantly informal. They dressed for dinner of course; an irksome habit for a man like Leachman whose dress whenever he could contrive it was an open-necked shirt and riding breeches, and whose favourite toilet was a swim in the river. But servants were plentiful in imperial India and there was always a newly pressed dress uniform ready for the wearer and a minion to help button and buckle it. Even for a lieutenant, service in India offered lordly compensations for the occasional hardships of military life.

For twelve idyllic months Leachman led the gentlemanly life of the remote hill station. Except in the short winter months its gardens and verandahed colonial homes were bathed in a warm sunlight and the air was scented by a host of roses. Shade, when shade was needed, was provided by pomegranate trees and the cheerful orange trees which descended from the well-watered gardens given to northern India and Kashmir by far-seeing Mogul emperors 600 years before. Distant peaks, snow-clad and majestic, were the backcloth of an enchanted world.

Each day was spent close to the girl he had seen at all-too-brief intervals in the past year, with whom he had corresponded affectionately, and who was now his constant companion.

Letters home in the summer of 1904 reflected a life of almost unalloyed pleasure in the populous hill station of Naini Tal. 'I row for an hour every morning before breakfast, and play polo in the afternoon and generally hockey or football afterwards . . . I am still everlastingly dining out . . . in fact, I never dine at the club.'

A month later: 'How do you think I shall look in an eau de nil coat?' His parents had been to Bayreuth: 'I hope father hasn't been flirting with any of the performers.' In October: 'I have been doing quite a lot of Freemasonry lately, and I am taking some of the other degrees.'

His mother wanted him to send a photograph, which was as good an opportunity as any to betray his poverty. 'I really haven't the money to get photographed, but if I can get somebody to give me tick I will see what I can do.'

Christmas came and went and he thanked the family for their presents; '. . . also thank you *very much* for the cheque, which is especially useful just now, as my tailor has gone bankrupt, and they have called in all his debts.' Only the slothful progress of army promotion cast a spell over an otherwise cloudless life. 'I don't see any prospect of being a Captain before I am grey headed.'

But another cloud loomed. The cold weather had sent all the civil servants and big-wigs scurrying from the hill station, and with them went his girl. He had said nothing specific about her in his letters so far; only hinted at her in his undulating moods of joy and remorse. But mother could read between the lines. 'It really is rather miserable in Naini just now and I am a little fed up.' A friend of the family, Winny Jones, had been out to India and paid him a call. 'What is Winny Jones so full of about me? Hope she isn't telling yarns!'

By March 1905 he was beginning to talk of globetrotting, and wondered if his father might not take a holiday in India. In April he was virtually the only available officer when the C-in-C called at his outpost in the United Province. 'Had to go all the way down to Kathgodam to meet Kitchener, I gave him lunch and went with him the twelve miles to the foot of Naini Tal hill, then he went on to Ranikhet. He was most affable, but is most awfully lame, he really can only just walk.' Things were looking up. The civil service was coming back for the summer. 'Our first dance is on Wednesday.'

Then came the revelation. On 25 May he wrote home: 'My

dear mother, Oh such a life we are leading. I have been making an effort to lead the quiet life, but alas! it is hopeless.'

The reason for the new note of exhilaration:

> Would you like me to marry an American with an accent you can cut with a knife? Everyone here thinks I am rather far gone, but I don't think so. Might do worse, you know, she is a niece of the Lieut-Governor's. If I write and say I am not going on leave, you will know it is a bad sign.

Mrs Leachman's response to an almost jocular question is not known. It was probably guarded. And there must have been other letters which told her more of the young lady in her son's life, but if so they have not survived. Philby in his unpublished biography was guarded in a most uncharacteristic way: 'It was on June 10th that, having lunched, presumably at Naini Tal, at the house "where the only girl I ever loved lives" . . .' (no further clue being given to the identity of the lady except the name of his host and hostess who shall remain nameless).

Bray was childishly coy about the matter:

> She *was* the only girl he ever loved and he lost her – not through any fault of his own, nor because their union would have been unsuitable in any way, but on account of one of those family misunderstandings which arise in spite of the good intentions of all concerned. It would ill serve the memory of Leachman to go deeper into the subject. There was no mystery about it – the facts were exactly as stated, no more and no less. Perhaps if Leachman had been less reticent in the days of his childhood, or more demonstrative, the bitter hurt would never have been inflicted.

It cannot be said that Bray or Philby did anything to lift the veil of mystery. Leachman never confided in Philby, but he did in Bray. Perhaps the latter's humbug provided a clue at least to what went wrong. 'Family misunderstanding'. Certainly Leachman gave his parents little information about the girl apart from skittish observations as to her nationality and accent. But his letters home do not suggest a gulf of hypocrisy between parents and son. He even alluded at times to his father's eye for a pretty woman in the musical world that he inhabited. Yet hypocrisy was deeply embedded in the Victorian and Edwardian social scene and it may be that Dr Leachman and his wife were horrified at the designation 'American' and the suggestion that her accent could be 'cut with a knife'. It is possible that they merely discouraged Gerard on financial grounds, for they were not vastly rich and their son was in constant need of money even in his single state.

Whatever happened to dash Leachman's hope of marriage at this time, it was surely not an ordinary matter of snobbery or class obsession, for the vivacious and attractive girl of Naini Tal whose name everyone involved seemed determined to hide, was Frederica Rothwell, the favourite niece of the Lt-Governor of the United Province, the Hon. Sir James Digges La Touche, and his wife Julia. Sir James was a charming and unaffected Irishman. Lady La Touche, who came from Bath in England, was devoted to her niece, the daughter of her elder brother Harry Rothwell who had emigrated to America in the 1880s and had become an American citizen. The La Touches were represented in many branches of the Indian administration from the civil service to the police force. Sir James's brother was engineering consultant to the Viceroy's Government. And the La Touches liked their young station officer, Lieut Leachman. Whatever it was that brought about the separation of the couple in the ensuing few months of 1905 it could hardly have been social disapproval. In any case Bray and Philby were wrong in believing that the couple parted for good in June 1905. They were still planning a future together. Leachman's posting to Naini Tal enabled him to enjoy the best of all possible worlds, and the gods smiled on him and the girl he inevitably came to know as 'Freddie' in the summer of that year. Leachman prepared for his first journey of exploration in June: an unapproved journey to the forbidden region of Tibet. And all was well at Naini Tal.

On Friday, 9 June he lunched at the Governor's residence, and went off happily to collect his caravan after bidding her a fond farewell, in strict defiance of the injunction of the Foreign Department at Simla that no such unauthorized journeys should be attempted.

He picked up his own pony at the village of Khairna and trotted north to Ranikhet for dinner with old pals at the garrison mess. On Sunday 11 June he set out on a hired pony, leaving his own in the care of his friend Lieut Greenwood who came from his home town of Petersfield. He had sent his baggage and kit on by coolie train to Lohba, a staging-post in the magnificent mountain country on his route.

From now on he and his pony had to take the strain in turns. The terrain was too difficult in parts for the pony to negotiate with a rider on its back. They staggered up steep inclines and down almost vertical descents; across frightening precipices. They were marching at a speed of nearly forty miles a day, sometimes covering fifteen miles on foot, the coolie train bringing up the rear. He bathed in the ice-cold mountain water of the Alah Namla river, sweltered in Karnaprayag and dined on chapatis, rice and dates.

At Narnpryag he wrote: 'slept in open as I could find no place level enough to pitch a tent'. Pipalkoti and Gulabkote were 'nice and cool'. At Satopanth, where he met a district surveyor at camp, and the fickle climate of the mountain regions began to play up as he marched north-east, it was 'rain and wind'; Serai Tota was 'very windy'. He had been going a week when he reached Juma, in sight of the mountain of Dunagiri rising to 22,000 feet on the white horizon. On Monday 19 June he was at the village of Martoli where he found a tent and an extra servant left behind by a shooting expedition from the King's Own Regiment.

Leachman was now at the forbidden crossroads of Asia. Younghusband's expedition had been to Tibet the year before and Candler's *Unveiling of Lhasa* had just been published to the joy of Britishers at home who saw in the deeds of intrepid young officers on the world's rooftop the highest manifestation of the spirit of empire.

Kim's men who went north, east and west through rugged passes and over high mountains to defy their Russian, French, German and Chinese counterparts, usually to arrive first, always to uphold the pre-eminent position of Britain in the remotest and most dangerous corners of the world – such men were the stuff of heroic fiction and of the most admirable patriotism.

To the army, however, and the Government of India, they had become an embarrassment. If India and its Viceroy looked with a jaundiced eye on the new alignments between the European powers which created the Anglo-French *entente* and gave rise to a new understanding with Russia over the long-disputed division of influence between the world's two great empires in Persia and central Asia, it remained a fact that there was a new balance of power. British and Russian intelligence officers would no longer compete for precedence in the great empty spaces of Asia and among the wild tribesmen and gurus and *ulemas* and princes of the East. Germany had become the competitor and old enemies who had pursued each other in the Gobi desert and across the steppes of trans-Caspia, over the Pamirs and beyond the Himalayas, would have to unite to confront a common danger. Kim and his like, pukka sahibs who had played their own game, the Great Game, would have to toe a line drawn by Whitehall and sanctioned by Kitchener, for the moment at least.

The country which Leachman prepared to enter without higher authority was a closed domain, ruled by a distant Chinese suzerain, though the Dalai Lama preserved his religious authority in his Lhasa stronghold. Some forty years before the Indian survey department had begun to map the region using agents trained at the secret service centre of Dehra Dun. Led by the agent 'A-K', Pandit Nain Singh, they followed the route which Leachman now took from India into the forbidden land, armed with wooden boxes with secret drawers containing their survey instruments, each with a prayer-wheel in which blank paper for making notes was substituted for the prayer-sheets, and a rosary for counting distances, one bead representing a hundred paces. Thus was the map of Tibet drawn up by the Survey of India.

Since then a procession of British and Russian travellers had entered and skirted Tibet, seeking to open trade routes, to subvert local chieftains, even to gain the support of the Dalai Lama for their various schemes. In 1903 news reached Simla that Russian arms had been imported into Lhasa and that Russia was about to take over the suzerainty of the country. Curzon sent the great explorer and intelligence agent Col. Francis Younghusband to investigate and a year later that soldier-mystic returned with an army led by Gen. Macdonald to subdue the Tibetans and warn the Russians. The Dalai Lama was forced to leave his capital and his countrymen ordered to pay an indemnity of £500,000 to Britain. A treaty was signed in which Britain insisted on Tibet's adhesion to China.[1]

Since that punitive expedition, the tempting territory which lay to the north-east of India with its highlands and snow-capped peaks and its vast game herds was forbidden to the men of the

Indian army and the British regiments, except with the formal approval of the War Office.[2] Such regulations were there to be observed in the breach by men like Leachman, with some of the finest and rarest game in the world roaming its hillsides and valleys unmolested. He would be among the last of the gentlemen invaders.

On 17 June 1905 Leachman stopped on the road to write a note to his mother:

> I am having a really hairy time. I should like you to see this place (Taboban in Garhwal), between 11,000 and 12,000 ft and snow all round. I only left Naini on the 10th and have done the 160-odd miles in eight days over most poisonous roads and in terrific heat. I have been travelling up the great Hindu pilgrim route, which goes to Badrimath where the Ganges rises.

He picked up his guide for the Tibetan journey at a village on the road to the Niti Pass, and men were sent to test out the route. They found it 'awful' and so they chose the Darma Pass to the south. The guide, Jai Singh, got very drunk on his first day and Leachman administered the punishment that he always meted out to servants who took to the bottle. He knocked him down, and took on a new *shikari*, Mukhan Singh. A team of yaks took over from the horses from here on; only they could negotiate the rock-strewn snow-covered terrain and the frightening ledges which led by a single false step to oblivion. On the first day out a yak fell from a path and broke its horn. And Mazir, Leachman's cook, became fevered and they were held up while he was fed with Bovril.

Leachman pencilled in the closely written text of his diary (kept on five sheets of scrap paper): 'Hard, bad day after bitter cold night [it was 15,000 feet]. It froze hard. Started at 5 a.m. for the Darma Pass – breath soon began to get a bit difficult . . .'

From here he could look along the pass to Tibet; at last put the initiative and skills learnt on the battlefield and at training camp to the test in 'a dam-tight place' or two, as Babu Hurree Chunder Mookerjee might have said, and perhaps cause the QMG's Department to sit up and take notice.

Burrel, 'a goatish animal of sorts', provided the first meal in

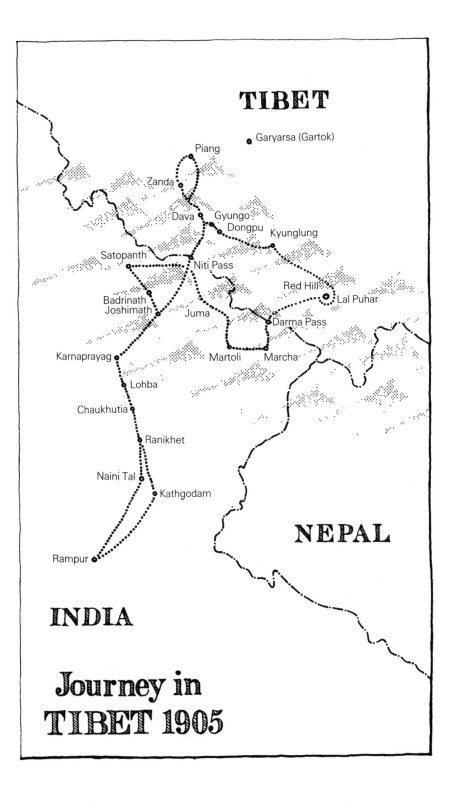

the Dalai Lama's kingdom. They left their first Tibetan camp at 4.30 a.m. on Saturday the 24th. By the afternoon snow was too thick to permit more burrel hunting. One of the coolies had to be given brandy to revive him after collapsing from cold. By mid-week they were at Lal Puhar, the Red Hill, renowned for the game in its vicinity, especially the wild sheep *ovis ammon*, a relative of Marco Polo's *ovis poli*. Tibetans were at camp near by and Leachman found the women 'quite handsome' and the men indolent, slouching 'like British labourers'. Wild duck added to the compensatory pleasures of Lal Puhar, and it was followed at the table by large and succulent hares.

The hunting was too good to allow a hurried departure. Leachman remained in the region of the Red Hill for nearly a week, moving off reluctantly towards Dongpu on Tuesday 4 July. They met an old man riding a yak to Kyunglung, turning a prayer-wheel for all he was worth as he made his way.

'Have run out of tinned milk, which is a nuisance as I can't have porridge now.' The expert traveller does not neglect his stomach if he is to survive the hazards of long journeys in strange lands and in foreign climates. Leachman needed no instruction in the art of survival.

They reached Dongpu after a day's travel and found a derelict fort, five old crones and a dog waiting to greet them. The devout old man on the yak had come and gone. Leachman was carried across the river by one of his *shikari* and they marched on to Gyangal. Snow and rain had given place to hot sunshine. They were joined by the brother of the chief *shikari* Mukhan Singh and his son: 'such a nice-looking boy'. More of Mukhan Singh's relations joined them as they went until almost the entire family was in train, including a villainous-looking brother-in-law.

Leachman was having bad nights. He was kept awake by thoughts of Naini Tal, and was exhausted by the niggardly air, for they travelled now at over 18,000 feet. And the yells and screeches of nocturnal creatures were magnified by his remorse. He wondered if something 'heavy' to eat at night would help him sleep and taught his cook Wazir to make beefsteak pudding and 'spotted dog'. He enjoyed the meal but his night was sleepless.

By Saturday 8 July they had reached the town of Dava which no European had visited for as long as any inhabitant could remember, and an old sepoy discharged from the 39th Garhwalis embraced the English officer who had come so far. The British trade agent at Gartok came to see him and asked him to take some 'despatches' to the Foreign Office at Simla. Contact with the 'news' and 'trade' agents strung across the world and feeding Britain's secret service with scraps of information which others fitted into a splendid mosaic, began for Leachman in the Tibetan wilds. He would have much to do with such men in the years to follow. They went on and up to Zanda.

By 9 July the caravan was on the road which led back to the Niti Pass. Mukhan Singh had taken himself off to meet old friends in Dava and he returned to camp a little drunk. 'Will have to give him what for tomorrow,' wrote Leachman before going to bed. His concern for the habits of servants was at times neurotic, though in this case it was informed concern, for the effects of alcohol on native peoples could be a cumulative tragedy as he had seen in South Africa and was to see again in India and elsewhere.

Snow greeted their return to India, still at a height of 17,000 ft, and a last camp at Patalpari where breakfast next day consisted of one small pigeon that had come too close. They were at Rampur on Sunday 16 July where Leachman paid off his yak-men and other helpers; 140 rupees for twenty-six days. A report of his arrival was sent to the Commissioner at Rampur. He returned to his post at Naini Tal and waited for the fur to fly.

In the event there was no inquest. Not, at any rate, on his journey. In mid August he was telling his mother that he had dined on several occasions since his return from Tibet with the Governor and that Sir James asked endless questions about his experiences. '. . . he talked and asked questions for about two hours about Tibet,' he wrote on the 17th. And jokingly added, 'I think I ought to get the CMG at least.' There were faint sugges-tions by this time of parental interference with his romance. Even after he had told his parents about Frederica, he never used her name in letters. Only 'the American girl'. He added in the letter of the 17th – again it must be supposed as a jesting aside – 'Perhaps if I bring it off with the American girl, I will get one.' He meant a CMG!

But there is no suggestion of any great difficulty with his parents, though perhaps his father was insisting on caution in view of his age and financial status. He was still living on a lieutenant's pay and a small allowance from home which hardly kept him in ponies and mess bills.

51

As for his own state of mind, he was in his own words 'having a most amusing time'. He had been made Cantonment Magistrate and was responsible for selling off cantonment land to Indian businessmen who all thought it necessary to bribe him as one of the better-established principles of life. They were astonished to find that he refused their offers, and even more surprised that he dealt with their claims impartially. 'I quite understand how some of the civilians out here make their money,' he observed.

On 21 September he wrote:

It is the final effort of the Naini Tal season, and everyone works pretty hard. There is a dance on Monday, large fancy-dress ball on Wednesday, and a Government House Ball on Friday, Civil Service Banquet Saturday, and theatricals the other two nights . . . In addition we play matches against the Civil Service at everything.

On 28 September:

My dear mother,
Such a week we are having. It is the Civil Service week, when everyone in Bengal finds his way to Naini . . . We had a most gorgeous dance last night . . . but as there were three hundred people and the room only holds two hundred, there was some slight discomfort . . . On Friday there is a big Government House ball. I spend my days trying to get hockey and football teams together.

He was trying to sell his 'crocked' pony to a 'deluded' colleague, and thought that he would have to sell the others as winter was coming on. He ended his letter, the last that was to survive from his days at Naini Tal:

Our official season ends on October 11th so we have not got much longer to gad about, but everyone seems to be trying to crowd a good deal into the time that is left. I think we have about eight dances in a little over a fortnight. Naini is looking up; there have been four engagements in the last three weeks; I call it a most dangerous place . . .

Your loving son, Gerard.

It was not the letter of a despairing or angry young man.

But winter had come, and the Governor and his household moved down to the plains at Allahabad. Frederica went too and then home to Chicago. Leachman never saw her again. He seems to have given his mind to other matters quickly enough, but he was never quite the same man after the year 1905 came to its poetic climax and, almost immediately, to its anti-climactic end. His taste for social life diminished, his temper, never far from the surface, worsened perceptibly. He spoke affectionately of Frederica – but only in the third person, the 'American girl' – to the end of his life. There was never another serious encounter with a woman, though there were flirtations in years to come. The La Touches retired at the end of the following year and their niece never returned. She never married either. The parting of the ways is marked only by a significant gap of some six months in the correspondence between Leachman and his parents. Perhaps they were not on letter-writing terms. Perhaps such letters as they exchanged were destroyed. The family never spoke of the matter.

6

The Long, Long Trail

A few months remained of station officer's duty in Naini Tal, where only dark clouds and cold nights circumscribed his life and the red pomegranates and green oranges and sweet-smelling poppies had faded from sight.

It was not until April 1906 that he was relieved and ordered to Changla Gala on the North-West Frontier, a fifty-mile ride from Rawalpindi. He was to take the musketry course which sickness had prevented him from completing a year earlier; six hours a day with rifle and machine-gun and long hours of private study and practice. If the exertions of the course came hard to some young officers they were pleasurable to Leachman. He was never happier than when his finger was on the trigger and man or beast challenged him to the draw. He was a bold horseman but not exceptionally skilled, according to his sister's family, the Parhams of Wiltshire. Observing him in the saddle, they judged that he had 'bad hands'. Of his ability with the rifle there was no doubt, however, and he passed the musketry course with distinction.

He was enticingly close to Kashmir at Changla Gala. Entitled to a short period of leave after his course he decided to make for the high regions which the Moguls believed to be the end of the habitable world. It was a legitimate journey this time, and he joined up with Capt. Butler, one of the several young officers whose enterprise and ambition matched his own and with whom he formed close friendships in his first three years in India. They met at Murree, at Ahran's, one of imperial India's finest restaurants set among the hills of the Hazara beyond the western border of Kashmir, and they stayed the night at the Curzon rest-house, a flea-ridden gift from a much-travelled Viceroy to weary voyagers who followed in his footsteps.

There were no difficulties, political or geographical, on this journey. The path to the beautiful capital of Srinagar across the Jhelum river was easy, with rest-places and eating-houses at Kohla and other villages on the route. The majestic scenery, 'perfect and utterly lovely scenery', brought rare bursts of poetic appreciation to Leachman's usually matter-of-fact diary. He glided down the Jhelum which wound its way through lotus and willow, to Sunbul at the foot of snow-capped and sunlit mountains. Capt. Butler had left him for an undisclosed destination at Srinagar; he was already on Simla's Special Duty List and he had special undercover work to perform. Leachman was still the apprentice, allowed to travel, encouraged even, watched and reported on to the Quartermaster-General's department. He would never meet Butler again, though their paths would come close in some of the remotest regions of the East.

With his party of coolies, a cook and a *shikari*, and six ponies, he made his way through the valley of Kashmir towards Mazar in the high north and noted a scene which many a traveller had looked on with enchantment; mulberry trees and cherry blossom, and bubbling brooks, fir forests and meadows, clear skies and a moon which rose over the white peaks in the distance. It was the route which old Abdullah of Bukhara had taken on his journey to Mecca by way of Delhi, to marry his son to the princess Lalla Rookh, *Tulip Cheek*. But Leachman went in the opposite direction towards the Zoji La pass, rising to more than 11,000 ft, and on across the Indus and the Shyok river to the hunting-grounds at the foot of the Karakoram mountains, to witness the break of day on the roof of the world.

He camped beneath the glacier peaks which fed the Indus with torrents of crystal-clear water and where only the cry of the jackdaw mingled with the splash and roar of the falls. The village of Abdan he noticed was 'full of pretty women'. But it was the pretty woman of Naini Tal whose far-off cry came to him persistently in the shadow of the Karakoram. Before leaving India two delayed letters had reached him from her exile and he read them

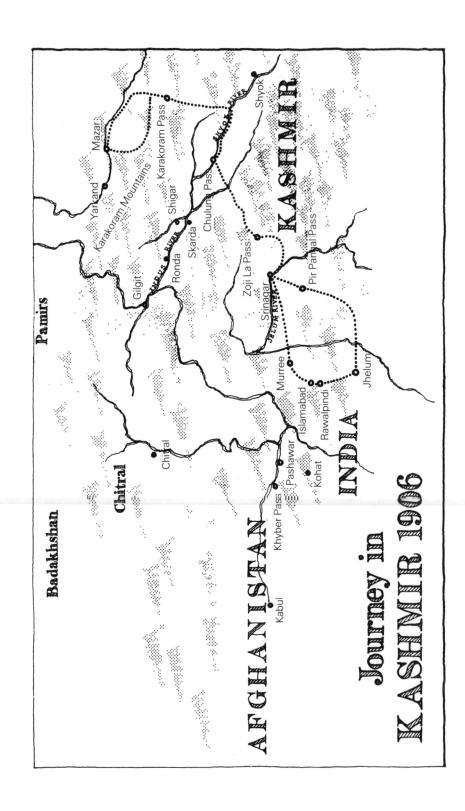

Journey in KASHMIR 1906

over and again on his journey, the last communications he was ever to receive from her, and then he went off in the footsteps of Marco Polo to stalk the great-horned wild sheep, *ovis poli* or the *shapoo* – that most familiar recourse of the young army officer in India at moments of crisis.

By Leachman's choleric standards it was a placid journey. There was only one show of temper when his guide, wilting under the strain of the sahib's relentless advance across beautiful but sometimes difficult country, lay down and declared that he was too ill to go on that day. To Leachman it was an example of native faint-heartedness. The unfortunate man was forced to go on. Leachman himself had been sick only a day or two before but with the tenacity that was to mark almost every journey and every privation of his future life he went on his way and concealed his pain and anguish. He expected the same resolution of others.

At the village of Tholti where his *shikari* was sent to bargain for a new supply of coolies, a heated argument started up. Angry words with the village headman led to an exchange of blows. Leachman hurled himself into the fray and lashed out at both sides indiscriminately. In consequence no coolies arrived at the camp and the baggage-train was waylaid. The angry Englishman who had been forced to sleep without so much as a blanket to cover him took the headman by the scruff of the neck on the following morning.

'I think they are a little alarmed at what I might do,' he noted. 'I certainly will create hell.' Baggage and coolies were soon on their way. Some who travelled in the wild places of the East sought to appease the natives in time of trouble with promises of reward and diplomatic words; others, and Leachman was prominent among them, relied on fists and in emergency on the gun. His bravery often bordered on the reckless.

By mid August he was back at Srinagar pouring scorn on the local salesmen who gathered round and the taxidermist who wanted to charge him exorbitantly to treat the animal skins he had brought with him. 'Sellers and swine of all sorts.' He paid off his guide and most of his coolies there. Settling accounts never left Leachman in good temper. 'I think the Kashmiri Hindu is the most loathsome beast . . . and the Musulman not much better.' At the end of August he returned across the mountainous route of Rattan Pir and the Thanni Mandi to India.

There were five months left of regimental duty, this time at Ambala, before he was due for home leave at the beginning of 1907. The apprenticeship was nearly over. Simla had taken notice of his ability to move fast and sure through different kinds of terrain and among all manner of people.

He had met a number of junior officers whose abilities and special qualities had also been noted by the intelligence department at Simla, though most were no more than names to him. He had been impressed by Capt. Butler who shortly after the Kashmir trip took up staff duties in East Africa. He had been taken, too, with Lieut Arnold Wilson, a young man of overflowing energy and patriotism whom he met at Ambala; and Wilson was greatly impressed by the tall, bony and somewhat brooding Leachman. He met but hardly noticed another young officer, Norman Bray, who had arrived in 1905 as a lieutenant on the unattached list, and who was to become his Boswell in a manner of speaking; to follow him admiringly and chronicle his exploits in lands about to be discovered.

He left his regiment on furlough on 30 January 1907 and arrived at Karachi two days later after 'a most disgusting journey' by train in the course of which he forcibly ejected a procession of intruders from his first-class compartment. When he reached Karachi he found that Thomas Cook had made a mess of his booking and that he would have to tranship at Bushire instead of going directly to Basra. He was 'pale with passion'. He visited the army staff offices and found nobody there at a normal working hour. His early enthusiasm for Kitchener's command of the Indian army had begun to wane. It was still too easy-going for Leachman's liking. His brief diary entries of this period suggest a distinct lack of humour. Perhaps the disappointed hopes of Naini Tal still rankled. Whatever the cause, he behaved on his travels like a petulant grandee, emulating the admirable Victorian Richard Burton in his readiness to swap words and punches with natives or indeed any fellow-countrymen who got in his way.

He had decided to return overland to England and he arrived at his first port of call, Muscat, on 5 February to be greeted by the pedantic, upright Political Agent of the Indian Government, Maj. W. G. Grey.

He found plenty to interest him in that rocky prominence and its desert interior where Omani tribal leaders plotted the overthrow of the Sultan, and German agents who had replaced the French and Russians as Britain's most powerful competitor in the area sustained an arms traffic which threatened the peace and stability of the entire Persian Gulf and even the security of India on its north-west frontier.

Leachman would learn the details of conspiracy in the region as time went on. Lord Lansdowne, the Foreign Secretary, had proclaimed in May 1903: 'I say it without hesitation – we should regard the establishment of a naval base, or a fortified port, in the Persian Gulf by any other power as a very grave menace to British interests, and we should certainly resist it with all the means at our disposal.' And Curzon, in the year that Leachman reached India, made a lightning tour of the Gulf states and Persia to tell each and every potentate 'We are the masters, the Royal Navy and the Government of India your protectors.' The great men had spoken.

It was the ordinary everyday signs of change, of discontent and conspiracy which Leachman noted in his diary: the chatter of the bazaar; the inscriptions on the great rock which guards the entrance to Muscat harbour where the name of the Russian warship *Giliyak*, sent to the Gulf in 1899 as a demonstration of the Czar's determination to find a warm-water port, stood out from the hundreds of other inscriptions made down the ages; the vulnerability of the Sultan if British gunboats should desert him, whispered in the tittle-tattle of the *suq*; the sight of the proud dhows of the Omani sailors and pirates as they prepared to make night time sojourns with the arms smugglers of the long, rugged Gulf coastline.

Only the inflexible resolve of Britain to retain its position in the Gulf could prevent the disaster of German accession, and Leachman and men like him could find little resolution in the British administration of the year 1907. Curzon had left India in November 1905 embittered and angry, accused by his own Conservative colleagues of bringing state secrets into open debate in his unseemly squabble with Kitchener. The sick and easy-going Lord Minto had taken over the Viceroyalty, and in the following month Balfour's Government had resigned in disarray, handing over to Campbell-Bannerman's Liberals without even seeking an electoral verdict. Sir Edward Grey was at the Foreign Office, Morley at the India Office. Home Rule, Gladstone's hobby-horse, was back in the political vocabulary.

The Indian Government and Whitehall were at each other's throat more venomously than ever. Britain had assigned to Germany the right to build a railway to the Gulf, the so-called Berlin–Baghdad line.[1] Turkey, on the verge of revolution, its young dissidents plotting the downfall of the tyrant Sultan Abdal Hamid from their secret enclaves in Salonika and Paris, had given Germany exclusive title to search for archaeological remains in Mesopotamia, and thus an open invitation to establish a sharp-eyed espionage system at the heart of the Ottoman Empire in Asia.[2] And in August 1906, just six months before Leachman set eyes on the Arab lands for the first time, the Hamburg–America liner *Candia*, gleaming in its new coat of white paint, had made a slow majestic way along that 'British lake' to the Shatt al Arab, to Basra and the Shaikhdom of Muhammerah where Britain's closest ally ruled. The crew lined the decks at attention and the band played 'Deutschland über Alles' as the immaculate ship slipped into port at Muscat and Lingeh, at Bahrain, Kuwait and Basra, and Arab and Turkish and Persian notables were piped aboard to salute the Kaiser and drink his health in champagne and orange juice.[3]

As Leachman made his way homeward matters which would play a crucial part in his career were being resolved, and sometimes confounded, at the fountain-heads of Europe and Asia. It was a confusing moment for men of Empire.

The long, long trail stretched out before Leachman. Empty deserts and forlorn mountain ranges merged with distant skylines, and tales were told of tribal conflicts which would decide the ownership of bleak lands which lay beyond the control of civilized governments; beyond the influence of western agents or the survey of western spies. His ship took on a party of missionaries of the Dutch Reformed Church of America at Muscat, men and a few brave women who were the first to take medical care to the Arabs. Leachman hoped that his language would not shock them.

Hormuz, the once splendid southern city of ancient Persia, now a sprawling red-oxide pit, was the next port of call. Then Bandar Abbas at the eastern end of the Persian Gulf coast, where he heard for the first time of another young English officer who was to share with him the vigil of the Arabian heartland, Capt. William Henry Irvine Shakespear.

Shakespear had joined the Indian Political Service while retaining his army commission in 1904 and since then had been deputy to the British Resident in the Persian Gulf, Maj. Percy Cox, whom the Arabs called 'Cokkus'; and Consul-General at Bandar Abbas.

Leachman heard tell of Shakespear's one-man war with the Russians in Persia and with recalcitrant tribesmen and decided that here was a man after his own heart.

Two years before, in 1905, Britain had been having trouble with tribesmen – egged on by Persian and Russian provocateurs – at its Gulf intelligence headquarters, Jask, further along the coast. It was decided that a telegraph station should be built adjoining the consulate on the sea-front. Again inspired by bribes and talk of British perfidy, the Governor of the Gulf Ports ordered that the station should be built inland. Shakespear waited until the new building was half constructed and then called in a party of Bluejackets who made the Persians pull it down brick by brick. It was eventually put up with a new consular building between the town and the sea. Leachman was impressed by the firmness of his fellow-countryman. While the Germans began the construction of their rail line from Anatolia through Mesopotamia to the Gulf, with Kuwait as its hoped-for terminus, the Russians proposed to build a line through Persia terminating at Bandar Abbas. But not if Captain Shakespear had anything to do with it, and Leachman scribbled in his diary a note of the danger posed by Russian ambitions in the region.

The missionaries disembarked at Bahrain 'rather to our relief, though they are a decent lot'. His ship, SS *Bulimba* was anchored off shore and Leachman had to while away the time aboard listening to the complaints of a merchant visitor who insisted that the British consuls in the region were a poor lot who had no commercial knowledge and who refused to learn Arabic. Prideaux in Bahrain and Grey at Muscat were noted Arabists, and Shakespear, though he had as yet only a fleeting knowledge of the Arab lands, had been a courts-martial interpreter in Urdu, Hindi, Farsi and Arabic before leaving India.

Leachman reached Bushire, headquarters of the British administration in the Gulf, on 12 February. The new Shah of Persia, the Russian protégé Muhammad Ali, had just been crowned in Tehran to the accompaniment of riots in Shiraz, Isfahan and Tabriz. The Persian navy was at Bushire, five gunboats and a sloop, dressed overall for the royal celebrations. They had been commanded in turn by Russian, German and British naval officers but all had resigned because the previous Shah had been unable to pay them, having dissipated the vast sums given him by Britain and Russia in the course of numerous sprees in Europe. The Residency itself was inland at Reshire and Leachman went there in the hope of finding Cox or his deputy Shakespear but both were away. He was generously entertained all the same and heard remarkable tales of German incursion in the region through the commercial firm known as Woenckhaus which had set up at the port of Lingeh eight years earlier and had since spread to almost every large coastal town on either side of the water on the supposed strength of a business in sea shells. British intelligence officers had followed the Woenckhaus men with amusement as they laboriously hunted the beaches for shells and made notes of shipping movements and the activities of other nationals. He heard too of the visit to Bushire a year earlier of a most imposing young German by the name of Wassmuss whose exploits, like his own, would become part of the history and the legend of the Middle East.

He transferred to the British India Mail Ship *Kola* for the voyage to Basra, passing for the first time over the silt bar of Fao where a Turkish fortress kept a desultory vigil, to Muhammerah, the independent territory between Persia and Mesopotamia which was presided over by the friend of Britain and the maestro of Freemasonry in the east, Shaikh Khazal.

At Basra he learnt that he and a French general who had travelled on the same ship would have to spend five days in quarantine on one of the off-shore islands. He also learnt that the Hamburg–America Line was paying the Turkish port doctor a hundred rupees every time a German vessel called and was offering free passage to Mecca to Turkish pilgrims.

The Turks, ever anxious to please visiting notables, sent a troup of young boys to Leachman and the General in their isolation. They made 'most indecent gestures' and the Frenchman was obviously delighted. Syphilis was the customary reward for those who availed themselves of the Turks' generosity.

As soon as he was released from confinement Leachman contacted the Tod family in Basra, managers of the famous Lynch company, owners of the Tigris paddle-steamers which ploughed the river between Baghdad and Basra, and many another commercial enterprise. He wasn't much taken with Mr Tod but was enthralled by his beautiful and vivacious Italian wife, Aurelia. It was with great reluctance that he left Basra and Aurelia Tod to join the little river-steamer *Khalifa* for the journey to Baghdad. He waved a fond farewell to the several friends he had made, especially to the little lady whom he had found such 'jolly good fun', settling down to observe places and peoples he would soon move among with the utmost familiarity. And of all the acquaintanceships of his first journey in the Arab lands none would have so poignant a place in his future life as that which he formed with the small, unpretentious boat on which he travelled to Baghdad. A few years hence he would see the *Khalifa* make an heroic journey.

For the moment the diary jottings revealed the fresh impulses of discovery, the first tentative observations of men and women and place-names which were new and foreign to him: Qurna, the reputed Garden of Eden, in the midst of date gardens and vast swamps; Amara, Shaikh Saad, Es Sinn, Kut al Amara; men wandering stark naked in the wild – the Sabaeans, followers of John the Baptist; nomadic tribesmen, the Badu, levelling their guns menacingly at the passengers as the *Khalifa* passed by; and townsmen, unskilled with the rifle and civilized, 'and therefore of poorer physique'. To starboard the distant mountains of Pasht-i-Kuh rose in azure beauty from the Persian plain. To port, as they approached Baghdad, the great arch of Ctesiphon stood as a reminder of ancient glory in the land of the two rivers.

A new Wali had just taken over in Baghdad when Leachman arrived, a Turkish ruler of unusual enlightenment. He quickly put in hand all kinds of improvements to the Beloved City and the first of them, a tramway, had already been commissioned. Others, including a suspension bridge and ferry, were soon to follow. For the time being, however, a string of boats slung across the Tigris was the only means of crossing. Leachman took the tram north to Kadhimain with an Indian businessman who took him to the roof of his house from where he was able to gain a perfect view of one of the loveliest of mosques, the Shi'a temple of the Imam Musa Kadhim. The *suqs* of Baghdad itself were teeming with goods and people. 'They are really wonderful, such as I have never seen in India. They are nearly all covered in . . . The street is about eight feet wide, but Turkish big people drive through with outriders regardless.'

On 3 March 1907 he crossed the river in a circumambulating coracle and met the missionary Dr Elliot on the other side, together with an assortment of servants, muleteers, mules, donkeys and pack-ponies. His first overland journey in the Arab lands was to be a picturesque if not entirely professional affair. The *zaptieh* – the mandatory companion of the traveller in the Ottoman Empire – turned out to be an arrogant 'dolt' who did not take long in rousing Leachman's ire. They stopped at the khan of Falluja overnight, on the road which led to the Euphrates. It was to be a significant place-name for the Englishman, but in March 1907 it was remarkable only for its barking, quarrelling dogs which kept him awake.

They were making for Aleppo. They went along the Euphrates in a *shakhtur*, a rectangular boat of tarred wattle, coated on the outside with bitumen: Ramadi, Hit, Jiba, Haditha, Khan Fahmi. Leachman was bitten and kicked by his 'vicious' pony, and greatly irritated by the Turkish gendarme in their midst. The party met two Armenians on the road, naked and without a possession in the wide world. They had been robbed by Arabs on the road. Their privations were only beginning, for soon the terrible persecution of that race which had begun at the end of the previous century would start up again in the Ottoman provinces and millions would die in an act of genocide with few parallels in history.

At Ana he noticed some pretty girls and at Khan Fahmi he photographed 'a most lovely girl'. Perhaps the memory of Naini Tal was diminishing at last and a youthful relish returning. His temper was as bad as ever, partly perhaps due to a cold caught in Baghdad. 'Must control temper', and 'mustn't use such foul language', he noted. And then, 'Cold better, but temper as usual bad'. He was an essentially honest man, and even in his most intemperate moods he tried to see the other man's point of view. Charity was sometimes beyond his natural resources, however, as on the Aleppo journey when he blurted out 'the *zaptieh* is the lowest, foulest coward on earth and would be a danger more than a protection'. Such sentiments were hazardous in the Turkish Empire.

His indignation could be self-righteous and astute, and he was quick to seize on the disguises and affectations of others. On one occasion when he was confined by a leg injury in India, he wrote home:

I don't know if you notice my hand is shaking, but I have just been bestowing summary punishment on my bearer. They have just opened the native bazaar again after it had been closed for cholera, and of course my bearer went down and marked the occasion by getting gloriously drunk. That I didn't mind very much, but I had warned him once before that he had better keep out of my way when he was in that state. Well today he didn't, and came and annoyed me so I hurt him.

A few weeks later his mother took him to task for his slapdash spelling in letters. He replied: 'You see I am rather handicapped in my spelling because I write so plainly that you can see how each word is spelt, which is not the case with everyone's writing!'

By the time they reached Nahiya Leachman and Elliot had been joined by assorted waifs and strays, including an Afghan mullah on his way from Kandahar to Mecca, and an Arab who had murdered a neighbour and was seeking refuge from the victim's relatives. On 12 March they reached Abu Kamal which was to become a boundary marker between Syria and Iraq in years ahead. Dr Elliot, a Presbyterian missionary, treated native sufferers from every kind of sickness and affliction as they travelled the desert path to Aleppo, and Leachman observed the usefulness of a medicine chest among people who looked on the European first and foremost as a heretic, then as a miraculous healer. Iodine, aspirin and ointments were to be his weapon of defence sometimes the only weapon at moments of danger.

The party arrived at Aleppo on 24 March and Leachman and Elliot put up at the Aziziya Hotel. The doctor retired to bed with a chill and Leachman met the consul, Longworth, at dinner, together with Percy Loraine, a young attaché at the Constantinople embassy, and Mr Jay, first secretary at the American embassy in the Ottoman capital. Men who were to become important contacts in the East had begun to gather round and to prepare their reports on the lean and purposeful soldier who moved among them: reports which would go to the military attaché at Constantinople for onward transmission to the War Office in London. Other anonymous agents kept watch on men such as Leachman who came out of the desert into metropolitan Syria; men working for the *Nachrichtdienst* of the Wehrmacht in Berlin and for the Eastern Bureau of the German

Foreign Office, presided over by Baron von Oppenheim.

Leachman went by train to Damascus on the newly commissioned Hijaz railroad, built by the famous German engineer who was known throughout the Near East as Meissner Pasha. He stayed at the Victoria Hotel close by the residence of the Ottoman Wali of Damascus and the resort of tourists and the world's spies and fortune-hunters. He looked from the top of Salahiya hill at the plain and the city, and at the distant snow-topped mount of Hermon which Arabs call 'Old Man Mountain'. He met a mysterious caller soon after his arrival, 'a sort of Englishman named Farli', according to his diary, who offered to accompany him to Najd and Kuwait. The same man, of indeterminate name and nationality, was to meet up with him again when he returned to pursue official tasks at the heart of Arabia.

He went on to Beirut, the rich and magnificent coastal province of the Empire governed by a Christian Pasha, its prosperous villages and vineyards, its cedars and clumps of fir, making a patchwork of red and green which merged with the emerald sea as he looked down on them from the mountains of Lebanon. He put up at the Hotel Allemand, teeming with Germans, where he was entertained by the vice-consul, a talkative young man whom he described as 'awful and verbose' and who told him of the growing conflict between Muslims and Christians in Syria. Some two hundred people had been killed in the previous three months. He heard too of conflict between the Turkish army and the strangely isolated people who occupied the mountainous region called Jabal Druse which rose out of the stony Hauran desert of Syria – people who were neither Christian nor Muslim, and who were generally disliked by both sects. His education in the complex affairs of the Arab lands was proceeding fast.

At the beginning of April he boarded the *Prince Abbas* at Beirut for the voyage to Mersin, a journey of idyllic days and troublesome nights, for the Turkish passengers lived up to their national reputation for sexual promiscuity, and they made constant approaches to his bedside, despite the hard lessons learnt by the importunate souls who went before. He arrived at the Asiatic coast of Turkey with fists raw from the punishment they had inflicted on his own behalf and on that of a fellow-traveller, Mr Stuart.

Constantinople was the next objective, reached by the marvellously constructed Anatolian railway which joined the Berlin–

Baghdad line then being built and which came to a number of dead ends where the engineers had been unable to find a way under or over the Taurus mountains. At such intervals the engine would simply run out of line and come to an agonized halt and the passengers were conveyed to the next stretch in flat-bottomed horse-drawn carriages. At one point the rain had washed away a segment of line and a relief train had to be backed up to take them on to Haidar Pasha station on the Asiatic side of the Bosporus, where Leachman arrived with Mr Stuart on 9 April. Fifteen minutes later the two men crossed the Galata bridge into old Constantinople and booked seats for *Rigoletto* the following night.

Leachman had arrived in Constantinople at the death-gasp of the old Ottoman Empire. Its last absolute monarch Abdal Hamid, Padishah, King of Kings, maintained his despotic rule with the aid of an army of spies and overworked torture-chambers. His enemies in his own army and administration plotted his overthrow from far-off strongholds in the Balkans and the Kurdish mountains, in Damascus and Basra, in Armenia and the hidden depths of Arabia; lands which for nearly half a millennium, on and off, had been governed by the Osmanli Sultans. The great powers of Europe coveted the corpse which must soon be dismembered and they hovered over the dying body like vultures at the scene of battle. It was easy enough for those powers to keep a vigil at Constantinople and Damascus, at Baghdad and Salonika, where consuls and military missions were able to establish 'sources' both official and clandestine. It was another matter to infiltrate the vast and largely unmapped deserts of central Arabia where two great princes fought for ascendancy, Ibn Saud of Riyadh and Ibn Rashid of Hail, and where the Sultan of Turkey claimed a disputed sovereignty. The secret services of Britain, France, Germany, Russia and Austria were all intent on finding men able to undertake demanding exploratory tasks in those regions. Britain had earmarked two men for those tasks, and they descended on the Ottoman capital at almost exactly the same time. Leachman arrived there in April and spent three days in sightseeing and casual meetings with embassy staff. Capt. Shakespear, at the end of his term in Persia and already singled out for sterner tasks, arrived two weeks after Leachman departed, at the beginning of May.

Shakespear had driven from the Residency at Bushire in a spanking new automobile, a Rover single-cylinder model which he had bought in India while serving as assistant to the Resident to the Nizam of Hyderabad, after being hurriedly sent away from Bandar Abbas following a blazing row with the Russian consul Ovseenko,[4] an officer of 'special ability'. He proposed to drive home to England in the car, and he had already travelled over some of the most impenetrable, roadless passes of Asia on his way to Constantinople, petrol cans strapped to every available space inside and out, for there were no garages or petrol pumps on his route in the year 1907. His arrival in Constantinople was a mild sensation. The motor-car was banned officially in the Ottoman Empire.

Both men met the military attaché Col. Surtees and the aristocratic 'honoraries' who buzzed purposefully around the embassy and disappeared every now and again on missions of great urgency and secrecy: Capt. Mark Sykes, George Ambrose Lloyd and John F. Lambton, heirs to baronetcies and peerages and to the power centres of British government. Sykes had fallen foul of the ambassador some little time before and had been given the task which befell many an aspiring intelligence officer who fell foul of ambassadors abroad, pasting up press cuttings. The introduction to the peppery and outspoken Sykes was to prove important to both the young officers from India. Leachman was not able to meet the ambassador, the imposing Irishman Sir Nicholas O'Conor whom Sykes likened to a character from Thackeray. He was aboard his yacht *Imogen* off the Golden Horn at the time. A pity, for Leachman would not have another opportunity to see the graceful vessel that was the ambassador's pride and joy until it turned up battered and unkempt on the Tigris serving gallantly under the flag of the Royal Navy amid the chaos of war.

Shakespear was able to meet O'Conor, to enjoy his Irish wit and charm and lavish hospitality for the first and last time, for the ambassador was to die in office a few months later, at the moment of revolution and the assumption of power by the Young Turks. It was the dragoman at the embassy rather than the ambassador who interested Shakespear, however, and who would certainly have interested Leachman had he stayed long enough to meet him. Fitzmaurice, short, red-faced, ginger-moustached was the real power in Constantinople. Another

Catholic Irishman who was dedicated to the spread of British influence in the world, but who, unlike the ambassador, was prepared to fight Turk and German tooth and nail. Fitzmaurice held on to his job by a hair's breadth. The Foreign Office had insisted two years earlier on the removal of the military attaché, Francis Maunsell, because of his anti-German activities. Now Fitzmaurice was being accused of standing in the way of Whitehall policy, though he was defended and even encouraged by the man who was to become the First Sea Lord and who had until recently been C-in-C Mediterranean, Admiral Sir John Fisher. The Admiral, Maunsell and Fitzmaurice had conspired to set up a network of secret transmitters and trustworthy agents in the eastern Mediterranean, with headquarters at Piraeus in Greece, using Admiralty money and reporting to the Admiralty's Director of Intelligence. But Sir Edward Grey heard of these and other matters, and Fitzmaurice was warned not to interfere in the affairs of Turkey or Germany.[5]

Leachman went home from Turkey on the Continental express, and found to his anger that he had to share a carriage with a German and a Turk, neither of whom liked fresh air. He opened a window all the same, and survived the journey to Ostend via Adrianople, Belgrade, Budapest and Vienna, arriving at Dover on 18 April. Shakespear motored to central Europe nearly a month later, calling on Maunsell in Macedonia, who commanded the gendarmerie there after being dismissed from Constantinople.

Leachman and Shakespear both spent the summer in England and returned to India in the late autumn. Their paths came ever closer, destined often to cross in city and desert, but never to coincide in time and place.[6]

7

Special Duty

Leachman returned to his regiment at Rawalpindi in November 1907, to be told on arrival that he had been put on the special duty list and was to report to staff HQ Simla.

It was a critical year. The year of war plans and talk of actual conflict, of disputes in Sinai, North Africa, Persia, and the Balkans; of upheaval in Arabia and the Persian Gulf. A dispute between the Shaikhs of Bahrain and Qatar in the course of which the Qatari ruler was murdered provided Britain with an opportunity to intervene along the Trucial coast and to gain what a Simla intelligence officer described as 'important knowledge'.[1] And in the fastness of central Arabia, cut off from the world by its great heat in summer and by its almost impenetrable deserts in all seasons, the young Amir of Riyadh, Ibn Saud, had inflicted a great defeat on the protégé of the Turks, the brave warrior prince Abdal Aziz ibn Rashid.[2]

A few weeks after that battle the Turkish troops which had occupied the central region of Kasim for two years past were compelled to withdraw. The Indian Government recognized an ascendant star in Ibn Saud and recommended to London that contact should be established so that his place in the Arabian firmament might be judged. But London replied, as it had replied to such requests for the six years since Ibn Saud had recaptured his homeland from Ibn Rashid, with a firm 'No'. Morley, the Secretary of State for India, told the Viceroy, 'The influence of HMG is to be confined strictly to the coastline of

Arabia. No steps . . . without my prior sanction.' If the world was at the verge of war over the occupation of Aqaba by a small unit of the Ottoman army, no disturbance of the peace must be risked in the vast regions of central Arabia whose ruling family was at loggerheads with the Turk and sought an alliance with Britain.[3]

Such was the state of play when Leachman arrived at GHQ Simla in December 1907, to share an office with Capt. Gibbon of the Irish Fusiliers. Leachman was to spend the next few months deep in the files marked 'Arabia', some 2,000 of them lining the walls in spring-clip boxes, and listening to Gibbon's tales of the adventurers who had gone before him into the wilds of Afghanistan and Mongolia, Persia and Arabia, to do the bidding of the quartermaster-generals of old; and to hear of the man who had devoted himself to the same files four years earlier, Capt. Will Shakespear. Leachman's role was ambivalent from the start. When he was ripe for action, filled with as much information as he could absorb in several months spent browsing through the Simla files, he would become a vital link between the intelligence departments of the army in London and India. He and Shakespear would invade the same deserts in unsuspected rivalry.

He spent the year 1908 in unaccustomed devotion to study, with only an occasional fling on the ballroom floor of Viceregal Lodge and shooting expeditions to keep him in physical shape. 'How is Jack?' he asked of his young nephew and godson, Jack Parham,[4] at the turn of the year, before suggesting to the child's mother (sister Mabel) that he should be encouraged into engineering, dam-building perhaps like the 'great engineers', or else into the army. But on all accounts to learn French and German and not to worry about Latin.

'Learn German', Haldane of MO2 had told Leachman in London, without hint of a reason, though it was obvious enough to any officer of the time who was the adversary elect, and the new recruit to the Simla staff was keen to impart this gem of wisdom to his nephew. 'I work many hours a day at German, when I might be employed very much better.' He studied Arabic too and began to make satisfactory progress though he found the language difficult. And he watched from his vantage point the comings and goings of the mighty in the year of renewed trouble in Afghanistan, the year of the ascent of the Young Turks in Constantinople and of Asquith in Downing Street.

In April he wrote:

> The whole place is in uproar with rumours of war. A very general idea is that the whole show is backed up by the Amir and that we shall find ourselves in Kabul before long if this cowardly government does what is right, which I suppose it won't . . . Simla is now full, the Viceroy and Kitchener having come up in a hurry on account of the show.

Cowardly or no, Britain had learnt hard lessons in trying to subdue the wild tribesmen of Afghanistan, and Asquith's Liberals were not anxious to add to the experiences of a very memorable past. The Amir Habibullah was persuaded to take hold of his tribes and Britain and Russia signed a Convention by which each renounced special claims on the territory, subject only to the Anglo-Afghan Treaty in 1905 in which Curzon had insisted on British intervention in the case of an invasion by another power. Simla returned to its quiet normality and Leachman went methodically through the 'Arabia' files and passed his preliminary examination in Arabic, complaining only, as fond memories came at intervals to blow dying embers to fitful life, that Simla wasn't a patch on Naini Tal socially.

He returned to regimental duty at Rawalpindi in October, his special duty stint at an end. Another year was to pass by before he could embark on the mission that had become his ruling passion.

Karachi, Muscat, Bushire, Muhammerah, Muscat. He had visited the same ports on his journey homeward in 1907, but now there was a bustling urgency about his travels, and a greater awareness born of the secret files to which he had been given access. Geography, the dispositions of Ottoman army units, the movements of foreigners in the Arab lands, rumour and the camp-fire revelations of Arab chiefs and tribesmen; such were the minutiae of the blue cardboard folders of Simla tied like legal documents with pink string, filling the gaps in the larger assessments of the political officers, mostly army men, with the brass tacks and ephemera of traveller and hunter, soldier and sailor, merchant and spy, the cumulative work of nearly two centuries, inherited from the East India Company which had ruled a large slice of Asia with its private army and navy, and with only a distant board of governors to impede its day-to-day endeavours, until the Mutiny spoilt everything and Whitehall and bureaucracy took over.

For men like Leachman the days of private enterprise would have been better by a long chalk, days of the great amateurs playing with the proficiency of the professional and twice as much zeal. But the day of the amateur was almost over. The Kaiser had seen to that. Leachman was about to meet up with men of his own kind and to begin his work in the shadows of the other kind, men trained in the hard professional schools of the Prussian and Viennese Military Academies, in the Eastern Bureau of the Berlin Foreign Office; men of high academic reputation and exceptional military skill. The telegraph ruled where once the camel-messenger sped. The motor-car and the armoured vehicle were on the way. Elaborate ciphers concealed political and military secrets as they were carried across thousands of miles of desert, mountain and water to their destinations in India, Constantinople, London, St Petersburg, Paris, Berlin and Vienna. Leachman's generation of political and special duty officers bridged the gap between past and future; and for a select few, of whom Leachman was one, there remained tasks to be performed in lands which were officially closed to travellers – tasks which would seldom be recorded anywhere but in the inaccessible files of MO2 and MO3 in London and Simla, and their equivalents in the capitals of the other powers.

His first tasks were on the periphery, in Mesopotamia and Syria, where others had hunted before him and where contemporaries were already on the trail. He must learn to mix with friend and enemy as an innocent among innocents, to live with Arab of town and desert, to identify Jew and Greek, Assyrian and Armenian, Turk and Chaldean among the milling crowds of the bazaars of Basra, Baghdad and Damascus and a thousand smaller towns between. And when he was ready he would undertake more vital journeys in lands where there were few bazaars and no protectors; not even Ottoman gendarmes.

The outlying regions had been well surveyed by the end of the first decade of the new century. Among Britishers, Mark Sykes had travelled in Syria, Anatolia and Kurdistan since his school years in the mid 1880s, accompanied early on by his father Tatton and causing a stir among Arab and Turkish hosts by a lavish style of living in the desert to which only the rich and eccentric *Ingleez* could aspire. Sykes was followed by Gertrude Bell, the wealthy and intellectually distinguished daughter of ironmaster Sir Hugh Bell, already far famed for her travels in the East, and like Sykes noted among easterners for her large and luxurious caravans, for her Wedgwood platter and crystal glass spread on Irish linen tablecloths, as though all the impedimenta of baronial homes in Yorkshire and Northumberland had materialized in the arid wastes of Arabia. Aubrey Herbert joined the adventurous spree, another of ambassador O'Conor's young honorary attachés at Constantinople who with Sykes and George Lloyd worked out his apprenticeship in intelligence gathering under the expert scrutiny of Maunsell and Fitzmaurice at the Ottoman capital. Herbert, half blind from his youth, myopic and of slender physical means, was a brave man; often ill on his travels, too ill to move on, he funked no journey however dangerous or remote, and he retained a touchingly genuine love of his fellow men, especially of Turks, as he stumbled among the wildest of their kind and came to know their perfidy and wickedness at first hand. They were the amateurs, the last of the privileged travellers who contributed their mites to the welfare of their country as they progressed through the Ottoman Empire in Asia, reporting their findings to the military attachés and first secretaries at Constantinople and Cairo, through the consular offices of metropolitan Syria and Turkey itself. The professionals crossed their paths of course. Col. Massy in Anatolia, Packe, Maitland and Newcombe in Syria working for Count Gleichen of MO2 and Lee Stack the director of intelligence in Cairo, and for Maunsell and his successor Surtees in Constantinople, under cover of the Palestine Exploration Fund, the Survey of Egypt and other such ploys.

Germany and the Austro-Hungarian Empire had been represented by two disparate men from the turn of the century: the German-Jew Baron Max von Oppenheim, and the Bohemian-Jew Alois Musil, the former an archaeologist with a taste for the high life, known from Cairo to Muscat as 'The Spy', the latter an academic of distinction whose twentieth-century journeys in Arabia were to win him universal recognition as an outstanding explorer of the desert lands, a brilliant scholar and an able intelligence agent.

Leachman reached Bushire on 16 November 1909. The Resident, Percy Cox, was away and so he went on to Muhammerah where he was received with warm approval by the political agent Arnold T. Wilson, the fiery patriot who remembered Leachman from their days in northern India together and who was quick to recognize a man after his own heart. And Wilson introduced his visitor to another of their kind, the young Ely Bannister Soane who had recently resigned from his job as manager of the Shiraz branch of the Imperial Bank of Persia. Soane had taught himself the language of the Kurds and was about to enter the mountainous territory of that warlike people, to move among them in disguise – an intelligence officer of almost incredible bravery and resourcefulness whose missions were cloaked in the darkest secrecy and of whose exploits the world was to know precious little. He was a man whose company Leachman savoured while he himself began to learn the arts of disguise and dissimulation. He described Soane in his diary as 'a most interesting man' and Wilson, the work-maniac of the eastern administration, as a man 'who is apparently above himself'. Wilson took him to meet the Shaikh of Muhammerah, Kazal, and there was immediate accord, for the ruler of that tiny principality which stood between Persia and the Arab lands on the right bank of the Shatt al Arab was the *éminence gris* of all Freemasonry in the Gulf region, Grand Master of the Mesopotamian Lodges. Leachman had retained his early enthusiasm for Masonry though he would have little time in the future to devote to its affairs. Shaikh Khazal was also privy to the innermost secrets of the political leaders of Persia and Turkey whose recent revolutions, inspired by merchants and disaffected army officers, had found succour in the lodges of Salonika, Constantinople and Tehran. And he was close to the powerful Shaikh Mubarak of Kuwait; the two men were seldom apart and differed over nothing except the relative merits of their yachts, about which they argued incessantly. Mubarak had been the guardian and protector of the young Prince Abdal Aziz ibn Saud and his father Abdurrahman when they were driven into exile by Muhammad ibn Rashid in the last years of the nineteenth century. Now Abdal Aziz was the master of Riyadh and of central Najd, a land closed to the outside world, and Leachman intended to penetrate to his fastness in the near future.

For the moment Basra was his refuge, the Marseilles of the East, with more than its share of wine, women and song, and air that was hot and humid and thick with the intrigue of a hundred nationalities. The land of Sinbad, of creeks and swamps and date-palms of which the Arabs say 'their feet are in water and their heads in hell'. It was the cosmopolitan tonic Leachman had been looking for since Naini Tal with its endless dances, dinner parties and unique companionship. He threw himself into the expatriate social life of Basra with fervour, dancing and drinking until three in the morning at the home of a French merchant, in the company of three ladies of 'doubtful virtue'. He was entertained also by Mr Mackie, one of several prominent Basra merchants with Anglo-German associations with whom he came into contact.[5] Days spent in practising Arabic were handicapped by a Baghdadi teacher whose dialect he found hard to understand as well as by the thick head with which he generally greeted the dawn.

In Baghdad, where he arrived on 2 December after a river trip by Lynch steamer, he met two remarkable men of the British administration. John Gordon Lorimer was the Resident, recently appointed in place of Col. Ramsay, bringing a Scottish wit and broad intelligence to the task of upholding British prestige and authority in the face of the German onslaught, of Turkish indifference to administrative efficiency and his own government's abdication of a once dominant role. William Willcocks, surveyor of Egypt and Mesopotamia, the great irrigation engineer of his time who was the progenitor of the Aswan dam project, traversed the twin-rivers of ancient Iraq with the impish charm and quixotic manner of a man who saw only too clearly the folly of tilting at windmills. His task was nothing less than to restore the canal system which the civilizations of Babylon and Assyria had created and which the horde of the Mogul Khans had destroyed utterly, and to find a satisfactory route for a railway through the country's swamps, mountains and arid plains.

While Willcocks surveyed Germany acted, gaining the sole right to build the rail line from Anatolia to Baghdad and on to Basra, as well as the sole right to dig for ancient treasures where once Layard and Rawlinson had dug and translated the earliest legends of mankind. Brilliant Germans – Koldewey, Andrae, Buddensieg, Preusser and a host of others from Berlin's university and State museum – had succeeded brilliant Englishmen, and they added to their scholarly work the role of espionage. Lorimer and Willcocks kept an amused eye on the newcomers.

And Leachman listened avidly to their tales of Ottoman misrule in a country where natives despised all government and rulers failed to pay their soldiers and policemen; where Britons, Frenchmen, Germans and Italians made and administered their own laws under the provisions of the 'Capitulations', imposed on the Sultan through centuries of improvidence and mounting foreign debt. He enjoyed for a fortnight the generous hospitality of the Resident and his wife, and the hilarious comings and goings of Willcocks, before leaving the quietly civilized British community of Baghdad for the fanatic company of the Shi'a pilgrims at the holy city of Karbala on the Euphrates. Life remained comfortable for a while. He lodged in luxury and splendour at Karbala at the home of the Persian Prince Majid Khan. But he prepared for his first journey into forbidden territory and the start of a life that was to occupy him in austerity and discomfort, with only brief periods of respite, for the rest of his days.

Muhammad Hassan, the British consul at Karbala, turned out to meet him and he was introduced to the Ottoman *mutasarrif*, Jelal Bey, who had been until recently a garrison commander of the Turkish army in Tripoli.

'He wished to create for himself such a reputation that he could meet the great men as well as the lesser, so that his knowledge might be complete and that he might not be lightly treated,' wrote Normay Bray, the earnest young lieutenant who followed Leachman to India in 1905 and was to follow his countryman's movements with adulation in the years ahead. 'So innocent, so correct was his behaviour that the Turkish officials failed to note that he had perfected his arrangements for an audacious move to be carried out under their very noses.' Seldom has a man moved with more open and transparent aggression in foreign lands, or with less careful planning than did Leachman. This would be the centre of his life's work, the territory of the Euphrates tribes and the religious fanatics of Karbala and Najaf and Kufa. Here men whipped themselves to a fury of anger, of domineering self-pitying militancy such as the world could hardly imagine until the late twentieth century when television cameras captured the frenzy of the Shi'ite mob as the mullahs and *mujtahids* vented a sense of injustice which originated more than a thousand years before in the struggle for the Caliphate of Islam.[6]

Leachman moved alone among the most fanatic of people, and few if any among his contemporaries could have done so with as much valour or ruthlessness. For the moment he travelled along the waters of Babylon as a tourist, forming impressions, making contacts, enjoying hunting expeditions in the tribal territory of the Bani Hassan, being received with politeness and with the generosity which characterizes all Arabs and Persians when they welcome a guest, though they may cut his throat after the lapse of a decent interval.

At Kufa Leachman was received by a mullah dressed in black tail-coat and wearing a glass eye, and the representative of the wealthy anglophile Jew of Baghdad, Manshim Danyal. At Hilla, near the site of Babylon, he visited 'a filthy hospital' and the Alliance Israelite School, where they sang 'God Save the King' at dinner. The mullah, 'a most objectionable' person, was rude about the charming gesture of the guests. In other circumstances Leachman might have taught him a lesson – 'hurt him' as he often said of his educational swipes at the opposition. For the moment an unaccustomed discretion held him back.

He returned to the Lorimers in Baghdad for the Christmas festivities of 1909, and the first days of the new year were spent in a breathless round of parties and jollifications among the European community. For part of his brief time in the city he stayed with the cosmopolitan Daud Bey Daghistani, son of the Ottoman governor of Mosul, and he practised the wearing of Arab dress, preparing for his first task in the Arabian interior.

While at Karbala he had contacted a reliable Bedouin messenger through the British consul, Muhammad Hassan, and sent him to Shaikh Abdullah of the Abda section of the great Shammar tribe which patrolled the northern deserts of Arabia on behalf of the Rashids, the rulers of Hail. Britain had recognized the sovereignty of the House of Hail, backed by the Turks, since the last years of the nineteenth century when the prince, Muhammad ibn Rashid, had ousted the Sauds of Riyadh from their capital. Now the Shammar tribes were ruled by a young and allegedly frivolous Amir who had been in the care of the Sharif of Mecca until his return to Hail a year before. Britain and the other powers were interested to learn about that prince, Saud ibn Abdal Aziz ar-Rashid (barely ten years old), and about the man who governed as his Regent, Zamil ibn Subhan.

Leachman set off on the first stage of a journey that was to take him to the Rashids of Hail on 13 January 1910, dressed in soiled Arab garb which had the look of authenticity, armed with just enough Arabic to convey essential greetings and the most abrupt instructions, and accompanied by a guide of the Bani Hassan, Khidr ibn Abbas, who could move with relative safety among the Shammar and their enemies.

8

Desert Encounters

Shaikh Abdullah had said that he could go to the Shammar encampment at Shuwaiyib a few miles into the desert on the east bank of the Euphrates. Abdullah's tribesmen would help him to reach the Shaikh of the Abda Shammar, Majid ibn Ajil, kinsman of Saud ibn Abdal Aziz the prince of Hail. Abdullah told Leachman to return to Baghdad and await instructions, for the Turks who were in regular contact with the rulers of Hail must not know of his intention to visit the Shammar capital. Neither must the princes of Hail know of the proposed journey until the Englishman reached them. A desert conspiracy was afoot in which two old enemies, the Shammar and the disciplined Muntafiq tribes under Ibn Sadun in the southern Mesopotamian region, were in uneasy alliance, aiming to subdue their common enemy Ibn Saud of Riyadh and his benefactor the Shaikh of Kuwait. Leachman was Britain's emissary to the pro-Turk Rashids but Britain was wary of commitment to one or other of the desert powers. As he waited back in Baghdad for word that he could go to Ibn Ajil, Shakespear, the newly appointed Political Agent to Mubarak, the redoubtable Shaikh of Kuwait, prepared to leave for inner Arabia to intercept Ibn Saud who was said to be moving with a large body of men towards Ibn Sadun's Muntafiq army. And to the north-west another Englishman, the naturalist and explorer Douglas Carruthers,[1] made a seemingly innocent passage through the lava-strewn crevices of Wadi Sirhan towards the township of Jauf which until recently belonged to the Rashids of Hail but had been captured by Ibn Shalan, the famous chief of the Anaiza, hereditary enemies of the Shammar.[2]

Musil, the agent of the central European powers, had marched with Ibn Shalan's army to the capture of Jauf, and now the Austrian explorer-spy kept a close eye on the Britishers who were invading the Arab heartland. So did the agents of the new regime at Constantinople.

The Turks kept watch on Leachman in Baghdad and he made a sightseeing visit to nearby Kadhimain to throw them off the scent. On 20 January he slipped out of his house at nightfall and made a dash for Karbala on horseback. Majid ibn Ajil had arranged for him to be met at his town-house there, and camels and servants had been stationed outside the city to await his arrival. Leachman's Arabic teacher, a well-off Christian named Aziz Azu, also had a home in the city and after discovering that the Turks had placed a police guard outside Majid's house he fled there. But the guard went with him. While the Ottoman gendarme waited at the front of Aziz Azu's house Leachman went through to the rear where a large, tree-lined garden swept down to a canal bank. He was wearing a dark suit and open-neck shirt. No one would have believed that he was on his way to central Arabia. He had to make his way along the canal to the encampment where his guide and the servants and animals were assembled. He hurriedly changed into Arab dress when he reached them and they made off across the shallow water of the Abu Dibbis lake and into the undulating desert which led to Tel Ibrahim where Majid was at camp. They reached the camp on the 27th. The Turks, alerted by the silence of Aziz Azu's home went inside to investigate. When they found that they had been hoodwinked they sent three mounted parties in search of the English visitor. One of them reached Majid's camp soon after Leachman, but the guest was hidden away and the Arabs assured the Turks that they had seen no one answering to the description of an *Inglizi*, improbably dressed in a western suit.

By the end of January Leachman was marching with Majid's Bedouin army through flat and unmapped desert in a south-easterly direction. Shakespear left Kuwait at the same time, heading south-west towards the Dahana sands which flicked down from the red dunes of the Nafud desert like an inflamed tongue until it disappeared in the wilderness of the Empty

Quarter far beyond the reach of any known traveller. Shakespear would turn sharp right at As-Safa, about 120 miles inland from Kuwait, towards the wells of Hafar and then march north-east along the Al Batin road. Leachman would keep going in the direction in which he had set out until they converged at a point where they could almost shout to each other across the silent waste. But neither was aware of the other's movements.

Bray, who came to know Leachman well, asserts that he was making for Hail the Shammar capital at this time. If so he was taking a strange path, travelling in the opposite direction from the Rashid homeland. In any case Ibn Rashid was coming his way with a vast army of tribesmen. It would have been pointless to have gone to Hail at that moment. The desert was in ferment. Armies were moving in all directions. London and Simla, Constantinople and the other centres of worldly ambition waited impatiently to know the outcome – to know which of the Arab princes would inherit the vast, unknown territory which their barely marked intelligence maps labelled 'Arabian Peninsula'.

By 3 February Leachman had travelled exactly 107 miles and was in the Wadi al Jarathim. A little farther on he came to the great dry wadi called Al Khur which had once, when Arabia was a well-watered land, carried plentiful water for more than 400 miles from its source somewhere close to Jauf into the Shatt al Arab. No European had ever recorded a sighting of the wadi at its extremity as it faded into the sands below the Euphrates. Leachman had made his first geographical discovery.

Majid's army met a party of Salaiba, the desert gypsies, on 5 February. The Salubba had their uses for the Arabs who otherwise despised them. They were the finest of all hunters and indefatigable carriers of gossip. They brought news that the Anaiza tribes were on the warpath, led in the east by their paramount shaikh, Ibn Shalan, reinstated at his capital Jauf, and in the west by Fahad Bey ibn Hadhal, a kindly old warrior who delighted in the company of his grandchildren in Baghdad when he was not leading his own children to battle against his hereditary enemies the Shammar.

Events began to take a strange turn. Majid's men moved cautiously, fearing an attack by the Anaiza as they marched towards the pilgrim route from Mecca to Baghdad, the Darb Zobaidah which was named after the wife of Harun Rashid of the *Arabian Nights*, its surface trampled to compactness by legions of the faithful over the past thousand years. But the ways of the tribal chiefs are not easy for the outsider to understand, and Leachman was surprised to learn that Majid had sent a gift of horses to Fahad Bey, the enemy chief, who was moving up on their rear while Ibn Shalan's Ruwalla tribesmen, the largest and most powerful section of the Anaiza, advanced on their right flank, hoping to intercept Ibn Rashid's Shammar force. By 6 February Leachman found Anaiza warriors wandering around the Shammar camp. By a curious courtesy of desert warfare, Fahad Bey had given Majid's men safe conduct in the Anaiza *dira* or grazing country through which they were travelling, and to show that his word could be trusted he had sent men of the Amarat, his own Anaiza tribe, to join their enemies in Leachman's encampment.

To the south, Ibn Saud was playing his part by raising a joint Saudi–Kuwait army to attack the Turk's other ally, Ibn Sadun, with whom the Shammar were in temporary alliance.

Such compacts are seldom reliable in desert war, and the cosy arrangement between Fahad and Majid was soon upset.

Leachman told the story a year later in the pages of the *Geographical Journal*, relating a stirring tale with commendable modesty.[3] His own part in the events of the next few days only came to light through the description given by Fahad Bey afterwards:

> On February 12, soon after dawn, we caught sight of the Anaiza moving parallel to our march, but unfortunately the Ruwalla, who knew nothing about the above-mentioned arrangement between the Shammar and the Amarat, were marching on the flank nearest us. Their horsemen soon swept down and by nightfall had seized the whole of the belongings, tents, camels, etc., of the Shammar after a running fight of several miles. My own small party of three managed to get away, and making a circuit to avoid the Ruwalla, succeeded in reaching the Amarat, whose Shaikh, Fahad Bey, received me most kindly.

It was a matter-of-fact account. And it was the first of only two essays Leachman was ever to write of his desert adventures.

He had been riding with Majid at the head of the Shammar column when the Ruwalla attacked. His companions Khidr and

Zawa were riding some distance away. The Shammar force had grown to several thousand men in strength as Bedouin bands joined it *en route*. The Ruwalla force was numerically stronger. Knowing that he could expect no protection from the Shammar he called his guides to him and the three of them galloped towards a depression where they were able to hide while battle raged and make their way gradually to the Anaiza camp some miles distant. Fahad Bey had promised protection and they would keep him to his word. In fact the old shaikh needed no persuasion. He treated Leachman and his friends with the greatest generosity. The Englishman had lost a camel and all his belongings in the flight to his camp. He replaced them ungrudgingly. But the conflict had hardly begun. Leachman learnt the details of the planned attack on the Shammar while he waited in the camp of Fahad Bey, where he was befriended by one of Ibn Shalan's men, 'a fine-looking ruffian', who had met the Austrian Musil.

Leachman had time, too, to assess the Amarat chief whose guest he was. Fahad had become cool. He knew by now, if he had not known from the outset, that he had an English agent in his midst, and he had no desire to upset the Turks who were his landlords in Baghdad, and protectors of his large family and large estates. He was old and nearly blind, said Leachman in his letters to his mother, ponderous on his feet but expert on horseback. He delivered his words slowly in a booming voice. He possessed a wide smile which would quickly dissolve when he was displeased or offended. When Leachman went to the old shaikh's tent on the Anaiza encampment soon after joining it he found his companions of the Abda Shammar, including Fahad, clamouring for restitution of their property. They had been promised *dakhala*, protection, during the battle. Instead, the Ruwalla had robbed them of everything. They complained of a 'great injustice'. Fahad had been forced to clear the harem of his tent to accommodate the complainants, while his womenfolk went off to separate accommodation.

Now in the chaos of Arab warfare Leachman was with the enemy of his former hosts and he had to march with the Anaiza from their camp at Lughatan.

His letters and notes, and his brief article in the *Geographical Journal*, provide a uniquely factual account of a desert army on the march, for the few explorers and soldiers who have travelled with such armies down the ages have usually been tempted to spice their stories with imaginative accounts of personal valour and sometimes romance. Leachman had neither the desire nor the ability to embellish his impressions. Writing did not come easily to him, and he was always careful, even in letters to his family, to avoid conjecture.

'The Anaiza, by far the largest tribe in Arabia, were at this time in exceptional strength,' he wrote. Only one *birkah* or reservoir was available on their route, at Jumaima – a stone structure 90 ft square with steps leading down to the water for the benefit of men and beasts. The column of men and animals was so great, however, that cruelty, as so often in the harsh places of the world, became the handmaid of kindness, and Fahad ordered that only *dhaluls*, riding camels, and men could be watered lest the *birkah* run dry. Baggage camels and women who did not have to work or fight could not be watered. The Bedouin disregarded the order until the shaikh's sons and chief men rode among them firing their rifles to warn off thirsty offenders.

At Jumaima news came that Ibn Rashid's main army was approaching, two days' march from Hail. The Anaiza pitched their tents in disciplined lines rather than in the haphazard layout of the usual Bedouin camp. Leachman counted some 3,500 black tents before he gave up his attempt to assess the strength of the force. Bands of tribesmen arrived by the hour from desert lairs, drawn irresistibly to the scene of battle by the promise of loot. The camp by the reservoir of Jumaima eventually covered the entire plain, stretching as far as the eye could see in an ocean of goat-hair black.

'These tribesmen are not true Bedouin,' wrote Leachman of the men who joined them from the Euphrates valley, Fahad Bey's irregulars. But they were better armed and carried Martini carbines of up-to-date manufacture. Most knocked the 'sights' off their rifles, having no use for such refinements. They were the Madan, part cultivators and part nomads, accustomed to defend their plots against the marauding bands of true Bedouin who lived by the raid, the *ghazzu*, and the theft of other men's possessions. As the Madan arrived they performed their war dances in front of the shaikh's tents, discharging their rifles in the air, leaping and chanting and generally making a colourful nuisance of themselves. The noise with which they announced their arrival was the undoing of the Anaiza army.

On 16 February heavy rifle fire was heard and Fahad's men thought that more Madan reinforcements had arrived. But it was the advance guard of Ibn Rashid's Shammar which came over the skyline, horse riders first, mounted on the finest mares in Arabia – 'drinkers of the wind' – followed by hundreds of *dhaluls*, fast she-camels, two men to a beast. Ibn Rashid had made a forced march and taken the Anaiza scouts by surprise. 'The Anaiza had but time to drive in their camels, and without much fight poured out of the opposite side of the camp, followed by masses of women and children on foot.'

It was dusk when the Shammar advance guard arrived at the camp and they rode straight through firing indiscriminately at tents and animals. When the alarm was given Leachman was seated in Fahad Bey's tent listening to the old shaikh's tales of war and desert history. Fahad was leaning against his camel saddle, his *khanjar*, the curved dagger of the desert warrior, resting on his thighs, his chiefs and guests seated in a semi-circle at his side, sipping coffee and listening politely.

As the Shammar burst on the scene Leachman ordered his servants to collect his camels and dash for Majid's tents where they would be safe. Though allied to the Shammar, Majid had agreed a truce with Fahad and took no part in the fight. Leachman stood with the Anaiza chief in the entrance of the tent and watched as the panic-stricken Anaiza rushed with their women and children to the shelter of wadis and desert hide-outs. 'It seemed odds on the Shammar,' Leachman noted, 'but I misjudged the speed at which the Anaiza could bolt.' He photographed the flight of his companions. Then, when the excitement was over he went to bed for a few hours. He knew that it would be as well to be up early next morning.

It was not until the following afternoon that the main army of the Shammar burst on the Anaiza camp. Led by horse-mounted cavalry and followed by camel riders they came like a tornado, cutting down the tents in their path, firing on animals and men. Most of the women and children had been sent to a safe area. But not a single tent of the Anaiza camp was spared and every possession of the forlorn army of Fahad Bey was taken. In the end Majid's men, camped near by, could not resist the temptation of so much loot. As they arrived on the scene they found their erstwhile companion Leachman sitting in his tent writing letters. The women left on the encampment had crowded into his tent

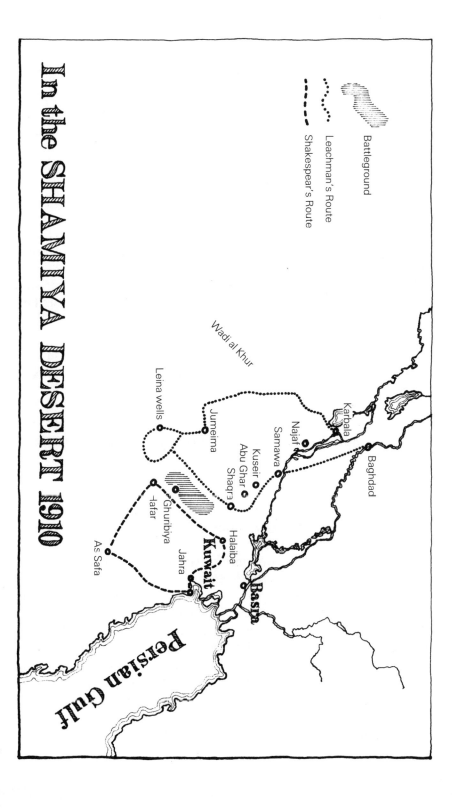

and pressed their jewellery on him before fleeing to the safety of a nearby depression. His tent was pitched among those of the shaikhs. After the pillage of the Bedouin tents the Shammar leaders came to Fahad, and then looked into Leachman's abode. He told them to stand away. They were in his light. Majid arrived on the scene to explain that here was the Englishman who had come to meet the Prince of Hail. Thus Leachman was led away from the desolate camp of the Anaiza to join their enemies at Zabala, twelve miles away by the Darb Zobaidah. Zamil ibn Subhan, the leader of the Shammar force, Regent of Hail and the only gentleman of that homicidal royal house, sent a message to Fahad regretting that he had not been able to pay his respects. A Shammar orphan who had seen his only adult relative, an uncle, killed in battle shot himself in remorse. The Anaiza buried their dead, surprisingly few in the light of their poor resistance. The women had collected their ornaments from Leachman before he moved off to join the Rashids.

The Shammar tents were white, easily distinguishable from the tents of all the other wandering tribes of inner Arabia, and made from canvas supplied to Hail by the Turks rather than from goat-hair laboriously woven by the women of the other clans. Leachman reached the Rashid encampment on 17 February at nightfall and the valley of Zabala glowed in the light of countless flickering camp-fires.

He was becoming accustomed to the way of life of Arabia's Badu, its noble tribes, competing for space and food in a wilderness as large as the sub-continent of India, fighting a daily battle for survival in stony, rocky, sandy regions where only the locusts could survive in the hardest times, sustained by the greenery devoured on their transcontinental journeys, to become a delicacy at the desert dweller's feasts.

Leachman was put to work bandaging wounds and treating sores, working by the light of hurricane lamps. The *Faranji*, the European, had one special virtue for the Badu. All were 'doctors'. All could treat the sick. And as he tended them he noted their devoutness, these men who had inherited none of life's riches yet thanked God for every small mercy and used His name in every sentence they uttered, though not always reverently.

He called at the royal tent the morning after his arrival to pay his respects to the young Amir Saud ibn Rashid and his uncle and Regent Zamil ibn Subhan. He was received splendidly by the hereditary standard-bearer of the Rashids, Abdullah Mubarak al Faraik, 'a gorgeous person' who took coffee with him while they awaited the call to the Amir's tent.

The handsome, unsmiling child prince sat silent at the audience. It was Zamil who received the Englishman with a firm grasp of the hand and the lengthy salutations of the Arab encounter. Nobody in the camp spoke English. Leachman's Arabic had improved to the point where he could follow the conversation reasonably well, though he had to ask the Regent to repeat to him some of the important details of desert politics and family history which Zamil related with mounting enthusiasm.

Leachman was to remain in the Rashid camp for five weeks, closer than any outsider had ever been to the Rashids. The chiefs boasted of homicide, relating as other men would relate the everyday happenings of the ghazzu the cut-throat deeds which had sent fathers and mothers to their deaths at the hands of their own children, and caused fathers and uncles to murder infants in their swaddling clothes. The English guest listened with rapt attention as the deeds of the royal house of Shammar were told to him by the culprits themselves, and embellished by their servants, especially by the standard-bearer Abdullah Mubarak who took a liking to Leachman and followed him everywhere. But even Leachman, close as he was to the sinister men of Hail, did not hear the full story of murder and intrigue which had surrounded the events of the past year, events which in some ways eclipsed even the bloodbaths of the more distant past, and which were to lead to more domestic slaughter.

Leachman had been preceded into the Arabian hinterland by Captain Butler, his companion on the first stage of the journey into Kashmir in 1906. Butler had been posted on special duty to East Africa shortly after the Kashmir exercise in which he was engaged. In 1908, due for home leave, MO2 asked him to team up with a fellow staff officer, Captain Aylmer, and to travel to England by the somewhat circuitous route of Baghdad and Jauf, where the Rashids were still in control, governing the town and its surroundings through a member of the family, Faisal ibn Hamud al-Rashid, and where much gossip connected with the shifting alignments of the Arab chiefs was to be picked from the grapevine.

Thus the two officers took the previously untravelled road from Baghdad to Jauf with guides from the Anaiza tribe, the brothers Muhammad and Abdullah al Mathi. Only one of them, Abdullah, would be permitted to enter the territory of the Shammar enemy.

When they arrived at Jauf they were led to an upper room of the Governor's mud-brick castle, Kasr Marid, where they sat cross-legged on the floor and sipped coffee with host and slaves, while the artful Faisal filched their possessions, asking casually if he could have their watches, compasses, binoculars. 'A system of polite robbery,' Butler called it.[4] Suspicion was engraved deeply in Faisal's features, and his heavily-lidded eyes lacked the lustre to which comparative youth entitled them. They heard the story of power-struggles in the Rashid family over recent years told with chilling candour, related by Faisal himself and by the slaves, relayed to them by Abdullah al Mathi in the halting English which he had acquired in the bazaars of Baghdad and Damascus.

The tale went back to 1906 when the Amir of Hail, Abdal Aziz ibn Rashid, died in battle with the army of his namesake and enemy, Abdal Aziz ibn Saud. The Amir of Hail was a brave warrior but he was so afraid of his murderous family that he never set foot in the capital after becoming the ruler. But he left three sons there: Mitab, Mishal and Muhammad; the eldest, Mitab, becoming the Ruler on his death. Another son, Saud, was just eight years old when his father fell on the battlefield, and to protect him from his brothers and cousins he was sent by his uncle Zamil to the sanctuary of the Prophet's city, Madina, where he was in the care of the Sharif Husain ibn Ali.

There were also three cousins of the Amir Abdal Aziz alive in Hail when he died on the battlefield. Their names were Sultan, Faisal and Saud, the sons of Hamud. One of them, Faisal, sat on the carpeted floor of the Jauf castle where Butler and Aylmer, fleeced of their belongings, listened.

After Mitab had been on the throne for about six months the three cousins decided to dispose of him and his brothers. They invited the three boys, including the Prince Mitab, to a picnic and rifle-shooting competition. The brothers took a friend on the outing, Tallal ibn Naif, and the four youngsters went off with their attendants to a prearranged spot in the desert, looking forward to a day of innocent sport. As they sat watching a display of horsemanship the cousins Sultan, Faisal and Saud stole up behind the boys and shot them in the back. Three, including the Amir Mitab, were killed instantly but the fourth boy Muhammad was carried badly wounded to his mother who, as it happened, was the sister of the murderers. The mother nursed her son back to life though he would probably have been a permanent invalid. But no male child of the line must be allowed to live and so, two months after the shooting, Saud Ibn Hamud with six slaves burst into his sister's home and cut the injured child to pieces before the eyes of its demented mother.

'Faisal's reputation is not too savoury,' noted Captain Butler.

Even more recently the culprit Saud had murdered his brother Sultan. And his brother Faisal lived in fear of retribution by the Regent Zamil, the maternal uncle of the infant Prince Saud who was taken to al Madina – the prince who was now back in his homeland under the wing of Zamil, Leachman's host at the Shammar encampment. Butler and Aylmer travelled from Faisal's lair through Wadi Sirhan, the northern gateway of the inner desert, to Damascus, and they reached England with two pairs of oryx horns, the parting gift of Faisal bin Hamud, who was generally called Faisal bin Rashid.

Leachman heard whispered revelation of the stories told to his compatriot at Jauf, and he made notes of the details of family strife and fratricide as he worked by lamplight in his tent at night. As he moved among the Shammar tribesmen he knew that an ill-advised question or gesture would probably be his last.

He described his first encounter with the princes of Hail.

I was called to the Amir, who was sitting in audience in a great tent with the regent, Zamil ibn Subhan, by his side. Saud is a handsome little boy with beautiful features and very fair. He is a fine horseman, riding being in fact his only amusement, and being but a child he becomes very weary of the long sittings in the *majlis*, where tribal affairs are discussed at inordinate length. He exhibits at times a most violent temper, which, with his features and other characteristics, he seems to have inherited from his father Abdal Aziz. Zamil ibn Subhan, the regent, is a man of thirty-four but, in spite of his youth, is probably a stronger man than the Ibn ar-Rashid Amirate have seen for many years. He is largely responsible for a very great change that is taking place in the position and character of this Central Arabian power.

These were the rulers whom Britain and the Ottoman Government saw as the stabilizing element in the peninsula and counterbalance to the ambitions of the Saudi Prince Abdal Aziz who had been at war with the Rashids constantly since he snatched his capital from them in 1901 after an occupation which had lasted for ten years.[5]

Leachman noted the current shifts of political allegiance. Zamil always referred to the Ottoman power as *dowlatana*, our regime. The Mutair, a tribe closely associated with the Shaikh of Kuwait in the past, was currently friendly towards Ibn Rashid, as were most of the central tribes. Sadun Pasha, shaikh of the Shi'a Muntafiq tribes, was an ally of convenience. Only Mubarak of Kuwait and Ibn Saud were at daggers-drawn with the princes of Hail, or so Leachman was led to believe.

The Hail folk were disciplined and devout as they went about their daily tasks in the great encampment: '*Muezzins* call at the usual hours in different parts of the camp . . . absentees are noticed and often beaten.' And he saw that piety did not embrace sectarian tolerance: 'They were fond of impressing upon me the fact that though they would eat food with me, they would not do so with Shi'a.'

He had been with them for five weeks, sharing the joys and burdens of Bedouin life, eating from the mountainous heap of the Amir's platter, drinking coffee in an endless round of social chatter, playing war games with the little prince who always led the proceedings on horseback, galloping among the tents with lance in hand, followed by his own horseguard. Arab guests at the camp were usually teamed with Leachman. It was the only time that Saud ibn Rashid ever smiled. At night Leachman visited the *divans* of the shaikhs to hear stories of war and the *ghazzu*, to listen to the unwritten history of the desert and to the unintelligible intonations of the camp poets. If the poets were not well recompensed they would go off to other tribal camps to make money by ridiculing their former employers.

He made repeated requests to Zamil to be allowed to march with the Shammar army and to journey to Hail with the Rashids. But Zamil had no intention at that time of inviting the English guest to his capital. He told Leachman that his life and his goods were in his hands, and he would have no hesitation in taking either or both if the occasion demanded. Leachman understood the message. On 23 February he had written to Shakespear in Kuwait to ask the new Political Agent if he would take delivery of his mail and to pass on the tittle-tattle of the Rashid camp. He was unaware at the moment of writing that the other Englishman was two days' march away in the desert, ploughing along the Al Batin depression in direct line with the Shammar camp and keeping an eye on the movements of Ibn Rashid and his temporary allies the Muntafiq.

23rd February 1910

Dear Shakespear,
I know your name from Gibbon in the Intelligence at Simla. I am here at camp with Ibn Rashid near Hail. Three days ago I was with a very large mass of the Anaiza on their way to attack Ibn Rashid. In the evening Rashid appeared and utterly defeated the Anaiza who got away with their camels only. Rashid's men looted thousands of tents. I took refuge with some of the Shammar who were prisoners with the Anaiza and with whom I had been for a few days before they were captured . . . They say civil war has broken out in Ibn Saud's kingdom, between his two brothers. I believe this is true. You know who the rival factions are so I won't bother you with details.

Sincerely, G. Leachman.

A few days later, having only recently arrived at the Rashid camp but already deep in the gossip of the warring tribes, he wrote to the Resident, Lorimer, in Baghdad, recounting again the events which led to his capture and his presence as a guest in the Shammar camp. And to Lorimer he divulged that the movement of the Anaiza force with which he left the Euphrates in late January had a larger purpose than he had indicated in his diary notes and letters: 'This movement of the Anaiza was concerted with Ibn Saud with the idea of utterly finishing the Rashid power. I came with the Shammar back to this place where Ibn Rashid is camped.'

His report to Lorimer was written in late March after he had been told by Zamil that he must leave the Rashid camp and make for the territory of the friendly Dhafir tribe in the direction of the

Kuwait hinterland.

A week before Leachman's letter was despatched to him Shakespear was camped at Halaiba, close to the deserted region to which his compatriot was ordered to proceed. And at Halaiba Shakespear had heard from one of Shaikh Mubarak's men the story of dissent in the Saudi camp. It was not quite as Leachman had been led to believe. Ibn Saud and the brothers who were supposed to be at odds with him were in fact on their way to Kuwait to meet the English Political Agent.

An attempt had been made to poison the Saudi Amir by two of his cousins, members of the royal family who were known collectively as the 'Araif', the lost ones, and who laid claim to the throne of Riyadh.[6] They had put the poison in his coffee but their work was frustrated by the sister of Ibn Saud who always insisted that his coffee should be tasted by a slave before her brother's was poured.[7] The slave had perished and the cousins made off hurriedly in the direction of the Hasa coast where they sought the protection of the Turkish garrison at Hofuf.

Shakespear arrived back at Kuwait on the last day of February to find Ibn Saud and his brothers waiting for him in the company of Shaikh Mubarak and Faisal ibn Rashid.

The deposed Governor of Hail had gone hot-foot to Kuwait after Hail had been taken by Nawwaf, the son of Nuri Shalan, in January 1909. The sullen-faced Faisal was eventually granted asylum by Ibn Saud at Riyadh, and on the last day of February 1910 he sat at dinner in Mubarak's unlovely palace on the Kuwait seafront. He was with his protector Ibn Saud, and the brothers of the Saudi leader. Shakespear was the other guest.

The Arab chiefs had planned an attack on Ibn Sadun's Muntafiq and their allies the Dhafir, and the atmosphere was conspiratorial. Shakespear and Ibn Saud got on famously. The other Arab leaders viewed the Englishman in their midst with frowning suspicion. The British Government, anxious to placate the Turks, would not look kindly on an act of open war against the friends of Ibn Rashid. And Ibn Rashid would make sure that at least one Englishman, Leachman, was given a ringside seat as the joint Saudi–Kuwait army made its incursion into the borderland region of northern Kuwait and Turkish Mesopotamia.

On 1 March the notables of Riyadh and Kuwait were entertained by Shakespear at the Political Agency. Afterwards Shakespear reported to the Government in London, through

Simla, that they spent a pleasant evening together and talked no politics, except for Ibn Saud's avowal that he would trust Britain and that his chief ambition was to rid his country of the Turks.

Next day the Arab contingent left for the oasis of Jahra due west from Kuwait town where a vast Bedouin army was camped around a single permanent building, the *kasr hamra* or Red Fort. Shakespear spent several days with the Saudi princes observing the comings and goings of a force whose discipline left a lot to be desired. They banged their war-drums incessantly and worked themselves up to a fever of excitement and then – as often as not – left the assembly ground to go off on a raid of their own. The generals never quite knew the size or composition of their force. Still, by the second week of March a unit of Ibn Saud's cavalry and a Kuwaiti army composed chiefly of Ajman and Mutair tribesmen was ready to move off.[8] Mubarak's official explanation was that his rag-tag army proposed to teach the Dhafir and Muntafiq tribes a lesson for recent raids on his tribes, and he explained that he was sending his eldest son, Jabir, to take charge of his contingents, though he had no great faith in his ability as a leader. As Leachman had noted, the raid had a larger purpose than Mubarak or the Saudis were willing to admit. It was part of the concerted effort of Ibn Saud and his northern ally, Ibn Shalan, with the help of Fahad Bey's Bishr-Anaiza, to subdue the Rashids of Hail and their temporary comrades-in-arms, the Muntafiq. It was a prospect which alarmed Britain as much as the Turks, for a victorious Ibn Saud would, they believed, threaten the entire Gulf region as far as Trucial Oman, and even beyond to the Yemen. For the moment, however, Britain's political representative on the spot decided that it was a domestic affair and reserved his official report until the outcome was decided.

Leachman's presence at the Shammar camp was reported to the Turkish governor of Basra in March. The Wali asked Britain's man, Consul F.E. Crow, what the Englishman was doing with Ibn Rashid. Crow replied: 'He's an English dervish studying botany in the desert.'

If the governor was deceived he was swift to take action to remove the 'botanist' from a stony desert in which few plants grew at the best of times.

During the third week of March news came to the Rashid camp which had moved to Jumaima of a battle at the nearby plain of

Ghuribiya. Zamil was told by a messenger from the Wali of Basra to expel his visitor, and on 25 March Leachman was packing his bags. The Regent's instruction was delivered reluctantly. Zamil was a broadminded man, worldly and, unlike his kinsmen of Hail, generous in his response to friend and foe. He had taken to the reckless Englishman and was sorry to see him go.

Zamil was secretly sympathetic to the rulers of Riyadh in whose cause – adherence to the religious precepts of Muhammad ibn Abdal Wahhab preached in the middle years of the eighteenth century – his ancestors had taken up residence at Hail.[9] Now a member of his family, Faisal ibn Hamud, was with Ibn Saud and a new alliance in central Arabia was rumoured. Leachman picked up the suggestions of intrigue and the rumblings of royal rivalry as he came to the end of his five boisterous weeks in the Shammar camp. More heads would fall before the Rashids departed the Arabian stage. Yet not all the tales were of murder and insane power mania. The Badu liked to retell the enchanting story of their ancestors' rise to power in the mountainous region of Jabal Shammar as they gossiped round the camp-fire. They told of the first true ruler among the Rashids, Abdullah of the family of Ali who recognized the authority of the Sauds, who was opposed in his youthful ambition to set up ordered government at Hail.[10] Foiled by local shaikhs he was forced into exile in the Syrian desert and there, so the story went, he was attacked by the Anaiza who left him for dead, slitting his throat and the throats of his companions before they left. But the destiny of Jabal Shammar could not so easily be disposed of, and while Abdullah lay in the hot desert, blood ebbing from the gaping gash, locusts gathered above the young chief and by the fluttering of a myriad pairs of wings blew a cloud of sand into his wounds until the flow of blood was stayed by the 'rude styptic' and his life stream began to flow. A flock of Kata, common birds then in Arabia, gathered over the reviving body of the prince and formed a giant shade to protect him from the sun.[11] Thus did Abdullah live on to become Ibn Rashid, the Viceroy of Faisal ibn Saud, until his death in 1845, according to the legend of the Badu, the wandering people of Arabia. And on his death, his son Tallal made himself absolute ruler and denounced his father's loyalty to the Ibn Sauds. That much at least is historically true.

Abdullah and his brother, Obaidallah, usually known as

Obaid, were together the suffragan princes of Hail from 1838, though Abdullah was the acknowledged ruler. Obaid's sons were noted for their bravery in battle. Since those days the rulers had come from the issue of Abdullah and his son Tallal, the politicians and military leaders from Obaid's side. Zamil ibn Subhan was connected by marriage to the latter.

The little Prince Saud and his uncle Zamil were a solemn pair when Leachman bade them farewell. The boy-prince had lost a playmate and his Regent had important matters on his mind. But there were many salaams, and Abdullah, the standard-bearer, planted a kiss on the Englishman's mouth. He marched off with a small party of Shammar towards Khamisiya on the Euphrates to buy food, on 25 March.

They travelled fast over unexplored territory to the Hajara desert and the tribal *dira* of the Dhafir. In gravelly, featureless country that was one of the great battlefields of Arabia, they found the war-camp of Sadun Pasha, paramount shaikh of the Muntafiq tribes. Sadun knew that the Englishman was on the way to his camp and there was a warm welcome. The shaikh was expecting another attack by the combined force of Mubarak of Kuwait and Ibn Saud of Riyadh. The battle planned in Shakespear's presence while Leachman was with Ibn Rashid had taken place on 18 March and the attackers had suffered a salutary defeat. When Leachman arrived at the scene of the fight the ground was littered with corpses of the joint army. The hyenas had done their work by night and by day the vultures and wolves stared disconsolately at bare bones and tore at the purple remains of human flesh.

It had rained heavily on the way to Ghuribiya, the scene of recent battle, and the journey across gravel and squelching sand had been accompanied by the strange metamorphosis of the desert when the wilderness becomes an instant garden of flowers and bushes appear as if from nowhere. Life is sustained by a sudden miracle and a day or two later it disappears from sight again and man is alone with his camels and sheep. Thus it was by the time Leachman reached Ghuribiya in the company of the man Zamil had sent to guard his caravan, Khadam ibn Faid, 'a delightful gentleman with manners such as I have never seen'. He met another of the great shaikhs of inner Arabia, Faisal ad-Duwish, chief of the Mutair, who was to become famous in the world as the leader of the fanatical religious revivalist movement known as the Ikhwan, 'The Brotherhood', the spearhead of Ibn Saud's eventual rise to power in the kingdom of his Wahhabist ancestors. Faisal al-Duwish's home was far to the south of Leachman's route, at Al Artawiya, but the grazing-grounds of his tribe stretched to the borders of Kuwait and the Hasa coast which the Turks had taken from the Sauds nearly fifty years before. Shakespear knew Ibn Duwish well and called him 'fat Faisal'; they hunted their hawks in friendly combat. But Faisal was to become too big for Arabia to hold and he was to suffer perhaps the saddest fate of all its leaders. At the time Leachman first met him he was a keen businessman who prospered by robbing the Buraida caravans which set out from Kuwait to central Arabia, and he offered to conduct the Englishman anywhere 'for suitable recompense'.

But it was Ibn Sadun who impressed Leachman most. He was 'a most delightful man' and Leachman felt more at home with him than with any man he had so far met in his life. Sadun spoke with some amusement of the recent battle. Ibn Saud's men had been badly let down by the infantry led by Jabir as-Sabah, Mubarak's son, it seemed. But the old man of Kuwait had made the most of a defeat signalled by the return of a demoralized army, its men riding sometimes four to a camel, its wounded left to die alongside fallen comrades in the desert. In fact Mubarak had complained to Shakespear that his men had been subject to an unprovoked attack by Ibn Sadun while on a shooting expedition. Shakespear, who had himself observed the build-up at Ghuribiya and nearby Rakhaiya, observed that an army of some 8,000 men constituted quite a large shooting-party. When he asked the shaikh why his men had suffered such a decisive and wholesale defeat, Mubarak – seldom lost for an explanation – replied: 'O my friend it was nothing. A dust cloud blew up at a critical moment and my men couldn't see.'

Shakespear had to tell the Resident at Bushire about the battle. Mubarak had become Britain's client and he was constantly being warned to keep out of trouble. On 22 March the Political Agent received a note from the Foreign Department at Simla which did not mince words: 'You will see that the Government of India direct that a warning be conveyed to Shaikh Mubarak, in terms of previous warning, not to enter into any operations calculated to involve him in difficulties in Najd or with the Turks.' When Shakespear went to find Mubarak to deliver the reprimand he found that the shaikh was back at Jahra with Ibn Saud preparing another raid on Sadun. But Britain's salvo had its effect. Ibn Saud called off the expedition, perhaps more gratefully than he cared to admit. The other Englishman on the scene waited in vain with Ibn Sadun for conflict to materialize, and townsmen came to reinforce the Muntafiq from the smallholdings of the Euphrates valley.

In April, Sadun took Leachman on a lengthy march, his standard carried behind him, his disciplined army an inspiring sight, and his English guest – ever precise in his observation of potential friend and foe – noted that they were less efficient in pitching their tents and the organization of their camp than Ibn Rashid's Shammar. And the daily *majlis* at which Ibn Sadun dispensed the justice of the desert was more businesslike than the councils of other shaikhs. Leachman met an *ageyl*, one of the Ottoman constables who escort travellers and caravans in no-man's-land. He had been in France, England and America, and asked the Englishman if he was 'a traveller'. When Leachman replied that he was, the man startled him by declaring 'You're a liar!'

The Arab leader and the Englishman camped together at Bir Shaqra as they marched northward, beneath a ruined castle, and they were brought news of the expected Saudi attack. It was a false alarm, but Sadun gave out battle orders with evident delight and his men danced in the flickering light of the camp-fires.

Leachman's servants had endured enough of the adventure. One of them babbled like a lunatic and the other admitted to shattered nerves. They sought permission to flee from what was still expected to be a battlefield to go to Khamisiya and on to their homes at Karbala. But by the time Leachman had finished with them they decided that war was better than the wrath of their master. On 4 April the army returned to Ghuribiya and the next day nearly 3,000 men paraded for their chief, each clan with its own banner, the white-clad soldiers brandishing rifles and sabres and shouting their deep-throated war-cries. They were joined by the Dhafir, their neighbours and allies, who galloped and trotted on to the parade ground. It was a spectacle Leachman would not soon forget.

He said farewell to Sadun Pasha on 7 April, 'this fine old man, so up to date and so courteous, very rich and a splendid soldier and a cordial enemy of the Turks'.

Within a year of that memorable meeting, Leachman's 'gentle-man' companion of the Shamiya desert, one of the finest of all Arab chiefs, would be arrested by the Turkish Wali of Basra through the duplicity of Sayyid Talib, the rogue son of one of the Province's leading citizens, the venal Naqib Sayid Rajjab.[12] Sadun Pasha was taken to Aleppo and gaoled there. He died of an alleged heart attack in November 1911, but according to British reports he was poisoned.[13] His son Ajaimi, in the tradition of Oriental arrangements, became a great leader in his father's stead and a loyal supporter of his enemy the Turk.

Leachman reached Baghdad on 21 April. The Turks, who by now were aware of his desert journey and his contacts in the hinterland, kept an eye open for him but they would not have suspected the unkempt ruffian who made his way on camel-back to the Tigris. He entered Baghdad at dusk and later that evening, bathed and dressed in the uniform of a lieutenant of the British army, he was entertained at dinner by His Excellency the Resident.

9

Through Kurdistan and Syria

By the year 1910 radical government in London had fed aspirant nationalism in the world with the succulent diet of Home Rule; and aspiration turned inevitably to revolutionary fervour. Trouble came to the streets of India as to Ireland and Africa, and assassination became the tool of the reformer. India's secret service chief, the massive and taciturn Charles Cleveland, began to record the setting-up of revolutionary organizations in Bengal and elsewhere. And Gulf intelligence at Jask became aware of a revival of the age-old gun-running sprees of the tribesmen and pirates of Oman who were being supplied with German and Belgian arms through Turkey and taking them across the Gulf to Baluchistan and thence to Afghanistan and the North-West Frontier.

India was alarmed. But the Foreign Secretary, Sir Edward Grey, maintained that the peace should be kept in Europe at whatever cost in the East, and he found a willing accomplice in Morley at the India Office who set himself to trim the wings of the viceregal authority to a point where *The Times* thundered that he was, in the so-called Minto–Morley reforms, acting 'unconstitutionally'.

It was the year of the Coronation durbar at Delhi, when the assumption of George V to the title King-Emperor, was marked for the first time by the appearance of the sovereign himself among the hundreds of millions of his subjects; the year of Morley's enforced retirement from the India Office and Lord

Crewe's accession, and of the appearance of Charles Hardinge, senior under-secretary at the Foreign Office, as Viceroy in place of the infirm Minto. Men of empire took heart, though one of them, Aubrey Herbert in Constantinople, saw in the promise of Home Rule, however tentative, 'the end of Britain's imperial reign'. His was not a lone voice.

The battle between Whitehall and India intensified rather than diminished under the new regime. The Foreign Office maintained its strict rule, 'no incursions into central Arabia'. But the secret service had its own priorities and if need be would keep up a surveillance of the Arab lands and the other provinces of the Ottoman Empire in defiance of Sir Edward Grey. Applications to travel in those lands, once dealt with by 'Foreign' Simla and the FO in London, became the concern of the C-in-C India and the Chief of Staff in London, and their directors of military operations began to decide who would travel and who would not. A battle royal ensued with the Foreign Office.

The Germans were running riot in Mesopotamia where their brilliant archaeological team surveyed the country for military purposes as it dug among the ruins of Babylonia and Assyria, and the chief intelligence officer among them, Conrad Preusser, appointed agents in every important centre. *The Times*'s man in Constantinople, Philip Graves, began to write about the activities of the German rail-engineers in Mesopotamia and Syria, where Meissner Pasha was putting the finishing touches to the Hijaz line. And as Leachman and Shakespear came out of the desert having between them made contact with the most important chiefs of Arabia and heard at first hand the rumblings of change and insurrection in their domains, the Austrian Musil arrived in Constantinople with the staff officer Thomasburger to receive instructions for his next journey to the Arabian heartland. But it was the application of a Danish mission known to have close contacts with German agents in Copenhagen to visit Arabia by way of Kuwait, and to make for Riyadh, which forced military intelligence in London and Cairo to act in defiance of the Foreign Office.

The file marked 'Travellers in Arabia' in the Political and Secret Department of the India Office grew thick as the new ambassador to the Ottoman 'Porte', Sir Gerard Lowther, began to tell the Foreign Secretary of Fitzmaurice's suspicions of conspiracies by French, German and Zionist agents, and even of

Freemasons, in the Ottoman Empire.

In March, as battle raged between Ibn Saud and Ibn Sadun at Ghuribiya, the Viceroy had asked the Secretary of State for India to obtain permission for one of his Indian army staff officers, Captain Fraser Hunter of the Survey Department, to travel in Arabia. He wished to travel across the peninsula from Madina to Kuwait and then down through the unknown Empty Quarter, the Rub al Khali, to Yemen. Part of the journey would be made in a motor-car. The official excuse was the map of Arabia on which Hunter and the Resident at Baghdad, J. G. Lorimer, were then working as part of the *Gazetteer of the Persian Gulf* which Lorimer was preparing as a secret guide to Britain's role in the area. But the possible need to transport men and materials in and around the Arabian deserts was in the minds of the Viceroy's military chiefs. Lowther in Constantinople recommended that the application be turned down and on 26 April Morley conveyed his official verdict to the Viceroy, regretting that no such journeys could be contemplated 'on political grounds'.

I am not staying at the Residency at present, as I have to dissociate myself from the British Government in the eyes of the Turks. I thought I should arrive back in civilisation to discover that I was a captain, but it does not seem to be so. I really think I shall have to abandon the profession of arms for a time and become a diplomatic servant in this country. I think I could get a consulship in Armenia easily, and there would be more chance of advancement.

Thoughts of promotion in the army doubtless gave rise to discussion of the alternatives at the Residency and it seems that Lorimer held out hope of a consulship in one or other of the less popular Ottoman vilayets. But Leachman's tasks were determined elsewhere and promotion would come in due course:

I shall go north to Mosul and round to Syria and do a touch in the Holy Land. I remember I was badly jumped on by father for not having gone to Babylon and Jerusalem when last in these parts. I have done Babylon, and must now do Jerusalem . . . I am enclosing a photograph of my beautiful self in Arab kit . . . Don't you think I am most Biblical in appearance? I am sorry the Liberals got in again. Things seem in a bad way in England. I am staying in a beautiful house on the river, with a select party of bachelors, and we have a never-ceasing stream of every nationality and seldom sit down to dinner with less than four different countries being represented. I am becoming quite a flyer at Arabic, as I should be after three months of nothing else.

He set off on 10 May 1910 on a journey very different from that outlined in his letter to the family. A remarkable 1,300-mile trek through the mountainous region of Kurdistan was the objective. He left in the shadow of a dispute about the journey of another special-duty officer, Captain Teesdale, who arrived in Baghdad from Anatolia while Leachman was making his preparations. Lowther at Constantinople had told Sir Edward Grey that the journeys of both Teesdale and Leachman had caused 'suspicion' in official Turkish quarters, and that the former must report to Lorimer immediately on his arrival in Baghdad. Lorimer was expected to read the riot act, even though the officer was travelling on behalf of military intelligence. But Lorimer was no supporter of Sir Edward Grey's policy of appeasing Germany and his reprimand was benign. Teesdale was sent on his way to Basra and Leachman wished God speed.

There was a condition of travel this time, however. Lorimer had to ask formal permission of the Wali, Nazim Pasha, and the governor insisted that Leachman should be accompanied by two Turkish gendarmes. Nazim was not lacking in humour. He sent the two mounted policemen who had vainly pursued the Englishman in the race for Fahad Bey's camp three months before.

By 1 June they were in the mountainous region of the Hamrin, at Kara Tepe, where the Turks kept a garrison which tried its best to maintain order among the world's most unruly tribesmen. Leachman was probably better equipped by nature than the entire complement of Ottoman soldiers to keep the peace in such a wild region. The Kurds were his kind, 'a fine lot of ruffians', and he was soon at home among them. He stayed overnight with the *mudir* of Kara Tepe and was greatly taken with his son whom he described as 'beautiful . . . really beautiful'. A few days later he was at Tauq where he found female beauty to admire, 'the most lovely girl I think I have ever seen'. The Kurds who were yet to become a thorn in his side were for the moment admirable.

Even the Turks seemed to be softened and made bearable by the mountain air and the eloquent charm of an ungovernable people. The arrival of the mail was a cause for celebration, for more often than not it was intercepted by booty-seeking tribesmen. And when they discovered that their English visitor who spoke better Arabic than most of them was unmarried at the advanced age of thirty they ribbed him unmercifully and made ribald offers of girls and boys to comfort him, using a strange mixture of Arabic and Kurdish and all manner of gestures to convey their meaning. At Kirkuk he met one of the Young Turk governors, imprisoned for years and tortured by Abdal Hamid's police, but now representing the new regime.

The Lesser Zab river was crossed on 6 June and a Turkish veteran of Plevna waited on the opposite bank to greet him – a fine old man whose body bore the scars of that famous siege. The old warrior and the youngster embraced and Leachman began to see that patriotism was not confined to Englishmen, and to understand that many a Turk still regarded the British as his natural and traditional ally. Some still talked fondly of the Crimea and believed that one day Turk and Briton would fight side by side again. On 8 June Leachman and his guards reached Mosul the capital of Kurdistan, presided over by Muhammad Pasha Daghistani, a man admired uniquely by Arab, Turk and Kurd. Daghistani's reputation went before him. He was said, in his youth, to have rescued a child from the mouth of one of the lions which roamed his house and lived on its rooftop. At sixty he was still one of the finest shots in the Empire, loved and feared by his people. He was a man who spoke Leachman's language and they spent eight days in each other's company, the Arab governor confiding freely in his guest.

Leachman left Mosul reluctantly on 17 June and went back across the Zab with his ever-present *zaptiehs*, towards the disputed Turco-Persian border (disputed to the present day though in 1914 Britain hammered boundary posts into the ground) and to trouble at the village of Darband where his foolish companions took him to the mosque and tribal fanatics gathered to protest. The infidel Englishman stood his ground as the locals declared a miniature holy war and they eventually dispersed, to the surprise of the Turks who took cover when trouble brewed. The Arbil–Rowanduz road led them to Balaal Zaqiq where in summer the fleas were so plentiful that all the inhabitants were driven from

Journey in
KURDISTAN 1910

their homes by them. They lost their way as they made for Rowanduz high in the mountains, and for the first time on this journey his temper was roused. The Rowanduz gorge, one of the most majestic sights in the world, was lost on him and he could offer his parents nothing better by way of description than 'beastly gorge with river running through it'.

The traveller's response to nature improved as they advanced through the vilayet of Van to the great plain of Urmi on the southern border of Armenia, where the Czar stated his claim to precedence with a large consular office and his private telegraph, though the world recognized the territory as part of the Ottoman Empire. Leachman wrote:

The place is full of missions, including that of the Archbishop of Canterbury to the Nestorians, and an American Presbyterian Mission which maintains a college two miles outside the town. There is a special quarter for Christians. The bazaars which are sun-roofed are splendid and are very clean and have magnificent shops and khans. The road from the town to the lake of Urmia passes through miles of beautiful orchards till it reaches the shore of the lake of Girmakhana. The lake itself is most beautifully blue and very salt.

A week's rest in that smiling land restored Leachman and his companions to full vigour after the weary march of nearly 300 miles from Mosul across some of the most rugged country and through rapscallion tribal regions.

'I had a most delightful week in Urmia,' he told his mother. The respite was short-lived. As they crossed the Persian–Turkish border (which then ran west of the lake) and made for the province of Van, nights were made sleepless by armies of fleas and Leachman contracted dysentery. There were shades of the South African war and of privations yet to come in the journey across the Khar plain, Mount Ararat emerging starkly in the northern sky. Ponies were lame from the long journey and rough terrain, and Leachman had to drag himself forward, unwilling to give in to pain or sickness, always obsessed by the need to move on to the next objective; knowing, in any case, that there was neither help nor shelter to be found in the wild. On 10 July they climbed the hill of Khushab, topped by a great derelict castle perched on a rock in the middle of the village at its summit. They looked down on Lake Van, the snow-covered Sipah Dagh forming a dazzling backcloth to Van itself.

'Van in this world, paradise in the next.' The Arab proverb expressed the sheer delight of his discovery, the sudden vision of a land made up of a patchwork of blue, green and white, fertile and washed by crystal streams and clean mountain air. 'I came out to Artemid where I am now. The camp is in a wood within ten feet of the lake, and except for bathing one does nothing but sit and laze, and berries and apricots drop off the trees into one's mouth.'

Yet even in this paradise the rich separated themselves off in a 'Garden City' – they used that name for their residential area, though Europeans were to call it their invention several decades hence – and Leachman found elderly Americans living out their last years in its isolated luxury in 1910. The Americans had done much in these distant lands to bring succour to the Christian minorities. They had lived through the terrible massacres of the Armenians in the last years of the old century, and as recently as 1907, and they told him about those acts of genocide. His response wasn't exactly sympathetic. 'I rather feel for the Turks, for the Armenians are a nasty people.'

He left Van after an idyllic week of rest and feasting, travelling along the lakeside to the great crater of Nimrud to the northwest. One of the earliest of Christian churches in the keeping of the Catholic Armenians brought forth another burst of anger. They imposed on his purse, modestly, but he regretted tipping them. 'They say it's for repairs but I should think it's for their stomachs.' Further on, at Nannakaṇ, he was confronted by 'a beastly little village with many staring, badly-behaved people'. His chronicler and apologist, Norman Bray, observed that the remark confirmed 'his personal impressions of the Armenians quoted in his previous letter'. The impression was none the more accurate or sensitive for having been repeated.

It is a rare man who lacks faults and shortcomings. Leachman had many. He was almost entirely without sentiment and was seldom moved by the suffering of the weak or the vulnerable. But his harsh judgements of others were redeemed in part at least by his ruthless self-criticism. Never for a moment did he display self-pity. Never, in pain, ill health or adversity, did he seek sympathy or aid. He was a man who admired wild men, and they him.

108

On 30 July he wrote home from Bitlis, and mentioned in passing that he was staying with an Armenian of whose hospitality he had no complaints. 'Bitlis is a big place built in a deep hole in the mountains. The Tigris rises, or rather has one of its sources, here . . . It is a bit hot but not unpleasantly so. It is one of the great massacre places, at which they usually begin; they killed over a thousand Armenians here a year or two ago.' He did not say, perhaps he was not told, that a thousand women, children and old men were herded into wooden churches and burnt alive.

There were brief moments of piety and vicarious generosity. He told his father: 'If you are itching to give away money to charity, there is a very fine mission in these parts called the *Archbishop's Mission to the Nestorians*. It is run by Canterbury and is doing a lot of good.'

He left Bitlis on 15 August, making for Diarbakr and Aleppo. Shortly after taking the road he found a group of Armenian villagers being attacked by Turkish militia. The Armenians were armed and were putting up a spirited resistance. He sat and watched the encounter from a hillside, until he was disturbed by a thick American accent: 'Say, there sure is some sort of a scrap going on down there.' Behind him stood a youngish man wearing highly polished brown boots, smart suit, white collar and straw hat. The stranger turned out to be an Armenian from the besieged village of Ziyarat below.

'I have just returned from the States,' he told Leachman, 'where I have been for fifteen years and made quite a nice pile. My ma and pa live down there . . . but it looks to me as if I shall have to wait a bit as I don't want to get my clothes spoilt.'

'Nonsense!' said Leachman. He took the man's arm and guided him carefully through rocks and boulders to make sure that his boots were not scratched, down to the village and into the middle of the Turkish squad. The fat NCO in charge barked at Leachman in Turkish. Since the Englishman did not speak Turkish and the Turk spoke no Arabic they were forced to converse in French, which was none too fluent on either side. The NCO eventually pointed to an officer some way off and Leachman went over to him.

'This man is going to see his mother and father after a long absence, and I am going with him,' he said.

'Unheard of,' said the officer.

'Kindly ensure that no one shoots us,' said Leachman. And with that he guided the Armenian exile to his home. He told the story to Norman Bray some years later as they sat and reminisced at Karbala in the midst of a holy war which the faithful were waging against the British. Bray asked him why he did not write down the story of his adventures, as he had been asked to do by many who had served under him and alongside him in war. 'One would feel such an ass!' said Leachman.

He reached Diarbakr on 5 August and on the 7th left on the last stage to Aleppo, accompanied part of the way by the Armenian dragoman of the British consulate. He visited Urfa on the way and struggled into Aleppo on the 14th, his horse lame and exhausted by a journey of 1,300 miles. He made for the Palace Hotel, 'a disgusting place', but it provided him with a much-needed bath. He arrived in Damascus on the pilgrim railway, the new Hijaz line, on 19 August, to find the Syrian capital infested with the spies and agents of his own and other nations, and the Turkish army on the warpath against an ancient foe, the Druses of the Hauran desert.

Everyone who was anyone stayed at the Victoria Hotel in Damascus, which backed on to the serai of the Governor's palace by the Abana river. Leachman's name appeared in the visitors' book alongside those of several British staff officers who by careful design were in Damascus at the same time: Majors F.E. Packe of the Welsh Regiment and Stewart Newcombe of the Royal Engineers, and Capt. C. C. R. Murphy of the Suffolks. On the parade-ground across the river Turkish cavalry were being drilled by German instructors provided by the famous Prussian soldier who was adviser to the Ottoman army and effectively its Chief of Staff, Field-Marshal von der Goltz. One of the German staff, Maj. von Hochwächter, was an intelligence officer of the Wehrmacht in Damascus. Occupying the Governor's palace was Field-Marshal Fetki Pasha, Wali and Commander-in-Chief of the Ottoman vilayet of Damascus, which covered most of the area known to the outside world as Syria. The Turks were determined this time to teach the warlike Druses a lesson, for they had been badly mauled in past encounters with those mountain folk who admitted neither to Christianity nor Islam though they worshipped the same God, and whose customs and precepts seemed strangely to have much in common with Freemasonry.

There had been other enquiring visitors earlier in the year as

110

Turkish troops began to shape up for a campaign that was to test the new army – an army fashioned by Germans and even dressed like their instructors in an oversize version of the *Pickelhaube.* Douglas Carruthers, the naturalist who had hovered around the Hijaz railway for several years and was in the region of Wadi Sirhan just before Butler and Aylmer made their journey, turned up at the garrison rail-junction of Ziza in February, to be followed by Musil. And just as Leachman left Damascus Lieut Bray arrived on the scene, on his way back to Simla after a briefing at the War Office in London. He was followed by the GSOs Capt. Knott and Maj. Leveson. It was a motley gathering and the Germans pressed on their British neighbours invitations to the club they had established on Straight Street by the German consulate. Hochwächter was the secretary of the club and a by-law laid down the strict ruling that 'no fez-wearing gentlemen' were eligible for membership. Cracks were already visible in the Turco-German *entente.*

The vaunted Ottoman onslaught fizzled out within a month of Leachman's arrival in Syria. The Druses, given ample warning of the attack, simply dispersed in their mountain fastness and offered peace talks after suffering some 400 casualties (and inflicting about the same number on the Turks) in outlying skirmishes. Their leader, Yahya Atrash, and the Christian Bishop of the Hauran went to the Ottoman General Sami Pasha with a white flag and were taken prisoner for their pains. But the Druses had the last laugh. They cut communication lines between Sami's HQ at Deraa and Damascus and thus facilitated an Arab attack on the Turkish garrison at Kerak. In a vicious assault at the end of the year tribesmen ransacked the fortress killing every one of the 800 or more Turks left to guard it and doing great damage to the Hijaz railway, setting trains alight, pulling up rails, and demolishing signal stations and tele-graphs.[1] Feeling had been roused by Sami's announcement of the Young Turks' decision to conscript Arabs and Druses, and so those warring factions of the Syrian desert found themselves in temporary harmony. The conflict and its consequences were kept secret from the world by Constantinople and by the Western powers.

Meanwhile, Leachman was skirting the area of conflict on his way to Baghdad where disturbances orchestrated by Arab nationalists had coincided with the Turkish build-up in the

Hauran desert. There had been disturbances too in the Yemen. And as the Turks began to withdraw to their barracks, having inflicted summary punishment on the Arab townsmen in their path, Gertrude Bell joined the throng at the Victoria Hotel. That lady of inexhaustible energy and means had recently visited the Anatolian and Armenian regions from which Leachman had just emerged, her notebooks full of measurements and archaeological details of the ancient churches which dotted her path. She, along with Professor Musil the academic Jew who had fostered the confidence of the great shaikhs of the Arab world, was the scholar among travellers – like Charlotte Brontë's Shirley made by wealth and education into the equal of any man, and in awe of none. She was the eyes and ears of the Foreign Office, where the friend of her youth, Sir Louis Mallet, was Sir Edward Grey's right-hand man. Another companion of her early days in London and Europe, Charles Hardinge, had been given a barony and was on his way to India as the new Viceroy. Her favourite uncle, Frank Lascelles, was ambassador in Tehran, Berlin and Bucharest in the years 1892–1914. She missed Leachman in Damascus but was in time to take dinner with Douglas Carruthers and to prick her ears to bar gossip, and talk to staff officers of all sides, before reporting to Constantinople.

Leachman left Damascus on 23 August, three days before a Turkish battalion departed for Jabal Druse. He was overjoyed by a letter from the Royal Geographical Society asking him to give a lecture at its headquarters in Savile Row, or alternatively to write a paper – 'I grew quite visibly on reading it' – and his thoughts were far from the brewing conflict which preoccupied fellow-officers in the Victoria Hotel. He made no reference in letters or diaries to the other officers, though many of them were engaged in much the same tasks as he; only to having upheld the honour of the Empire 'by force of arms' when confronted by 'a not very sober bespectacled German' at Aleppo just before he set out for the Syrian capital. He had no wish to stay behind for the Anglo-German high jinks that accompanied the Druse affair, though he did manage one game of polo with Turkish officers. 'The game consisted of riding an untrained pony over small species of ditches in company with seven other untrained, kicking ponies. I was in cold perspiration all the time,' he wrote.

From Palestine there were long letters home designed to prove to father that his son (who would shortly be in pressing need of an advance on his annual allowance) was not entirely without Christian conviction or an interest in antiquity. On 30 August he wrote:

> You see I am now a pilgrim. I left Damascus a week ago, and came down by the famous Hijaz railway to the Sea of Galilee. I crossed the lake of Tiberias where I stayed in the Franciscan monastery. Tiberias isn't much of a place, but stands out rather nicely with Crusader towers into the lake. The lake is most picturesque. It is surrounded by hills on all sides which take beautiful colours upon them at different hours of the day.

He sailed across the lake to Capernaum and the ship sprang a leak and nearly sank.

On by horse to Nazareth, by carriage to Haifa and Mount Carmel, the view 'magnificent', the people 'loathsome', though he thought himself better off than most visitors by virtue of speaking Arabic, albeit the Arabic of the Bedouin which was colourful in its expletives and largely unintelligible to the town Arab.

A coastal steamer took him on the overnight voyage to Jaffa and he was immediately caught up in a fight. An Arab aboard the ship demanded money of him and as he went to deliver a sharp lesson to the man a knife was produced and Leachman's leg gashed. A rough-and-tumble followed in which several other Arabs took the side of their friend. Ship's officers joined in and one of them fell down the gangway into the sea. The sailor was rescued from the water and Leachman's assailant was badly battered by the end of the exchange. 'I think,' wrote Leachman, 'I have never had a more uncomfortable journey.'

He stayed at Fast's Hotel in Jerusalem, much favoured by the Germans. Leachman thought it 'peculiarly beastly'. He expected to find Jerusalem an unpleasant place and he was agreeably surprised by the reality. 'It's really quite a nice place.'

He went down to the Dead Sea, to Jericho and across the mountains of Moab to Amman, and returned by train to Damascus on 9 September. The fires of war blazed on the mountain tops of the Hauran and could be seen for many miles, a warning to Druses far and wide that the enemy was approaching. But that was a matter for the other staff officers milling around

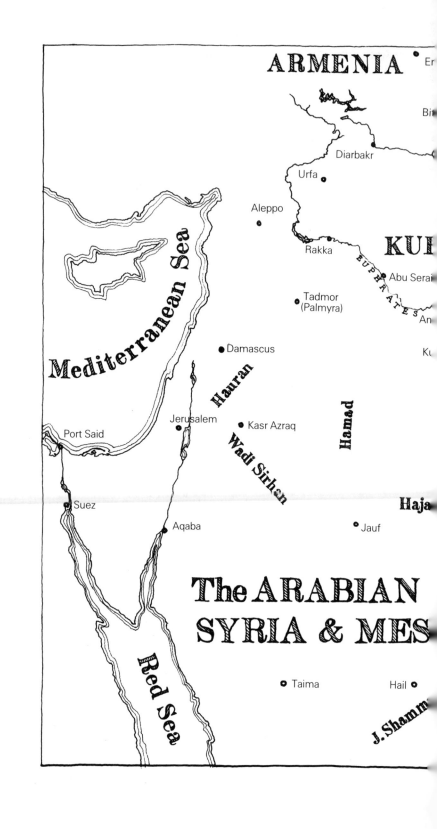

Van

Caspian Sea

Mosul

TAN

Sulimaniya

Tehran

Kirkuk

Hamadan

Kermanshah

TIGRIS

Falluja

Baghdad
Ctesiphon

Isfahan

Karbala

Dizful

Kufa

Shuster

Najaf

Ahwaz

Qurna

Nasiriya

Basra

Muhammerah

Abadan

Kuwait

Shiraz

Bushire

NINSULA

Persian Gulf

OTAMIA

Al Hasa

Katif

Riyadh

the city. Germans and their British counterparts seemed to be equally in the confidence of the Turks, and Murphy, Simla's man who would shortly take over as chief of military and naval intelligence in the Gulf, was called to Sami Pasha's HQ to be briefed on the Turkish army's plan of campaign. Leachman was concerned with the arrangements for his journey to Baghdad which he planned as a record-breaking dash along the old post-road. He had to arrange for *ageyls*, and for fast camels. The Druse campaign was a desultory affair as far as he was concerned and hardly deserved comment.

He drove from his hotel in Damascus in a carriage and pair as far as Dumair, the village outside the city which marked the end of civilization and the beginning of the desert. His *ageyls*, Hamdan and Abdul Razzaq, were waiting for him with camels and Bedouin companions. He had been sick at times on his Palestinian wanderings, wracked by the fevers and pains which had now become familiar to him and which would dog him for the rest of his life, offering the doctors no clues whatever in their attempts to diagnose a cause. But he was in good spirits as he mounted his camel and made once more for the open spaces on 26 September 1910. He intended to reach Baghdad in ten days by camel at a speed unknown over such a distance, 540 miles. His route, the *Darb Asai*, the old post-road was well worn by the mail-carriers and messengers of a thousand years, though it had been abandoned in 1906 in favour of the Baghdad-Aleppo route because of constant attacks by tribal robbers.

He was attacked by fever soon after setting out but he went on doggedly. Only packed dates could be carried in their saddlebags to keep them going. Only water collection at the wells marked by rings of loose stone, and occasional stops for sleep, could be allowed to hinder their progress. There were few landmarks and no habitations for hundreds of miles. The camels began to flag – though Leachman had obtained the finest beasts available from Muhammad Bessam, the Damascus merchant who supplied the shaikhs of the desert and their visitors with almost all their needs. The *ageyls* began to doubt the wisdom of the journey: Saba Abyar, Bir Mulussi, Mahainir, Kubaisa; 200, 300 miles, 400 miles. Leachman was red raw on his rump and dripping day and night with perspiration. The guides at last began to break and threatened to leave the mad Englishman. He taunted them with the label *imrat*, women! – a jibe no Arab of the desert can endure, and so they raced on, lamenting and cursing as they went. Kubaisa marked 440 miles, an average of 63 miles a day. They were within a hundred miles of their objective.

They crossed the Euphrates on 4 October and reached Baghdad at dawn on Thursday the 6th. On the final day of the journey he wrote in his diary the enigmatic lines from Kipling's 'The Winners'.

> Down to Jahannum or up on the throne
> He travels fastest who travels alone.

Sick and sore, he got only as far as the Royal Navy gunboat moored on the Tigris by the Residency steps. He flung himself onto a bunk and slept for two days. Nearly a fortnight later he told his mother 'I am jolly glad I did it . . . but I shall think a good lot before I do it again.' The feat had never been equalled as far as any Arab knew, nor was it to be bettered until the old post-road from Damascus to Baghdad became a motorway. They had averaged 60 miles a day, with only three drinking wells between them and disaster.

10

Mission to Ibn Saud

The Arabian adventure was over for the moment. Leachman rejoined his regiment at Rawalpindi at the end of 1910, having arrived at Bombay aboard the SS *Kola* a few days ahead of the new Viceroy Lord Hardinge.

He would soon be back. He had proved himself to the Staff in London and Simla. The dictum of the late ambassador, O'Conor, 'No entanglement with Wahhabees', still held sway in Whitehall where the Foreign Office continued to refer to Ibn Rashid of Hail as the Amir of Central Arabia and refused to accept Shakespear's assessment of the Amir of Riyadh as a leader of incomparably greater stature.

There was a pithy significance in the timing of Leachman's return to India. As the new Viceroy took over, so Morley resigned from the India Office and the more malleable Marquess of Crewe succeeded. Within three weeks of Leachman's arrival at Bombay, His Imperial and Royal Highness the Crown Prince Wilhelm of Germany turned up as the guest of the Viceroy, in the aftermath of a meeting between his father the Emperor and the Czar of Russia at Potsdam.

There was rebellion in the Yemen and along the Trucial coast – 'Wahhabi to the core' according to the *Times of India* – and Bluejackets were landed by the Royal Navy at Dubai.

The year 1910 ended with an ordinance from Army HQ at Fort William to administrators of all districts under the jurisdiction of the Government of India to take strict precautions in entertain-

The family crest and motto.

Parents, Albert Warren Leachman MD and Louise Caroline
Blandford Leachman, née Singer.

'Fairley', the Leachman home at Petersfield in Hampshire from a painting c.1890.

Leachman as a child.

Leachman's sister Mildred.

Leachman the cadet, 1898.

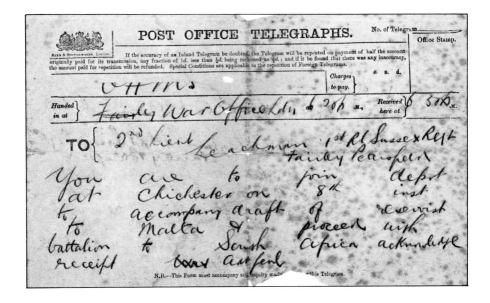

War Office telegram calling Leachman to service in the Boer War, January 1900.

Subaltern in South Africa, 1900.

The Military Secretary presents his compliments to M. Leachman, and begs to acquaint him in reply, to his letter of the 26th instant that it is regretted that there is no information available as to the whereabouts of 2nd Lieut Leachman, Sussex Regiment. It is indeed, possible that this Office never went into hospital on account of his wound, and in any case, all communication telegraphic or otherwise, addressed to Lieut Leachman, Sussex Reg; Capetown will be forwarded to wherever that Officer may be.

A. W. Leachman, Esq.
Fairley, Petersfield

War Office
28th August 1900

Letter to Dr Leachman from Military Secretary, in response to an enquiry as to the whereabouts of Gerard in August 1900. The black-bordered notepaper was in standard use for dealing with enquiries regarding missing personnel.

In charge of the Regimental football team in India, 1903.

At home in Petersfield with sister Janet's dog.

At home, on leave from India.

In *mufti*, India, 1904.

In regimental uniform, 1905.

Leachman incognito in Arab dress.

Tent of Sadun Pasha photographed by Leachman when he camped with the Muntafiq chief at Bir Shaqra in April 1910.

Fahad Bey ibn Hadhal, Chief of the eastern section of the great Anaiza tribal federation, Leachman's first host in the desert and his wartime ally, with grandchild. (Photographed by Gertrude Bell.)

Leachman with the Muntafiq, waiting for Ibn Saud's army to renew the attack in April 1910.

rinces and retainers of the House of Saud at Riyadh, photographed by Leachman in December 1912. lis were the first photographs ever taken in the Saudi capital, though Shakespear had taken pictures of the Amir and his brothers at Kuwait and Thaj in 1910 and 1911. (Reproduced by permission of Royal Geographical Society.)

The Hasa Gate at Riyadh, photographed by Leachman as he left the Saudi capital in 1910.

Watering the camels on the record-breaking journey along the old post-road from Damascus to Baghdad in September – October 1910.

Leachman's house at Karbala where he spent much of the years 1917 and 1918, when not in the desert, and the beautiful gold-domed mosque of the martyr Husain near by.

Leachman rests up in his Dodge automobile while his Turkish prisoners, brought in from the desert, contemplate their new life.

Picture taken by Lance-Corporal Jack Summers as Leachman hauls away the Halberstadt German fighter stolen by the two men from a Turkish aerodrome near Shergat at the junction of the Tigris and Zab rivers, October 1918. And a close-up of the captured plane.

Leachman leads envoys of Ali Ihsan Pasha, Turkish commander at Mosul, to armistice conference with General Cassels, 3 November 1918.

Leachman's 'Avenger' with
Corporal Wing and (left), the
Rolls-Royce 'Silver Dart' which
he used in the latter stages of the
campaign, with his American
pilot Lance-Corporal Summers.
(Photographs taken by Capt.
Kermit Roosevelt.)

Khan Nuqta, the caravanserai between Baghdad and
Falluja where Leachman was murdered.

The re-interment of Gerard Leachman at Baghdad on 1 March 1921; gun-carriage, and lowering of the coffin.

The simple headstone of the grave bears the essential facts of life and death.

ing and talking to the representatives of foreign powers. Parliament in London began to reassess the Official Secrets Act. Military intelligence in Whitehall was reorganized once more; MO1 took over India and the British Empire; MO2(b) retained Arabia and the Ottoman Empire and added Austro-Hungary to its territory. The lands of three great desert travellers – Musil, Leachman and Shakespear – became one to the army staffs and the secret service, and their dominion of the inner deserts of Arabia was to be challenged by only one man. The courageous young Dane, Raunkiaer, had decided to make the journey to Ibn Saud alone in defiance of a ban imposed by Britain on the expedition of the Danish geographical party which had been mooted two years earlier.

The return to the North-West Frontier was eventful enough. But its compensations were few for a man who had become accustomed to the astringent life of the Arabian wilderness. There was the usual social round of the European in India: endless dances and 'at-homes'. He wrote, 'We have been most gay here lately, but I get very tired of it. We are *At Home* so often that one has to be very much on one's best behaviour and run around continually feeding old ladies and gurrls.'

At times he was so depressed by life in the officers' mess that he took himself off with a tent and slept alone in the open spaces, but he felt the cold badly 'after the toasting I have had'. A row with his father, who accused him of extravagance, enlivened the first months in India after his adventures among the Arabs, Kurds and Armenians. He had lost much of his kit on his journey, and white ants had bored holes in the clothes he retained. He needed parental help to rig himself out:

> I received your most severe and a little uncalled for letter concerning my great extravagance. You jump to conclusions. Because I happen not to have paid a bill for a long time, does it follow that I have been very extravagant? The bill in question has not been paid for the simple reason that it is not correct . . . By the way, with all my faults, if I say I will hand money into a person's account on a certain day, I do it and not eighteen days later.

If his own predicament was easy enough to understand, so was his father's concern.

The British officer was still expected to pay for the mandatory pastimes and pleasures of service abroad, and for journeys however valuable they may be to King and Country. Many a father in Britain of comfortable but not unlimited means had to stretch his resources to enable a dutiful son to serve in the open spaces of the Empire. Dr Leachman was such a man, and every now and again he protested. In any case the son was utterly dependent on his parents' goodwill. He soon decided that discretion was the better part of valour. By April 1911 he was telling father 'I wish I could get home for a bit', and by June he was asking a familiar question, 'I wonder if you are feeling particularly rich?'

His official reports on the journeys of the previous year had been delivered up to Lorimer in Baghdad. When he reached India he occupied his time in the monsoon by writing an account of the expedition into Najd with Fahd Bey's Anaiza and his subsequent experiences with Ibn Rashid's Shammar and Ibn Sadun's Muntafiq for the *Geographical Journal*. In March[1] the journal came out with his article, and an accompanying announcement that he had been awarded the Gill Memorial Medal for his 'survey of a difficult region not visited by a European for some twenty years'.[2]

In the post which brought notification of the Gill Memorial Medal – and a cheque for forty pounds – there was a spirit-warming invitation to visit Kasim at the heart of Arabia, and perhaps Riyadh, at the Royal Geographical Society's expense. Things were looking up. He went to a race-meeting at Rawalpindi and according to a letter home 'made a lot of money'. Presumably he had speculated with his RGS cheque.

Too much should not be made of Leachman's exploratory work. His contribution to the map of Arabia was small, and the authorities in London and Simla were well aware of his strong points and his weaknesses. He was impatient in most things. He made no route notes on his travels and he never mastered the techniques of the surveyor. Had he surveyed carefully he could never have covered the vast distances which he traversed in record times. His objective was to make contact with the chiefs of the interior and to report back with the utmost speed. All the same, he mapped one or two areas of desert with remarkable accuracy, using only a prismatic compass. Having done so he would race on and forget to mention a single topographical detail of his route for hundreds of miles. Blessed with a less impetuous and volatile temperament, he would surely have been one of the finest of all desert explorers and map-makers. In the event he was probably the most ruthlessly efficient, and certainly the fastest, of all the remarkable men who wandered across the central deserts of Arabia in a hundred years or more. Col. Hedley, the chief of MO4, the topographical and map-making section, was soon pursuing Maunsell (now Leachman's contact in London) for any tit-bits of information that might help with the War Office's urgent efforts to update its Arabian maps. Maunsell explained that as Leachman had returned to his regiment after the 1910 journey he, Maunsell, had compiled the map of his route, using detail from the maps of Wallin the Swede and Huber the Strasburgian compiled in 1848 and 1884 respectively. Maunsell's 'Leachman' map was supplied to Carruthers, then working in the map room of the Geographical Society and liaising with Hedley's department at the War Office. Maunsell told Carruthers: 'Leachman's work was carefully done with compass and timing the rate of his camel. He had no astronomical instruments such as sextant or theodolite, but his compass work was good.' And he told Hedley: 'Leachman furnished no route books. He only sent . . . a sketch-map.'

The close collaboration between the Royal Geographical Society and the War Office in the early years of the present century enabled a number of secret journeys to be made with dual geographical or academic purpose, thus providing the most convenient cover for the officer on special duty. It was a device used by all the major powers. Musil travelled under the auspices of the Imperial Military Geographical Institute of Vienna; the Germans chiefly under the banners of the great Prussian universities and museums. One of them, Professor Zugmayer of Berlin, was a familiar sight to the British in Baluchistan, dressed in shorts and floppy hat, armed with a butterfly net. He was one of the world's great experts on the *lepidoptera* – and on the activities of Indian and Persian revolutionaries in the border territories.

Leachman's call from the RGS to revisit Arabia had War Office approval. But the Foreign Office was inevitably obstructive, having just begun conversations with Constantinople on an

Anglo-Turkish treaty.[3] The matter was urgent from the army's point of view however. Revision of the old maps of Syria and Arabia was vitally necessary in the light of the completion of an Anglo-French war plan. There was need, too, to update files on Arab leaders.

On 29 June Leachman told his father confidently:

> The RGS has written to me that I must certainly try to get to Riyadh or Al Kasim next winter as to do this would be a feat of the first geographical importance and the Society will certainly reward me. This is a reward in the money line . . . Now I wonder if you could let me have a cheque for a whole year's allowance, i.e. from next October's. If you could manage it I should be much obliged, but otherwise I shall have to borrow out here at an exorbitant rate . . . By the way they babbled a lot about a difficult and dangerous journey. It was neither, provided one didn't look for trouble.

Father obliged and he whiled away the summer months at 'Pindi' in dances and parties, and in anxious contemplation of the row going on in official quarters over his journey.

Towards the end of August he wrote: 'I don't know what has happened about my leave, but I imagine Lord Crewe is at present contemplating it and intending to refuse me permission to travel. In which case I shall have to revert to subterfuge.' And a few days later, on 31 August: 'I feel extremely like resigning my commission . . . This foul Government have refused me permission to travel, though my application was most strongly supported by the C-in-C and the Indian Government who know a lot more about these things than a lot of traitorous counterjumpers. So I have been put back a bit but I will do them in the eye yet.'

Do them in the eye. Political and military authorities in Britain had become accustomed to dancing a kind of Mephisto waltz now, in which a decent pretence of peacekeeping was offset by a sharp awareness of the need to keep abreast of the Emperors Franz Josef and Wilhelm. In the last resort the War Office would decide the matter; Whitehall under the Asquith administration was careful, but not suicidal.

Leachman arrived in Basra on 11 November.

The next day a pale, insignificant young man left Copenhagen bound for Baghdad, Basra, Kuwait and Riyadh. Barclay

Raunkiaer, consumptive and slight of build, had assumed single-handed the task that was to have been undertaken by a large and well-financed Danish geographical expedition, had not the British Government refused to sanction it.

Events which followed Leachman's arrival at Basra can only be described as bizarre, though they must be seen against the background of the activities of the other European powers in the area. At the end of the previous year when Leachman arrived in Damascus along with a bevy of British staff officers, when the Turks were demonstrating to the Arab world the strength of their German-trained army, the Sharif of Mecca launched an attack on Ibn Saud. The Sharif was aided by Ibn Rashid's Shammar tribesmen. Ibn Saud drove off the invaders but only after submitting to a bargain which, according to the world press, recognized the supremacy of the Meccan chief; a bargain which was wrung from the Saudi leader in return for the freedom of his favourite brother, Saad, who had been captured in the battle.

In March 1911 Captain Shakespear had met Ibn Saud on the Kuwait–Hasa border and afterwards told the British Government that Ibn Saud denied any such bargain. He also reported that after the battle there had been correspondence between all the Arab chiefs, including the Sharif and Zamil the Regent of Hail, in which an uprising against the Ottoman power was proposed with Ibn Saud at its head. The suggestion of an Arab coup had come in the first place from Arab officers serving in the Ottoman army who had formed a revolutionary committee which they called *Al Ahad*,[4] or the Covenant, based at Damascus but with important followers in Baghdad and Basra. At the same time German activity in the Gulf reached a high pitch with a vast network of agents working through the Wönckhaus company and the very respectable archaeological team of Professor Koldewey, the Deutsche Orient Gesellschaft. At the beginning of 1911, as the Liberal opposition in the Ottoman Government planned a coup against the Young Turks and simultaneously proposed negotiations with Britain, Sayyid Talib of Basra made a hurried journey to Constantinople. Talib, at first a supporter of the Young Turks, had become a leading light of the Arab independence movement. Russia invaded northern Persia and British reinforcements were sent to Shiraz in the south. A suspected German agent was on his way to Central

Arabia. Military and naval intelligence chiefs in London and Simla began to take matters into their own hands.[5]

On the day of his arrival in Basra Leachman wrote to his father: 'I have been extraordinarily lucky and my affairs are prospering. I leave, all being well, in two days time with a great party of Arabs and shall be very safe so you need not be disturbed.' On the night of the 13th he went to a wild party and arrived after midnight at the home of his host, the British merchant, C.F. McPherson, much the worse for wear. 'He would dine with you and say "Good Night" and that was the last that would be heard of him for perhaps months,' wrote McPherson some years later. He added, 'Leachman was indeed playing the "lone hand" and carrying his life in his hands.'

A letter written on the day of his departure told a slightly different story. He was to make *incognito* for Kuwait and was to pick up the Arab party in the desert, on the road from Zubair. 'I am going with a type of Arab well known for their straightness and broad-mindedness so things should be alright.' More precisely: 'I am leaving tonight to go down by desert to Kuwait . . . and go down to a place not very far from Riyadh in the centre of Arabia.'

He had not informed the Political Agent in Kuwait of his intended visit, or at any rate the naval surgeon Lieut Kelly who was standing in for Shakespear while the latter attended the Coronation durbar for King George V at Delhi. Indeed, Leachman appeared with an unruly Arab mob on the 16th, proceeding through Mubarak's domain like berserk dervishes. Leachman was disguised as a Levantine pedlar of cheap jewellery. His companions, though not identified by their English leader, were almost certainly the ruffians who gathered around Sayyid Talib in Basra and subjected that city to a reign of terror. Whatever their purpose, Shaikh Mubarak expected them. They were hauled before him at his serai on the sea-front and given a dressing-down such as Mubarak was uniquely qualified among Arab leaders to deliver. Next day they were back in Basra. Leachman offered a somewhat lame explanation of his mission when he next wrote to his parents.

> I got away from Basra very easily. I went south for three days to a place where I expected to meet the men who were going to take me into Central Arabia. I found that through the abso-

lute rottenness of the Arab who was my companion, that they had left already. The consequence was that I had to go into Kuwait and there I was hauled in front of the Shaikh who was rather offensive and sent me back to Basra.

For the first time in his adult life Leachman had taken a reprimand without fighting back. It can only be supposed that he was under orders to get to Ibn Saud before the Germans could make overtures and that Sayyid Talib had double-crossed him by warning his erstwhile friend Mubarak of the journey. Sayyid Talib himself, fresh from talks in Constantinople, met Ibn Saud a few weeks later. Mubarak went off to Muhammerah to join Shaikh Kazal aboard one of HM ships to toast 'Their Imperial Majesties King George V and Queen Mary'. Leachman went back to India.

He returned to his regiment on the North-West Frontier for Christmas 1911, and remained there for the first three months of the following year. He took his promotion examination in March 1912 and in April set out for England and well-deserved leave. He had made his captaincy in his thirty-second year.

The journey to Riyadh proposed by the Royal Geographical Society at the instigation of Carruthers and Hedley of MO4, loomed large during his six months' furlough. The visit of the Dane Barclay Raunkiaer to Riyadh had proceeded while Leachman was back in India licking his wounds after the Kuwait débâcle. Meanwhile, the Indian Government, in defiance of the Foreign Office, had facilitated Raunkiaer's trip. Shakespear gave him a letter of introduction to Ibn Saud, as did Shaikh Mubarak. But they took the precaution of informing Ibn Saud of the courageous young visitor's purpose, discussed with the Turkish and German officials in Basra, to offer the Saudi leader precedence in Arabia and financial support, if he would renounce his pro-British policy. After an exhausting and dangerous journey in the course of which he was subjected to insult and humiliation, he arrived at Riyadh in March 1912 to find that Ibn Saud was conveniently absent – away on a raid. He was received hospitably by the Amir's father Abdurrahman, 'this amiable but austere old man with eagle eye and white beard'. The Dane could only 'confirm the chieftain's deep-rooted belief in the hegemony of the British Empire'.

Sir Edward Grey personally rebuked Shakespear and the Indian authorities for assisting Raunkiaer.

Now it was the turn of London to find out at first hand what was going on in that closed region of Najd to which, as Mubarak had told his 'son' Abdal Aziz ibn Saud, 'the door must remain closed'. Leachman was the chosen agent, and the now customary farce must be played out in which Capt. Leachman of the British army, whose regiment was serving in India, applied to the Resident at Bushire for Indian approval for his journey, in the knowledge that the Resident would refer the matter to London where the application would be rejected. The battle between Whitehall and Simla surpassed in subterfuge the efforts of the two power-centres to hoodwink the Germans and Turks. As it happened Sir Percy Cox, the Resident (knighted in the Coronation honours), was on leave in England at the same time as Leachman. Sir Richmond Richie at the India Office suggested that they should seek Shakespear's opinion on the proposed journey.

On 26 October 1912 Arnold Wilson, who was acting for Cox at Bushire, wrote to the Political Agent: 'Dear Shakespear, We have had a request from Leachman. Cox thinks we should do everything possible, privately, to help him, but before doing anything he (Cox) thinks we should mention the matter to you as he knows that you have ambitions in that direction.' It was a personal letter but Shakespear's reply was official and terse.

I don't exactly burn with affection or admiration for Leachman after his masquerade here last year . . . Judging from Leachman's previous trips and what I have heard of him (I have never met him) he will probably attempt the present trip again in disguise . . . as to which I have the strongest objection so far as the badawin tribes around Kuwait are concerned. They trust me more-or-less and have become used to me knocking about the place as a 'sahib' who doesn't seek to pinch their country . . . Raunkiaer . . . though he admittedly wore khaffiya and abba, could not be disguised and did not speak Arabic.

In December Cox himself wrote to Shakespear supporting Leachman's cause: ' . . . one necessarily has a fellow feeling for these wanderers, and realises the Quixoticism of discouraging

126

our own men, while we assist foreigners.' By the time that letter reached Kuwait, Leachman was practically at Riyadh, armed with the authority of the War Office and the Indian General Staff.

On 22 December, curious as to what was going on, Cox wired the consul at Damascus, George Devey, to ask if he had any news of Leachman. Devey replied that Capt. Leachman had left the city on 3 December making in an easterly direction, 'whence he goes SSE to map the route between Najd and Basra'.

It is interesting to note that either the consul made a mistake of exactly a month in his telegram to Cox, or he was party to an attempt to pull the wool over the eyes of the Indian Government. Leachman had arrived in Damascus on 25 October and left for Riyadh on 3 November, accompanied by an Arab, Saleh Mutawah, with whom he had travelled before with Fahad Bey's Anaiza, and an *ageyl* and two youths from Kasim. He wrote home just before leaving, on 2 November:

> I am off on my travels tomorrow. I was having great difficulty in finding anyone to go with, but to my delight an Arab walked into my hotel one morning, whom I know well. He had only arrived from Baghdad the previous day. He was agreeable to go with me anywhere . . . Things are in a bad way here; no news at all of the severe Turkish defeats is out here, but I heard the first news tonight privately . . . Unless anything unforeseen happens, I doubt if I shall be near enough to Basra or Kuwait to get a letter there . . . If all goes well I should be 'off' Basra or Kuwait in about three weeks' time . . . It has been raining here like anything and the roads are in an awful state . . . PS: This will not go until I have left Damascus.

Caution was mixed with confusion; perhaps deliberate confusion. Neither the Damascus consul nor his parents could have known that he was making for Central Arabia and Ibn Saud or that he intended, if he could obtain the Saudi leader's permission, to go on not to Basra or Kuwait but to the unexplored Empty Quarter far to the south of Riyadh.

But his estimate of time was remarkably correct. No man ever travelled faster in the desert come wind or high water. He made easy work of regions which other intrepid men looked on with awe, and he made light of the gravest adversity. He had advanced only a few hours into the desert from Dumair north of Damascus when the cry went up *Silahkum, silahkum!* (To arms, to arms!) 'This seemed hardly wise,' said Leachman, 'as we had only three rifles among us, and the other side, who were not more than a hundred yards off, heard the cry and responded by firing into the black mass of camels.' (He had picked up a camel caravan which left Dumair at about the same time.) His men changed the cry to *ageyl, ageyl,* and the firing ceased. The raiders turned out to be the Wuld Ali, a branch of the Ruwalla Anaiza, lords of the Syrian desert, Ibn Shalan's men. They were pursuing an allied tribe, the Amarat, with whom they had a temporary quarrel. Next day they encountered another group of the Wuld Ali returning from a raid 300 miles away at Dair-ar-Zor, complete with herds of looted camels. They touched the Damascus–Baghdad road which he knew well from his record-breaking journey of 1910, and from there turned off towards Najd.

They went to the wells of Ghara into the region known as Al Wadiyan, and met a party of Salaiba: 'There is no certain knowledge of the origin of these people, though various theories have been put forward, one of which is that they are descendants of the Crusaders, *salib* meaning a cross.' He heard that Dr Musil had recently 'threaded through this mass of wadis, which even the Bedouin have difficulty in naming'. They went on for six waterless days, and almost impossible privation for most men, until they came to wells at Aghar, where more Salaiba were in occupation, one of them a former companion of Musil, or Shaikh Musa as the Arabs called the Austrian Jew. One of them composed a poem in Leachman's honour and recited it to Saleh, and then to the master, on a cold and cheerless dawn. Leachman was not as appreciative as the cheerful Salaiba poet would have wished.

They were now crossing the route of Aylmer and Butler, his early companions in India, on their 1909 journey. They sighted innumerable birds and dined off the *hubara*, which he called the 'great bustard', though it is the lesser bustard. Wadi al Khur, the central Arabian arm of the landmark he had discovered in his first real journey on the road from Karbala, brought them to the wells of Hazil. He thought that the wadi must form a route known only to the Bedouin and *ageyls* from Jauf to Najaf on the Euphrates. Single riders could cover the 300 miles between the

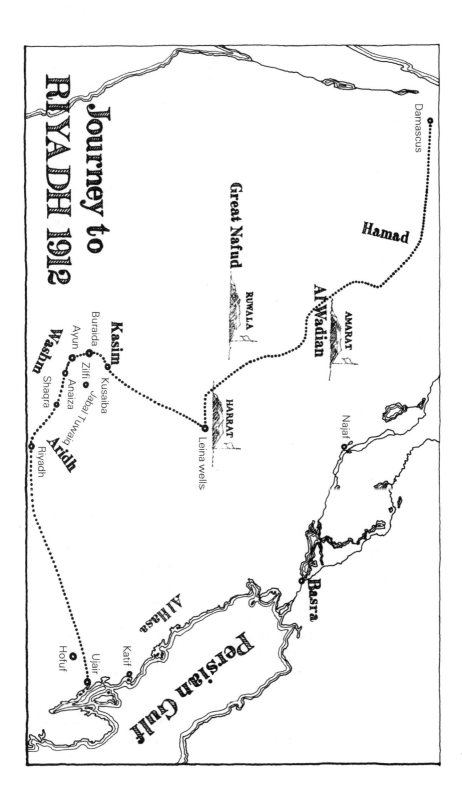

two places in five or six days, he learnt, halting only at the wells of Aghar. He heard too that Jauf had fallen to Ibn Shalan, a fact which Musil had reported to his masters months before when he marched into Ibn Shalan's capital after the latter's son Nawwaf had captured it from Faisal ibn Rashid.

Leachman noted his camels' delight when water was found. 'Here the camel drinks . . . in the most leisurely fashion, and he appears to taste the full joy of a long drink in the manner of a gourmet born.' He added, 'The Bedouin is extraordinarily kind to his camels, and in return the Arabian camel is a very different animal to the ill-mannered, treacherous variety encountered in India. The Arabian camel never bites or kicks.' On the fourth day they left the Nafud, the great desert of flaming-red sand-dunes which the Blunts had described graphically when they crossed the same ground on the way to the Darb Zobaida in 1879. Then on to the wells of Leina, which were the south-easterly limit of Leachman's 1910 journey. 'Now not a blade of grass or desert bush was visible.' The Bedouin repeated their saying: *Leina, leina, mithal ajine, gada b'il leina, asha b'il Basra.* ('The traveller refreshed at Leina will go so fast that he will dine at Basra 250 miles away.') Now they were in the Dahana, the long sand-belt which stretches from the Nafud in an arc between Najd and the Gulf hinterland until it disappears in the uninhabited Empty Quarter.

From the Dahana they approached Kusaiba, mounds of stone arranged in a great megalithic circle guiding them to their destination. 'The origin of these stones[6] is difficult to comprehend, unless some public-spirited person in olden times endeavoured to form a track of loose stones. The Arabs say it must be the work of Zobaida, Haroun ar-Rashid's queen, the great benefactor of this part of the world.' By 3 December they had reached the gravelly border between the territory of Ibn Rashid and the disputed land of Kasim which Ibn Saud had taken back from its Turkish and Shammar occupiers in 1906: 'The border-line between the Shammar kingdom and Kasim runs north of the towns of Kusaiba and Kuwara. These two towns change hands constantly according as Ibn Saud or Ibn Rashid are in the ascendancy.'

By now they had marched for 300 miles without mishap. But conditions became dangerous from Kusaiba onward. The Ataiba tribe was on the warpath and only a week before had attacked

Kusaiba itself and robbed the shaikh of the town. They needed an Ataiba *rafiq* to see them through, but none was available. Leachman decided to leave without one. They mounted a high cliff at the rear of the town before sunset, and remained there with their camels concealed in a hollow until it was dark. At nightfall they pushed on rapidly, and two hours before dawn they stopped by the wayside outside the town of Ayun, to sleep and rest their camels. They were on the road which leads from Hail to Buraida, and Saleh's provenance began to emerge; it transpired that he was the brother of the Amir of Ayun, a town of some 4,000 inhabitants.

Saleh had left his birthplace for Baghdad as a youngster but the natives were delighted to see their lost son return and he and Leachman were led triumphantly to the Amir's house. Saleh whispered that his companion was an Englishman who was on his way to meet Ibn Saud, the Amir's liege, and Leachman was told *sotto voce* that in the divided territory of Kasim he must pass himself off as a Musulawi, a resident of Mosul. A lavish feast was put on for the visitors, and a lump of meat went the wrong way down the Englishman's gullet. There were fifty or so men squatted round the table, and they remarked in unison that it must be difficult for a civilized man to fall in with their savage ways. Cultured people, one of them remarked, used a spoon rather than their hands to guide the food to their mouths. Leachman found the inhabitants 'broad-minded, business-like and travelled', and he observed that their community was a very happy one. There were few old men, a consequence of the never-ending wars between Ibn Saud and Ibn Rashid.

At Ayun, Leachman heard that Ibn Saud, the great Amir of Najd, was at Buraida. The last thing he wanted was to meet the Arab chief there and thus be refused entry into Riyadh, but the Amir of Ayun, whose name Leachman is careful never to mention in his notes, dared not send the party on a westerly route which would have avoided Buraida. It is clear, although he doesn't say so in his public account of the journey, that the route through Najd had been agreed beforehand with Ibn Saud, probably through his agent in Damascus. They went through date plantations and a desert of white dunes to the walled town of Buraida, and were pleased to find that the warrior prince of Riyadh had left in the early morning, some hours before their arrival.

'A great wooden door stood open in a lofty gateway in the wall; we entered and crossed a wide-open space, at the north-east end of which was a stronghold of Ibn Saud, where he is said to keep an armed force to cope with risings of the turbulent tribesmen.' Ibn Mu'amer, one of Ibn Saud's lieutenants from Riyadh, had been installed as governor. He was a difficult man, 'an obscene individual' according to Shakespear, and Leachman was left for an hour or more in the courtyard of the palace, his camels couched at the doorway, awaiting an invitation to enter.

Leachman and Saleh were eventually shown into a dirty house which formed part of the mud-brick palace, where they were left without refreshment for further hours until, in late evening, they were ushered into the presence of Ibn Mu'amer. Leachman told his host that Ibn Saud might not be entirely pleased with the reception given him at Buraida, whereupon the atmosphere became friendlier. It became apparent that the governor was a weak character who was constantly dictated to by the Negro slaves who attended him and who were devoted servants of Riyadh.

'A ridge of white sand two-hundred feet high, driven by the wind into curious shapes, protects the town on the west, while intervening between it and the houses of the town is a long strip of dense date-gardens and cultivation.' There was not much else to note of the place which Palgrave, Doughty, Huber and others had described before him, all of whom had mentioned the bigotry and fanatical nature of its people. 'It is one of the few towns in Najd in which I met with any discourtesy,' Shakespear was to write.

The governor had sent a messenger to catch up Ibn Saud and ask him what should be done about the Englishman. The order came back to send him straight to Riyadh, and Leachman found that the great man had left instructions all along the route that he was to be assured every comfort in the towns and on the road. He took the little-used road along which Capt. Sadlier of the East India Company had travelled in pursuit of Muhammad Ali's army when the Egyptians and Turks came to destroy the Wahhabi empire a century before – the road through Shaqra in the district of Washm. He went on to another Ayun, Ayun as-Sirr, before entering the white-sand plain which leads to Washm. They stayed one night at a *kasr* in a village called Murabba, where an hospitable and fervent old man bade him repeat time and again the sacred *kalima* of Islam:

La illah ilallah wa Muhammad ar-rasul Allah.

'There is no God but God and Muhammad is his messenger.'

At Shaqra he was received by the brightest of all the local chieftains *en route*, the Amir Muhammad ibn Saud, no relation of his distinguished namesake but an impressive young man of great charm who spoke to him of world politics, aeroplanes, wireless telegraphy and trade. He entertained Leachman with good food and urbane chatter and provided his party with beds for the night. Leachman's caravan moved on to Jabal Tuwaik, the backbone of Najd. They ascended to the top of that narrow tableland and went on for some ten miles until they came to the watershed at the head of Wadi Hanifa, which leads down to Riyadh and in those days carried what little water the Saudi capital could boast of. They passed the old capital, Dariya, its ruins standing as a monument to the invasion of Muhammad Ali's army in 1818 and the slaughter which took place. Leachman thought that it must have been larger than the present-day capital which 'suddenly springs into view, having been hidden in a dip in the ground'.

He described his arrival in Riyadh:

Across the open plain Saleh and myself wended our way, both of us in some doubt as to what the nature of our reception would be in this stronghold of Wahhabism, recounted to us as the most fanatical sect of Islam in the world. Entering the town by a high gateway having iron-studded wooden doors, we passed through a number of quiet by-streets and then suddenly emerged into a broad square with a bazaar, in which business was at its height at this noontide hour of the day; as we passed through many curious eyes were fixed on us, and then we came to a large open space flanked on the right by a lofty castle, which proved to be the palace of Abdal Aziz Ibn Saud, the Wahhabi Amir of Najd.

They parked their camels and took their places on a mud bench, to answer the questions of townsmen and slaves who gathered round them, and to await the call of the Amir.

133

Leachman made no diary notes during his trans-Arabian journey, kept no route log and wrote no letters. His own description of the journey, written over a year later for the *Geographical Journal*, gave no dates or details of his mission. But we know from the Political and Secret records of the India Office that Shaikh Mubarak and Shakespear in Kuwait were keeping a close watch on his movements.

On 23 December Mubarak told Shakespear that Ibn Saud had sent horsemen to meet Leachman and escort him to Riyadh. Shakespear commented: 'I hope he doesn't play the fool or disregard what Ibn Saud tells him. He will certainly get into trouble if he does.'

On Christmas Day Mubarak told Shakespear that his fellow countryman had arrived at Ibn Saud's camp, suggesting that he probably arrived at Riyadh on Christmas Eve.[7]

By New Year's Day Shakespear was singing a different tune. He wrote to Cox: 'You will have seen Leachman, I suppose. It's a jolly fine journey and I am awfully pleased that Ibn Saud did him so well, though I rather envy all those other travellers going to Riyadh when I am the only one who really knows the king.'

Envy would not serve Shakespear's cause. Leachman had gone to Riyadh as the emissary of London, in the early stages of Anglo-Turkish talks designed to produce a treaty which would recognize once and for all Ottoman suzerainty over central Arabia. Shakespear and the Indian Government regarded Ibn Saud as the rightful king of the territory. London was to confirm the Porte's nomination of him as *mutassarif* or governor of the Turkish province of Najd.

Leachman was impressed by the chief, whatever title the outside world might devise for him: 'He is a man of about forty, six feet high and broad in proportion, with a strong though kindly face and the simplest of manners. He shook me by the hand and put me at my ease at once by the friendliness of his greeting, and a long conversation ensued on the Turco-Balkan War.

Inevitably Abdal Aziz told him the convoluted story of his family's and his own rise to power, telling him with special relish the story of his own accession after the storming of Riyadh in 1902. Leachman's version read:

Muhammad ibn Rashid having died, the Shammar power grew weaker, and Abdal Aziz left Kuwait with a following of only forty men, riding two on a camel, and made a dash across the desert to grasp the power again in Riyadh. He reached the place, and leaving the camels in charge of two men outside the walls, the remainder of the party entered the town by night and made for the castle of Rashid's governor. In the open square they happened to find an old woman, and discovered from her that the governor did not inhabit the castle by night, but usually came there early every morning. They then managed to effect an entrance into the castle and locked the great gate, leaving a small postern in it open. In the morning the governor came with an escort only to be cut down as he passed through the postern door, a fate which some of his followers shared. Abdal Aziz then went up on to a tower of the castle and proclaimed that Rashid's governor had been killed and that Ibn Saud had returned.

It was a story that was to become enshrined in Saudi folklore. Much the same tale had been told to Shakespear at camp at Thaj a year before, though it differed slightly with every time of telling.

Leachman was given lodgings in the royal palace and received a constant stream of visitors, all of whom showed him the greatest courtesy. Stories of Wahhabi fanaticism were as ill founded as was the belief of his country's politicians that it could conduct an Arab policy in concert with the Turks which discounted the Amir of Najd. When he went into the town he was accompanied by Abdal Aziz or by the slave who had been deputed to look after him. When an old man asked Ibn Saud why he entertained a Christian in such style, the Amir replied: 'Any Englishman, whether Christian or not, is my friend, and dearer to me than many Moslems of other sects.'

One of the notables Leachman met was Ahmad ibn Thaniyan whose mother had been a Circassian slave-woman. Educated in Constantinople, he spoke excellent French and had many discussions with the English visitor on the geography of Arabia and the politics of the world. Leachman estimated the population of Riyadh at that time to be some 25,000, based on the information that 7,000 men had attended prayer at the great mosque during the last 'Id' or festival. The bazaar was small and the prices of food and other articles dear. Though smoking was frowned on and drinking alcohol forbidden, there was much smoking in private and he was often asked by visitors to his house for a little of the 'shameful'. The Amir regularly attended prayers five times a day and enforced the attendance of the townsmen 'with the rod'. At night a mullah would read the Koran to Ibn Saud in his private apartments.

It was an enjoyable stay. Ibn Saud had already put his case for an alliance with Britain to Shakespear and his proposals had met with a stony silence, broken only by sarcastic remarks in the margins of official documents, when they reached the Foreign Office in Whitehall. It was unlikely that anything which passed between Leachman and Ibn Saud would have diverted the Saudi ruler from his chosen path of working, if necessary with other Arab princes, to eject the Turks from his territory, or to relinquish his aim of obtaining British protection for the lands over which he laid claim.

Ibn Saud refused Leachman permission to travel south to Jabrin and beyond. After a week's residence in Riyadh he left with a Bedouin escort of the Ajman, Duwasir, Bani Hajr and Al Murra tribes. The latter were the great trackers of Arabia, able to pick up the footprints of man and animal with uncanny skill. Leachman's party made for Turkish-occupied Hofuf in Hasa, a town of 30,000 inhabitants, many of them Wahhabis, who bitterly resented the Ottoman occupation of Ibn Saud's coastal province. But the Turkish officers received Leachman with open cordiality. They went on to the almost deserted town of Ujair with its custom-house and ruined Arab fort, arguing fiercely among themselves. Leachman's companions were 'bigoted and fanatical, miserable in appearance, and capable of lying in a manner unknown elsewhere in Arabia'. They arrived at Bahrain at the end of December, after a stormy journey in the Gulf in an Arab dhow which nearly capsized. He went to the consulate to report to Maj. Trevor who was away, and then to his friend McPherson, who had business interests there as well as at Basra.

McPherson recorded the meeting: 'Entered a long, cadaverous and altogether filthy-looking Badu, who greeted me with "Hullo! got anything to eat?"'

War by the Waters of Babylon

The journey through central Arabia had not been notably productive of geographical or political results. There were a few detailed projections of unmapped landmarks in the Kasim region, made with the aid of a compass only but remarkably correct, and he had struck up a friendly if somewhat wary relationship with Ibn Saud. He was impressed by the Arab leader, but not bowled over by him as was Philby in later years or caught in a web of mutual admiration and dependence such as was woven by Shakespear and the king-to-be at Kuwait and Thaj in the two preceding years. Yet once more he had shown himself to be perhaps the most brilliant and tenacious desert traveller of all time. He had covered some 1,300 miles of the most difficult and notoriously inhospitable regions of the world in just fifty-two days. He had commanded respect and acceptance when the need was there, and had melted inconspicuously into the Arab crowd when there was no need to assert himself. He had made valuable contacts, and was able to report, as no one since mid-Victorian times had been able to, the mood and complex relationships of tribes and leaders in a part of the world which had become strategically important yet was less well mapped or recorded than the Gobi desert or the outer regions of Mongolia.

For the moment it was back to India and his regiment on the North-West Frontier. On the way he called at Bushire to report to Cox. Wilson, now first assistant to the Resident, observed: 'He was bronzed and lean almost beyond recognition, and nursed two great sores, "as big as dish-plates" he assured me, where the badly upholstered framework of the camel saddle had come into contact with his almost equally ill-covered frame.'

When he arrived in India he was called once more to Simla. He disliked the work of the desk-man, the 'staff wallahs' as he called himself and his companions as they laboured among the intelligence files, and he added to them details of his conversations with Ibn Saud and Ahmad Thaniyan and the petty amirs he had met on his way. After ten days at Simla he went off with a pile of staff work which he would complete at leisure while he resumed the battle with warring tribes from the other side of the Peshawar hills.

On 29 January 1913 he wrote to his parents: 'I got back here from Simla yesterday. I *did* have a strenuous ten days up there and I wouldn't have let them work me so hard for nothing, as is the case, if they hadn't been a nice lot. I have brought any amount away with me which will last well into summer.'

There was a letter dated 12 September in which he reported to his parents that he had just completed another journey in Kashmir:

> I managed to get away at last and endured the two hundred miles to Srinagar. I really didn't mind it very much as it only takes two days and there is lots to look at on the road. Kashmir is perfectly glorious. The very clearest of air with just a bit of bite in it, and the whole place a mass of apples . . . I have just come down the Jhelum in a houseboat – a lovely journey.

It was his last carefree journey. His last holiday.

At some time during his duty at Rawalpindi and along the length of lawless frontier which separated India from Afghanistan and Baluchistan, he wrote for his own amusement the story of a typical pursuit of tribesmen and professional trouble-makers. It was a naïve acount. Leachman had no natural facility as a writer. Nevertheless his 'Story of one of the Small Frontier Affairs' as he called it, was charged with a significance which often resides in understatement.

It told of two Pathan brothers, Silghai and Janghai, rascals even by the standards of the North-West Frontier. They had taken over the mountainous no-man's-land between the frontiers of India and Afghanistan where they instituted a Mafia-like regime of murder and terror. The Political Resident at Peshawar put a price of 3,000 rupees on the head of each of the brothers, dead or alive, but it had no effect, and a punitive expedition was sent in. The Pathans were eventually holed up in a fortress, though the Sikhs and Bengal Lancers who surrounded them had no idea of their number. When the battle was over it became known that six tribesmen, including the brothers, had held out for seventeen hours against 500 soldiers equipped with two field-guns. The enemy had their women with them, and when the fight was over, the ladies of the fort, 'white and pretty as any English-woman' went through the pockets of their dead menfolk and made off without a word. Silghai was killed, but his brother was captured and 300 tribesmen gave themselves up when their leader was arrested. The British colonel in charge of the engagement was seriously wounded and died on the stretcher journey to Bannu on the Indian side. Leachman's essay concluded: 'So ended this small affair, which is only one instance of many of the same kind which take place every year but are never heard much about.'

It was the kind of engagement which occupied Leachman and his companions of the 1st Battalion Royal Sussex for nearly two years after his return from Arabia, up to the declaration of war in August 1914. There were no more ruthless fighters in the world than the Pathans, and Britain was to make full use of those who joined her in war.

It has been suggested that Leachman's employment in the war was delayed unaccountably, and that had he been sent earlier to join his tribal friends in Mesopotamia he might have caused early havoc behind the enemy lines, assessed the Turco-German strength more accurately than was the case, and generally helped to avoid the disasters which marked the initial stages of the campaign.

According to Bray: 'It becomes astonishing to see what happened to him between January 1913 and the beginning of 1915.'

Philby suggested that he was in need of a rest, 'both for body and mind'. The historian of the Sussex Regiment, G.D. Martineau, wrote: 'When war broke out, there was at first an unaccountable delay in employing Leachman's remarkable genius.'

In fact, the General Staffs in London and India were by now well aware of Leachman's particular abilities and knew exactly how they proposed to use them. The question was *where*?

While he was serving as brigade-major at Peshawar his Commander, General Young, wrote of Leachman in his annual report for 1914: 'Shows remarkable aptitude for staff work. Has performed duties of bridgade-major with much success, being quick, reliable and conscientious.'

The divisional commander General Blomfield added: 'I have a very high opinion of Leachman's value as an officer. He is very hard and active physically and possesses sound judgement, and has a very level head. A fine horseman with an excellent eye for country. A very good selection for the special service list.'

Praise indeed. The nature of the work he would be called on to perform was clearly set out by the time war came in 1914.

For the moment, however, he must wait on events. And there was a shock from home as he occupied himself on the North-West Frontier with his regiment and fed voraciously on horrific stories of death and disaster from the European fronts. On Christmas Eve of that year his father died. He and the 'old man' had known times of acute and even angry difference, especially over money matters and over the girl of Naini Tal. In many ways they were birds of a feather, and by and large father and son understood each other well. They shared the same volatile temper; the same ability to forget and forgive. 'Hope you didn't throw a book at him,' wrote the son to his father on one occasion when he heard of a dispute in the local council chamber, appreciative of his parent's ability to display his own kind of paddy.

Men of Leachman's volatile temperament cannot expect universal approval or popularity. Quick, reliable, hard, conscientious, as his superiors said, and as ruthlessly tough with others as with himself, he is sure to make enemies as well as friends. Already the military secretariat at the India Office in London was compiling a dossier on the man who, though strictly speaking not one of its own, was to become by adoption one of its prodigal sons; a report which had about it some of the qualities of the curate's egg. Everyone admired him. Not everyone liked him.

'It seems almost incredible . . . that Leachman remained in Peshawar till March 1915,' wrote Bray. 'We may well imagine how he fumed with impotent rage during these weeks and months as he read the vague and garbled accounts of what was

140

happening on the shores of the Gulf he loved so well,' wrote Philby.

Nothing of the kind. He was in constant touch with the General Staff offices at Fort William[1] and Simla, where his eventual employment was under anxious review. Problems of place and time were posed by the long delay in Turkey's expected decision to enter the war on the side of the Central Powers, by events in Persia, and by a change in the balance of power in central Arabia which followed Leachman's journey with the tribal armies in 1912.

In the month of January 1913 when he returned from Bushire to India, stirring events took place in the Ottoman Empire. On the 4th the *Times* correspondent Philip Graves reported disturbances in Constantinople accompanied by a movement led by Arab officers in the Ottoman army to establish an Arab empire. At the time of Leachman's sojourn with Ibn Rashid's Shammar force at Abu Ghar and Ghuribiya in the Shamiya desert. Zamil the Regent had been in correspondence with Ibn Saud regarding an Arab uprising which was to be instigated by Arab officers at Damascus and Baghdad and led by the Saudi chief. French agents had picked up the scent of revolt and, fearful of the consequences in Syria where they had long-standing territorial ambitions, the Quay d'Orsay and the French secret service decided on a policy which was to lead to the betrayal of the Arab conspirators.

On 15 January 1915 M. Bompard, the French ambassador at Constantinople, told the Foreign Ministry in Paris of the plans of the 'Arab Reform Party in Syria'. At the same time the French consular-agent in Beirut, M. Picot, was instructed to meet Ibn Rashid's agent in Damascus, and to offer French protection for the rulers of Hail if they opposed the plans of *Ahad* and Ibn Saud. France was acting through the newly appointed chief minister of the boy-prince of Hail, Saud ibn Subhan, the nephew of the Regent Zamil, a revolting young man with pug nose, harelip and squint eyes which fixed their victims with a hideous, bloodshot glare. When Britain heard of the French negotiations, and heard too that the old liberal rearguard of Kiamil Pasha had finally been defeated in Constantinople, it greeted the emergency with another bout of war between the Foreign Office and India, with military and naval intelligence intervening. The Ottoman emissary Hakki Pasha was, after all, in London talking to Sir Edward

Grey. Britain's bargaining counters were substantial, even in dealing with so ruthless an organization as the French secret service, and so mercurial a situation as prevailed in the Ottoman regions. But events began to overtake the negotiators in London.

Enver, the pro-German leader of the Young Turks, began to take charge of the Committee's fortunes in Constantinople, though the strongman of the old guard, Shevket, took over as grand vizier. Jamal Pasha, who would come to be known as the 'Butcher of Syria', was made military governor of Constantinople and a few weeks later the city went up in flames after revolutionary slogans had appeared on the walls of the mosque of St Sophia. Azmi Bey, the bully among bullies in the Committee hierarchy, was made chief of police and subsequently governor of Adana, where new outrages against the Armenians and Greeks started up. Disorder and murder spread throughout the Near East. In Kuwait, to which principality the Indian Government sent a deputation to search for oil and seek a concession from Shaikh Mubarak, two of Shakespear's agents were murdered. Mubarak was away at the time, talking to the oil men. When he returned the culprits were taken to the bazaar district where their crime had been committed and flogged before being garrotted, as a warning to others who might be tempted to take up the Turco-German cause. Three Arabs had earlier started a fight outside the Political Agency in Kuwait while Shakespear was away, and others had joined in until the place was under siege. At almost the same time the Viceroy was the subject of a bomb-throwing attack in Delhi. Such events were not necessarily connected, but India's secret service chief, Cleveland, suspected strongly that they were, that a wide conspiracy was receiving support from Berlin and Constantinople with the aim of destroying the British Empire.

In May 1913 came the affair that was to force the hands of Whitehall and Constantinople in deciding who to back in Arabia. Shakespear went to Khafs where Ibn Saud kept his horses and was at camp, collecting an army of his most reliable tribes and tribal leaders. The Foreign Office, deep in talks with Constantinople's emissary, Hakki Pasha, knew nothing of the journey. Two weeks after Shakespear left the camp, Ibn Saud marched on the coastal region of Al Hasa and won a decisive victory over the Turks whose garrison withdrew in disarray, despite reinforcements brought in from Basra on a British ship.

The news of Ibn Saud's victory arrived in London just as Sir Edward Grey and Hakki Pasha reached agreement on the question of suzerainty in central Arabia and on the matter of the Berlin–Baghdad railway. The Indian Government and its Political Agent were castigated by Grey when he found out what had happened.

At the end of the year, after a long squabble between the Foreign Office and Simla, it was agreed that Shakespear should be allowed to proceed on a journey across Arabia which would take him via Riyadh to Hail and on to Sinai. His mission for the General Staff was to survey in detail the route along the northern Nafud region which Leachman had traversed in 1912, to ascertain whether, in the event of war, motorized vehicles could accompany cavalry on the road from Najaf by the wells of Labba to Wadi Sirhan and the back door to Syria. But he took on another and even more secret task. He travelled from Buraida to the region of Jabal Shammar with a deputation from Ibn Saud to Zamil the Regent. Zamil was in great danger and Shakespear was preceded by none other than Saleh al Mutawah, Leachman's guide on the journey to Ibn Saud and brother of the Amir of Ayun, who had gone to warn Zamil of an expected attempt on his life. On Sunday 19 April Shakespear was camped at the wells of Hayaniya, when news was brought to him that Saleh, the emissary of Ibn Saud, was safe in the desert but that he had not been able to reach Zamil in time. The Regent had been murdered by slaves of Saud ibn Sabhun, the minister of the young prince, as he rode outside the royal tents.

The threatened Arab rebellion was effectively over. Ibn Saud could not act without the support of the Rashids, and with Zamil out of the way he had no friends at Hail of any consequence. Hail became the unquestioning ally of the Young Turks. But the Arabian situation at the end of 1914 was more complex than even the strange affair of Zamil's murder suggests.

On 18 April as Shakespear waited for news at Hayaniya, eight days after Zamil's murder, Abdullah, the second son of the Sharif Husain of Mecca, called on Lord Kitchener, the Resident at Cairo.[2] Abdullah's father had been party to the plot among the Arab princes to rise against the Ottoman power, though he had challenged Ibn Saud's leadership and was, in any case, a salaried vassal of the Turks. Abdullah wanted to know if Britain would support the Sharif in a holy war declared from Mecca, but he was given an evasive answer by Kitchener's secretary and right-hand man, Ronald Storrs, the old Carthusian whose schooldays overlapped Leachman's.

Two days later, on 20 April, Crow, the consul at Basra, reported that the Turks, those 'genial and agreeable exponents of paternal despotism and *dolce far niente*', had sent a delegation to Kuwait to see Ibn Saud.[3]

The Indian Foreign Department reported on 10 May that a meeting had taken place between the Saudi leader and the Turks at which Ibn Saud was told by Grey, Shakespear's successor, that he could expect no further help from Britain and that he must sign a treaty with the Turks which was proffered to him by the arch intriguer of Basra, Sayyid Talib. According to the Viceroy in a note to the Secretary of State the meeting nearly ended in a free fight, with Ibn Saud refusing to sign, Grey and Talib telling him that he must, and Ibn Saud and his followers threatening Talib and the Turks with physical violence.

Sir Louis Mallet had gone to Constantinople at the beginning of 1914 to take over from Lowther and make a last bid to procure Turkish neutrality. Negotiations went on for three months after the declaration of war between the Entente and the Central Powers in August 1914. But the ineptness of Britain was overwhelming. Helmut von Moltke, the German Chief of Staff, had said that Turkey would be 'no asset' to the Triple Alliance, but Britain drove the Ottoman regime into the arms of the Kaiser, and Turkey entered the war on 3 November 1914.[4]

In January 1915 Shakespear was sent on a mission to Ibn Saud to seek his support for the allied cause, even though his help and allegiance had been spurned so recently. The Englishman obeyed orders from London to join with Ibn Saud as Britain's Political Officer on special duty, and so followed the Saudi army on to the battlefield around al Artawiya which both he and Leachman knew from their Arabian journeys. He joined in battle with the old adversary Ibn Rashid and was killed on a hillock at Jarab, near the spot where Zamil the Regent of Hail was murdered.[5]

The Indian Government appointed Leachman successor to Shakespear on 4 March as special duty officer assigned to Ibn Saud. But Ibn Saud wanted nothing more to do with Britain for the moment. He had lost his bosom friend Shakespear in battle, he had been officially abandoned by Britain, and though he promised the Resident at Bushire that he would do nothing to help the Turks, he made it clear that he had tired of Britain's duplicity.[6]

In making the new appointment, the Viceroy told the Secretary of State in London: 'Captain Leachman has travelled considerably in Arabia, sometimes in disguise, and though not of the same calibre as Shakespear, he may do well under Sir Percy Cox.' It was not a fair judgement of Leachman, and it was not shared by the General Staff in London or Simla. He had so far had no real opportunity to show his paces in negotiation, apart from the very difficult mission to Ibn Saud, but it is probably true that he could never have taken the place of Shakespear in the Amir's affection or esteem. In any case the need did not arise. Ibn Saud disappeared from the scene, and Britain through its Arab Bureau in Cairo took up the cause of the Sharif of Mecca.

Yet another factor contributed to Leachman's prolonged exile on the North-West Frontier. Persia, even more than the Arab lands, had become a cauldron of German intrigue and tribal unrest, and threatened Britain's vital oil installations at Abadan and Ahwaz and beyond to the Bakhtiari country of northern Arabistan. By October 1914 a party of Germans had left Berlin under the leadership of Herr Oskar Ritter von Niedermayer. They were to join up at Aleppo with Wilhelm Wassmuss, the Adonis of the German political service, whose task was to infiltrate the Persian tribes and stir them to holy war. By 1915 he was well on the way to achieving his aim. Mobs roamed the streets of all the main cities and the few British-Indian troops in the country were in grave danger. The military consul at the holy city of Meshed, Col. Percy Sykes, was under immediate threat.

Sykes himself was on the supernumerary list by this time, though he was yet to lead one of the great expeditions of the war across Persia. Other officers were available for the special duty tasks which confronted the army from the Caucasus to the Gulf, from the North-West Frontier to North African Tripoli, the Yemen to German West Africa, to say nothing of France and Belgium. But men of the calibre needed – able to speak the necessary languages and to operate alone from within enemy territory – were few and far between. Leachman was one of a select band who would be capable of contending with the Persian fanatic and the Arab tribesman, roused to uncontrollable fervour by calls to holy war, and to acts of premeditated violence by promises of reward made by the most unscrupulous agents of the other side. There was delay in deciding whether to use his particular brand of grit and nerve in Persia or Mesopotamia. At the end of 1914, following Turkey's entry into the war, he was earmarked for Persia. The debate went on into the first weeks of 1915.

Both the DMO in London and Simla Intelligence wanted Leachman to join Sykes in Persia as a special duty officer, with particular responsibility for dealing with the elusive Wassmuss and the German missions to Afghanistan which had set out from Berlin on the long and hazardous overland journey in October 1914. But Sykes would have none of it. He and Leachman had met in India and had taken an instant dislike to each other. Sir Percy Sykes, the senior officer, of serious disposition, an able historian with a fondness for Persia where he had served for long periods, was not impressed by the impetuous and aggressive young officer of the Sussex Regiment. But his view was not shared by the General Staff in London or Simla. In October Sykes told Hirtzel, the head of the India Office Political and Secret Department, that he was 'having some difficulty', but was opposing moves to post Leachman to Persia. But, he added, 'vested interests in England are very strong'. The concern of Maj.-Gen. Callwell, who took over as DMO from General Henry Wilson in August 1914, was to ensure that round pegs were hammered into round holes. Specially qualified staff officers were desperately needed in France and only the most essential could be spared for the eastern theatres. In the end, Sykes won and Leachman was posted to Mesopotamia. He was on board a crowded troopship which inched its way over the silt-bar of the Shatt al Arab on the morning of 11 March 1915. By the afternoon Leachman was being briefed by the Chief Political Officer, Sir Percy Cox, at Basra GHQ.

Expeditionary Force 'D' had come to southern Mesopotamia not to fight a war but simply to guard the oil installations in Shaikh Khazal's province of Muhammerah and in the region of south-west Persia known then as Arabistan. But it had become embroiled in a campaign whose tactics were dictated by the old Prussian von der Goltz and the War Minister of the Young Turks, Enver Pasha, whose uncle Khalil was field commander of the Turkish 6th army.

From the moment that troops landed at Fao on 5 November 1914 under the command of Brig.-Gen. W.S. Delamain – they seemed to be engaged in a 'promenade'.[7] The fleet carrying Delamain's men had anchored off Bahrain on 23 October to await War Office and Admiralty instructions before proceeding to the mouth of the Shatt al Arab, and while there one of the intelligence officers with the force, C.C.R. Murphy, went ashore with a small force to arrest the German agents of Wönckhaus. By the time they burst into the Bahrain office the managing director, Herr Harling, had sent details of the British force to Basra. The Turks knew that an army was on the way. They knew its strength and make-up. But they did nothing to hinder its progress. Fao was taken almost without resistance. Within a few days of that initial success, a new commander was sent from India, Lt-Gen. Sir Arthur Barrett. On 15 November, Saihan was occupied, and then Sahil. On the 22nd a victorious British army moved into Basra and Sir Percy Cox read a declaration to the populace telling them that the British were there as their friends and allies and that their religion and holy places would be respected. The only cloud on the horizon when Leachman arrived in Mesopotamia was the activity of the Turco-German wreckers on their right flank in Persia.

Auxiliaries had made a successful raid on the pipeline at Ahwaz, and the tribes of Arabistan had joined with the pro-Turkish Bani Lam led by the ruthless Anglophobe Ghadhaban al-Bunaiya. Wassmuss had defeated an attempt by British intelligence officers to trap him at Bushire on 22 February. His confederates, including the consul, Dr Linders, were arrested (illegally, for Persia was a neutral country), but Wassmuss escaped to wreak havoc among the tribes. There was danger, too, on the British left flank beyond the Euphrates where the Muntafiq tribal federation under Ajaimi Sadun was the formidable carrier of the Ottoman flag. Since Leachman's journey in 1910 with Ajaimi's father, several attempts had been made to pull the Muntafiq out of the Turkish camp. Shakespear and a political officer, Robert Money, had visited Sadun soon after Leachman's reports reached London, in clandestine attempts to secure his neutrality in any 'unforeseen' conflict.[8] But Ajaimi, who had himself been arrested on the orders of the Wali of Basra only two years earlier following more skulduggery by Sayyid Talib, was a paid servant of the Turks and a man of loyalty.[9] When war came he hoisted the Crescent flag and became a constant thorn in Britain's side. Leachman would become his fiercest adversary.

Leachman's briefing in Cox's office was attended by Arnold Wilson, by Murphy of Intelligence who had taken over the Jask station before the war, Campbell Thompson who had worked with Hogarth, Lawrence and Woolley at Carchemish (from which vantage point they kept an eye on the German builders of the Baghdad railway), and Gribbon who had come down from Intelligence Branch Simla to join the Mesopotamian staff under Col. Beach's direction.[10] The deputy head of the Indian secret police, E. C. Gregson, was also there. He had taken over responsibility for the civil population of the country and Leachman's intimate knowledge of the Arabs of Basra, gained in some of its sleaziest backwaters, was invaluable to him. The task assigned at that meeting was simple enough. Leachman would be working for both civil and military intelligence and would set up his own 'news' network among the Arabs. He would be responsible for pacifying the tribes, and where possible would work behind enemy lines. He was to be the freelance among warring factions of the military and civil powers as the British-Indian army made its way, at first steadily and then at a hurried pace, towards Baghdad. Politicians in London quickly saw in the initial successes of the force an opportunity for propaganda to counter enemy victories elsewhere. As the 'Mespot' army moved gradually north, the fatal blunders of the Gallipoli campaign began to come home to roost, and Whitehall's 'easterners' looked ever more insistently towards Baghdad.

He resumed a few old friendships in Basra, visited the famous American missionaries, Mr and Mrs Van Ess, whom he had met on previous visits and who helped him in earlier days with his Arabic, and contacted notables who had been privy to the secrets of earlier missions – men like Ibn Saud's friend Abdal Latif ibn Mandil and Muhammad al-Sha'aina. One 'old friend', Sayyid Talib, had been sent back from Ibn Saud's camp to Basra by Shakespear, and Cox had sent him on to India as the involuntary guest of the British Government. Leachman visited one or two night-spots where British and enemy agents and staff officers kept watch on each other as they had done in peacetime, usually dressed as Arabs and looking like advertisements for Turkish delight as they sipped coffee or whisky and toyed with the ladies of the town. Leachman's sister Mabel, perhaps with a presentiment of war's finality, told him that it was 'time he was married'.

'I am obliged for your incitement to marry,' he replied, 'but it would have to be a Basra Jewess, and most of them weigh 18 stone when they are fifteen, with a face on top like an angel, which is sad.' His assessment of Basra's women was not quite accurate. Tod's beautiful wife was still there and he saw her often enough to maintain his interest in women. And Basra still teemed with the exotic ladies of the East – Greek, Armenian, Persian, Arab and Jewish. They and the bars and coffee-houses were consolation for troops who were there for a few days before they went into battle.

In April he was sent to Shaiba where Gen. Fry was holding that 'godless spot' which had nothing but dust and filth to give it a definable character. He waded through six miles of flooded desert to reach the place, yet within a day or two it had become an arid desert fortress, and as he took up his quarters in the fort he witnessed cavalry patrols being driven in from the desert by Sadun's Arabs, who were mostly fellahin, small-time cultivators who took to their camels and horses when called upon by their leader to mobilize for the *ghazzu*. It was a state of affairs which Leachman was determined to put a stop to, especially when he saw the Arab horsemen careering impertinently round the British occupied fort. Leachman went out at night to reconnoitre the Turkish garrison at Nukhaila and realized that an attack was imminent. It came on the 11th and for three days there was heavy fighting. As a staff officer it was not his business to take part in the affair, but inevitably he was in the thick of the engagement. The Turks retreated on the night of the 14th, abandoning their own camp and leaving the ground carpeted with dead and wounded. Their commander, Col. Subhi Bey, who had been GOC at Basra when the British took the city, was captured and sent to India. The Basra vilayet had been more or less cleared. Sister Mabel, delighted to learn that Gerard was seeing active service at long last, wrote to congratulate him and to suggest higher things in the diplomatic service. Just after the battle on 15 April he replied:

Thanks . . . but I'm not sure the job suits me very well. I don't think I'm a diplomat, I have too bad a temper. I was lucky to come in for *the* show of this part of the world, and it was a great fight. I have never had such a shelling, and we had to sit in the open instead of being in the trenches. The British regiments are wonderful.

He acknowledged the lack of diplomatic tact which the Viceroy had pointed to when he compared him with Shakespear. After the battle of Shaiba he had to return to Basra and he was not at all happy in the Political Office or at Staff HQ where he was with men of his own kind; Gribbon, Murphy, the erudite and courageous (and inordinately mingy) Scot Campbell Thompson, and, of course, the chief, Col. Beach. All conversation now was centred on Persia where a force had been sent in to deal with the tide of pro-German feeling engendered by a visit from Field-Marshal von der Goltz, by Turkish armed success at Kermanshah and the capture of a joint Russian-Indian guard. There was talk as well of political events at home where Lloyd George had told Asquith that the War Office was incompetent, and the Prime Minister had met the Conservatives with a view to coalition and the First Sea Lord, Admiral Fisher, had resigned in the wake of mounting disasters in the Dardanelles. Churchill, the architect of the early disasters, had been put out to grass as Chancellor of the Duchy of Lancaster. Closer to the cauldron in which Force 'D' found itself, they spoke at dinner of the arrival of Gen. Nixon from India to take over from the ailing Sir Arthur Barrett.

The time had come to set up a desert 'news' chain. Each day Leachman sallied out to the tribal districts and took special care to befriend the children, the intelligence gatherer's best friends. He took them sweets and occasionally gave them small sums in return for running errands, or just as a gesture of goodwill. He would appear at the encampments to offer his salaams to the shaikhs and sit around with groups of youngsters. Gradually they gave him their confidence and became his principal source of news. With their help he was able to follow the movements of the tribes, and assess the strength of Turkish forces. He became the Pied Piper of the swamps and deserts above Basra and along the Euphrates and Tigris. But such tactics could not remain secret for very long. It was soon reported to GHQ at Basra that the Turks were aware of his disguised visits on their flanks and behind their lines. A petty shaikh had informed the Turks of one of his visits. Next night Leachman mounted his new pony 'as wild as sin and goes about the country shrieking', and set off for the Arab's home with some of his pre-war Basra companions. The shaikh was dragged down from his parlour, and dressed down in a loud voice so that any of his companions lurking near by could know the seriousness of his crime. He was then dragged back to Basra and dumped in the bazaar district.

Leachman's philosophy was simple, and it was to prove effective. In tribal war you either dominate or submit to treachery and almost certain death. There are no comfortable compromises.

His work now was in the desert. He knew that given time he could bring the most important tribes to Britain's side, or at least ensure their neutrality. He was aware also that time was not on his side. At the time of his arrival at Basra in March, the redoubtable Musil was on his way to the Euphrates from Najd, where he had been with Ibn Rashid's army and had witnessed the clash in which Shakespear died. He went to Najaf, Kufa, Falluja and Baghdad, before returning to Damascus, skirting the contending armies and appointing agents as he went for the Austro-Hungarian secret service. Austrian consuls were still at work in all the major towns. More importantly, the masterly German agent Conrad Preusser, left behind by the archaeologists who had returned to Berlin on the declaration of war, was working in competition with Leachman among the tribes. Preusser spoke perfect Arabic and like Leachman could merge into the Arab community, in desert or *suq*. The two men were to fight tooth and nail for the allegiance of the tribes throughout the war. They acquired a grudging mutual admiration in the process.

At a critical moment Leachman was called away from the vital work he had been set by Cox and the General Staff. With the consolidation of early gains in the Basra province, and with hair-raising defeats being reported daily from other fronts, Whitehall began to put the heat on the Mesopotamian commanders. Germany knew, or guessed, what was passing through the 'secret' channels of a London administration whose differences were regularly aired in the press.

At the end of May, the Cabinet in London began to discuss impatiently the question of an advance on Baghdad. Between April and July Gen. Gorringe had led an Indian cavalry force in a sweep of lower Mesopotamia and Arabistan, occupying Ahwaz in April and posting friendly tribesmen along the pipeline. On 25 July his troops entered Nasiriya on the Euphrates. At the very start of the campaign, in December 1914, an advance force had taken Qurna, the reputed Garden of Eden, at the juncture of the two great rivers and the point where they merge into the Shatt al Arab. Thus the Anglo-Indian army of Gen. Nixon held an unchallenged line stretching from the Karun river in Persia to the Euphrates. Staff reports showed that the strength of the Turkish 6th Army was below scratch. There was almost as much dissension in the enemy camp as in Whitehall, with Liman von Sanders and von der Goltz fighting for command of the Turkish First Army. An attempt to buy off the Turks by the Director of Naval Intelligence in London, Capt. 'Blinker' Hall, had recently been foiled by Admiral Fisher who thought the sum being offered, £4 million, was too high. Had an advance on Baghdad been decided on in August when the enemy was at his weakest there may have been a chance of success, even though Townshend, the general in command of the Tigris front, had warned that he would need massive reinforcements to make victory certain. The General Staff in London were pressing for Indian troops to be sent to the Western Front. London needed a victory, however, and the Mesopotamian army would have to take Baghdad with whatever resources it could muster.[11]

In May 1915 Gen. Townshend, commander of the 6th Division made up of Dorsets, Norfolks, Rajputs and Mahrattas, led his force up the Tigris from Qurna towards Amara. The *Lewis Pelly*, Shakespear's beloved agency yacht, was sent ahead to sweep the river of Turkish mines.

On 15 May Leachman wrote to his mother: 'I am getting very fidgety again. I would like to go off into the wilderness, but I am afraid that is out of the question at the moment.' Like the *Lewis Pelly* he went on ahead of the main army, to sound out the tribes on the route, to purchase animals and supplies, to report on the strength of the enemy forces. Gen. Townshend's flotilla made its way up river, the commander aboard the sloop HMS *Espiègle*. The Turks massed along the Tigris front were three times as strong numerically as the British force, and a new commander, Nureddin Pasha, had taken over in Baghdad. War Office telegrams conveyed the news that Nureddin was being reinforced with units of the crack Fire-Brigade Division based at Constantinople. But the British force pushed on relentlessly driving the Turks before them. Amara was captured on 3 June, Sir John Nixon, the C-in-C, following the victorious army and establishing his advance HQ there. London was jubilant, particularly since a renewed assault on the Dardanelles had failed to penetrate the Turkish lines. Expeditionary Force 'D' moved on. In August the advance along the Tigris continued towards Kut al Amara, a little township at the junction of the Tigris and the Hai river. Townshend regaled fellow-officers with the strategic theories of Napoleon, Clausewitz and Moltke. 'Throw your principal mass at the enemy's weakest point which is his line of communication, which in higher tactics is that flank nearest his natural line of retreat.' He talked too of his hero Belisarius, the Roman general who conquered most of Mesopotamia in AD 541. But von der Goltz, the adviser to the Ottoman army, and Nureddin in Baghdad, were also students of the military strategists of the past.

On a more prosaic plane it was Leachman, always ahead of the army, moving in disguise among the Arabs and Turks, who contributed as much as anyone to the tactical jigsaw of the moment: 'Our forward intelligence is good,' observed the commander. Leachman had to punish Marsh Arabs on the road to Amara who cut a field-telegraph he had established. Kut al Amara was occupied on 28 September. Townshend had been taken ill after Amara and sent to India to recuperate before returning with the congratulations of the Viceroy ringing in his ears to continue the push to Baghdad. But the Viceroy had warned London time and again of the inherent dangers of the campaign and had stressed the wastefulness of 'side-shows'. The war would be won or lost on the Western Front he said. But few listened.

Nothing had been heard from Leachman during July and early August while the army rested and Townshend was reviving his health and spirits at Viceregal Lodge. He had melted into the enemy territory north of the army's line of advance. From his reports and from messages transmitted by agents in Baghdad, Beach's intelligence department had been able to piece together a detailed picture of the Turkish army on 3 June: at Baghdad itself only one regular battalion and two reserve battalions (inferior); at Kut, one regular batallion (escaped from Shaiba), four Arab battalions, two reserve battalions (inferior), twelve guns from Shaiba; between Kut and Amara, the remnants of Halim Bey's defeated Qurna army, the remnants of a force of Arabistan tribesmen sent to Qurna by Leachman's host in Kurdistan, Daghistani; and two Fire-Brigade units, escaped from Amara. Practically all the Turkish artillery had been lost or captured in the campaign up to that date. The omens were good. But Townshend was having doubts. He had not devoted his life to military strategy for nothing. 'Where are we going to stop in Mesopotamia?' he asked the Chief of the General Staff in London, Gen. Wolfe Murray, on 8 August. 'I stayed with the Viceroy last month but could not get anything out of him.' Wolfe Murray had no say in the matter. Kitchener the War Minister called the tune, backed by the 'Easterners' in the coalition Cabinet and in Cairo. 'We have certainly not good enough troops to make certain of taking Baghdad, which I hear is being fortified,' said Townshend.

But there was no stopping now. By the first week of October Aziziya had been taken.

At last Leachman came into view again. He wrote from Aziziya on 10 October: 'this is the farthest north for the moment; I have been fifteen miles further on myself, and I came back with the Turkish army after me. But that was some time ago and we are now sitting looking at each other at close quarters.'

He told his family that the first aeroplanes had arrived, an old Voisin and three Henry Farmans, junk from the Western Front, sent as a token to the forgotten army of Mesopotamia and somehow kept in the air during every available daylight hour by a small group of Royal Flying Corps officers. And he observed that there were many Englishwomen still incarcerated at Baghdad, the Turks having refused Gen. Nixon's attempt to exchange them for Turkish prisoners.

> It has now changed from horribly hot to bitterly cold [he wrote]. I am full of work from morning to night. It extends from buying sheep for a whole division and straw for about ten thousand animals up to paying a thousand pounds to an Arab shaikh to do some dirty work . . . I thought I was overpaid, but I'm not. The day is a twenty-four hour work one.

The wounded and sick from the battlefronts were being sent to base hospital at Amara and Leachman spent his time going back and forth between there and Aziziya during the enforced halt at the latter town. And while he and others of the Mesopotamian army went about their tasks, there was more argument and more vacillation between London and Delhi (to which city the Indian High Command had removed from

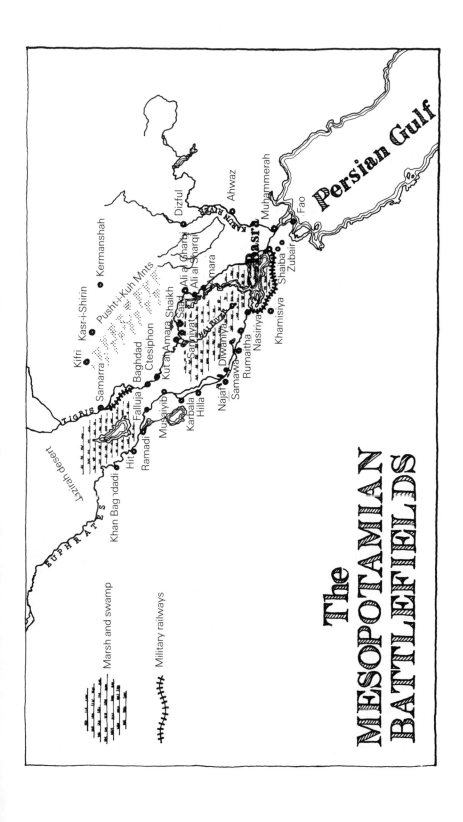

The
MESOPOTAMIAN
BATTLEFIELDS

Persian Gulf

Marsh and swamp

Military railways

TIGRIS

EUPHRATES

Jezirah desert

Khan Baghdadi

Ramadi

Hit

Falluja

Baghdad

Ctesiphon

Samarra

Kifri

Kasr-i-Shirin

Pusht-i-Kuh Mnts.

Kermanshah

Kut al Amara

Musaiyib

Karbala

Hilla

Najaf

Diwaniya

Samawa

Rumaitha

Nasiriya

Khamisiya

Zubair

Shaiba

Basra

Sad

Saniyat

Sannaiyat

EL HANNA

Amara

Ali al Gharbi

Ali al Sharqi

Shaikh Saad

Dizful

Ahwaz

KARUN RIVER

Muhammerah

Fao

Simla and Calcutta following the decision of 1912 to make it the new capital). Doctors and ambulances were in short supply, and as an aside to all that was happening in Mesopotamia the advance party of Niedermayer's Afghan mission had arrived in Kabul along with Indian agents in July. The Indian Government was threatened with war on its own doorstep and was trying to keep back troops and medical facilities.

Townshend was the hero of the British army at the moment, though he would shortly become the black sheep. It is as well to heed his words at the moment of decision, for historians were to ignore them studiously afterwards:

> Of our two divisions in Mesopotamia mine, the 6th, is complete; the 12th division (General Gorringe) has no guns! or divisional troops – and Nixon takes them from me and lends them to Gorringe when the latter has to go anywhere . . . All these offensive operations in secondary theatres are dreadful errors in strategy: the Dardanelles, Egypt, Mesopotamia, East Africa! I wonder and wonder at such expeditions being permitted in violation of all the great fundamental principles of war.

But if Townshend was the darling of Whitehall and the High Command, Capt. Leachman was the hero-figure of the troops. It is Arnold Wilson, the strong man of the civil administration, who tells us virtually all we know of him at this time:

> During these years (on the Tigris line) he made for himself a unique position, and a reputation among all classes for bravery, energy and outspokenness that was enjoyed in like measure by no other Englishman of whatever rank. His courage – displayed on many occasions, in tight corners and in open battle – earned him the respect alike of friend and foe; his tireless energy was a precious asset to a harassed staff, a tonic to weary regimental officers, and an example to all.

There are glimpses of what was happening in the few letters he had time to write, though he seldom spoke of his actual work. In the middle of October: 'Still in the same place you see, and all very fed up . . . They have just told me to enlist a large number of

Arab horsemen – I lightly suggested that I should command them myself.'

The letter was unfinished. Four days later he resumed it: 'I had to go down river to teach a lesson to some Arabs who had fired on our ships . . . a lyddite shell in the middle of the shaikh's tent probably taught them the error of their ways.' On 10 November the 6th division was preparing for the final onslaught. Leachman again went ahead of the army with a small and trusted band of Norfolks: 'We marched all night in the piercing cold, and at dawn found the Turks just gone. We got on to their trail, though, and gave them a nasty start.'

On 10 November he wrote: 'Still here, but not for long I hope . . . We have surprised the Arabs a bit lately and killed a certain number of them, with the result that my flock are behaving themselves better than they did. With our arrival in Baghdad I hope they will really settle down.'

He told his sisters that he was aggrieved at the lack of warm things in parcels from home. 'I expected showers of socks and warm things and sweets etc., but they never came . . . We get nothing to eat now, I suppose because we are a long way away.' It was his last aside before disaster struck. The army moved off on 11 November towards Ctesiphon, the ruins of the great city from which the Sassanians ruled Persia and ancient Iraq, the last outpost on the journey to Baghdad.

Townshend's army reached Ctesiphon on 21 November. They were a stone's-throw from Baghdad. On 26 November Leachman wrote to his parents:

We have had a very big battle at Ctesiphon since last I wrote. The Turks had a very strong position and a large number of troops. Our men were splendid. I could not have believed that men could have faced such a blaze of fire, shell and rifle, without an atom of cover – you will have seen an account in the papers, so I need tell you no more about it . . . It is now the day after the fourth, so excuse me if the letter isn't all it should be. I have had so many friends killed.

Leachman's letter was written during a brief respite at Lajj as the reinforced Turkish army forced the exhausted British back along the banks of the Tigris. Next day they were at Zor, the next at Aziziya, Leachman riding out on the flanks of the retreating

157

army to keep rapacious tribes at bay. Seeing the defeated army making hurriedly for cover they sensed rich pickings and waited on the side-line like the vultures which hovered overhead.

On 3 December 1915 Townshend led his sick, hungry and demoralized army into the village of Kut al Amara whence it had started out less than six months earlier. The Turks encircled them, their gunboats dominating the river, their guns commanding the banks. The longest and bitterest siege in the history of the British Empire had begun. The new Secretary of State for India Austen Chamberlain, Hardinge the Viceroy, Beauchamp Duff the C-in-C India, Nixon the GOC and Townshend himself would be held to blame. The 'Easterners' in London – Kitchener, Churchill, Lloyd George, Amery and a compliant Asquith – would escape the reproach of history, though they had insisted on the adventures and side-shows of which Kut al Amara was, with the Dardanelles, the spectacular manifestation. As Field-Marshal von der Goltz and Khalil Pasha inspected the Turkish lines in front of the encircled British force, its commander hoping against hope that a relief force would be able to break through to them, Whitehall finally decided on the evacuation of the Gallipoli army. There were further humiliations in store, and Leachman, who had gone off to the Amara base ahead of Townshend's men, was to bear witness.

Kut undid all Leachman's good work among the tribes, as it undid the prestige of the Allies in the world at large. German and Turkish propagandists naturally made the best of the British army's headlong dash for shelter pursued by the gallant and victorious Turks. Arab tribes, pacified and in some cases actively coming over to the army's side, turned to murder and large-scale looting.

On 5 December Gen. Nixon wired the War Office with a summary of Townshend's plight, and of that commander's view of the situation: 'Townshend reports: I shall expect him (von der Goltz) to turn this place, putting off a force of observation at Kut . . . I have shut myself up here, reckoning with certainty on being relieved by large forces arriving at Basra.' Nixon ended the telegram which the Secretary of State for India circulated to the Cabinet: 'I have approved his proposal, and shall now make my concentration at Amara.'

Townshend had written in his diary during the engagement at Ctesiphon, when his 'Invincibles' were driving the enemy before them with fixed bayonets and the battle was going his way: 'The Turks, when entrenched, are the most formidable soldiers in the world.' He thought that when fighting from a fixed position they were better than the Germans.

Leachman, almost alone among the officers present, believed that a break-out was possible. But Nixon would not listen to his plan. Nevertheless, he was given permission to go to Kut in the first days of the siege to assist an escape and to see if he could rescue some of his Arab servants who were trapped there, one of them his guide in 1910, Khidr ibn Abbas. Another was a young Indian servant boy, Hassan, taken on during the northward advance, who had become his devoted and almost inseparable companion.

According to Khidr, who thought the story should be 'written with a pen of gold', Leachman made his way through enemy lines to guide a cavalry force in an attempted escape. The details of his mission were never made known officially since his movements were unobserved. Only his Arab guide, Khidr ibn Abbas, and a passing reference in one of his own letters tell of an action which many believed would have won him the VC had there been a witness to his courage. At any rate he somehow penetrated the Turkish positions, in Arab dress, found his Arab friends who were taking shelter with natives of the village, and then made contact with the cavalry. He led them in a mass break-out and took them on the road to the village of Ali Gharbi where they were able to join the force gathering to relieve their comrades. It is said that 5,000 troops, many of whom would have died of slow starvation had it not been for Leachman, were enabled to escape in those first days when, admittedly, the Turks had not quite closed all the gaps. They were even able to take two gun batteries with them.

Al Khidr, an articulate Arab who spoke English well, wrote: 'One stands astonished before this man of genius, and certainly there are very few in military annals who could have accomplished these dangerous deeds.'

Leachman's own account, written on 13 December, was modest indeed:

You must excuse the very bad typing, but my typewriter has been in the war, like master, and we are both feeling a bit old . . . I came out of Kut with a crowd of cavalry to nurse them down to Ali al Gharbi, and then could not get back again owing to the enemy on the road, so I am now going to Amara as Political to a new army corps commander, and I am writing on my launch, which I managed to get hold of again . . . If I told you all that I would like to, my letter would not survive the censor.

A few days later he told his parents, 'My stay in Amara is only likely to be temporary, and I hope to return to the front, with the full intention of handing over every Arab I can find to summary justice. They are brutes, and for the last fortnight I hardly remember a moment when one was not being shot at by them.'

At least when he returned to Kut he would have the services of his 'excellent' boy Hassan, whom he had left behind with the British force at al Gharbi.

Now it was back and forth between Kut and Amara, and his launch became a familiar sight on the river. He ran aground on Christmas Day 1915 and arrived at the mess at Amara, where his corps commander was Gen. Aylmer, in time for plum pudding, 'better than nothing'.

'Most of my friends are in Kut, where I wish I could be.' Footwear was his only personal problem. Boots sent out from Petersfield where they were made for him by the local cobbler had to be reinforced locally with stronger stitching before they would stand up to wear in desert and marshland. Occasionally homesickness came to him, as it came more insistently to those who were less familiar with the treacherous conditions of Mesopotamia. 'I am longing for a visit to civilization and shops. I don't often get taken like this but there are limits even for the most cheerful person.' Gen. Aylmer arrived 'green' from India with no knowledge of the country and Leachman was deputed to 'inform' him. Arabs were loath to go with him on his sorties into the surrounding country, as were Muslim troops of the Indian army: 'They think I am a fire-eater and get them into danger, which is quite incorrect.' Soon he would have his companion Hassan back. Their father-and-son relationship was to prove the highlight of the campaign for many a soldier. Hassan was an agreeable young man who had somehow acquired a liking for liquor. Knowing the inherent danger of alcoholism among the Arabs, Leachman at first reprimanded him and then resorted to more abrasive punishment. Hassan proved to be a Jekyll and

Hyde, devoted and loyal at one moment, unreliable and disobedient the next, and like his master inclined to fall among
thieves. When he was particularly difficult Leachman would
shout at him and beat him over the head. Hassan would shout
and fight back, and sometimes run away. It was a non-stop Punch
and Judy show and the troops loved it; a rare diversion in the long
months of suffering and dashed hopes which marked the siege of
Kut al Amara.

The first attempt to relieve the beleaguered men came on
6 January 1916 at Shaikh Saad. A few days later the battle of the
Wadi ended in failure to break through. The first attack at Hanna
fizzled out on 21 January. Leachman was always there, going
from one battlefront to another to keep marauding Arabs at bay,
to lecture their shaikhs, and to guide the army in difficult terrain.

Nixon was the first to pay the price of defeat. Two months
earlier he was being congratulated by London and India and was
on the point of inheriting Mesopotamia. In January Lt-Gen. Sir
Percy Lake succeeded him. Aylmer, who had been leading the
relief attempts went too, within six weeks of the GOC's sacking.
Leachman had formed a high opinion of Aylmer, the VC who as
a young major had relieved the Chitral expedition in 1895, an
expedition in which Capt. Townshend had distinguished himself
and been commanded afterwards to dine with Queen Victoria.
As commander of the Tigris Corps, Aylmer had made his HQ at
Hanna, from where he had conducted no less than six relief
attempts up to 8 March in response to deadlines set by
Townshend.

But it was the attack on the Dujaila redoubt on 8 March which
sealed the fate of the trapped men of Kut and of Aylmer. The
position called *Dujaila* was on the east bank of the river, Kut at
its head. If it could be taken a bridgehead might be established
over the river. Argument has proved endless as to the culpability
of Aylmer and his subordinates for the events which took place
that day. Kemball, the general chosen to lead the assault,
delayed action because his heavy guns were not in position,
having been told by Aylmer to 'stick to the programme' of
attacking only after a heavy bombardment. On the evening of
the 7th, in gathering gloom, Leachman had been sent in to
establish the enemy strength. He crept from the British position
to the redoubt in 'strange, brooding silence'. He eventually

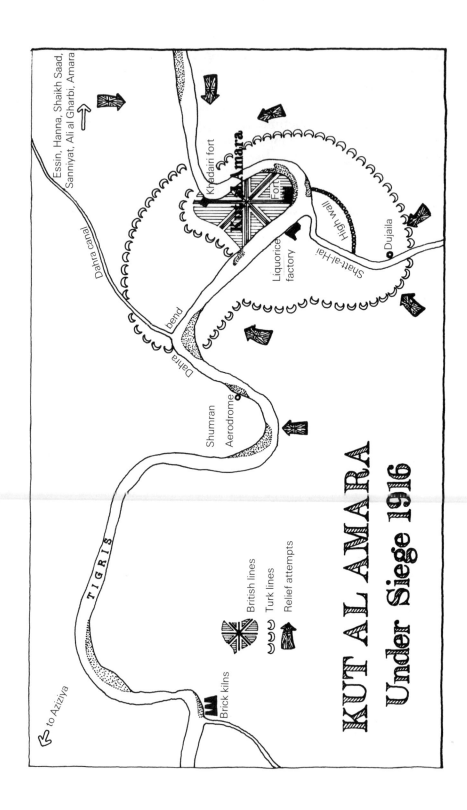

KUT AL AMARA
Under Siege 1916

British lines
Turk lines
Relief attempts

TIGRIS

to Aziziya

Brick kilns

Shumran
Aerodrome

Dahra

bend

Dahra canal

Essin, Hanna, Shaikh Saad,
Sanniyat, Ali al Gharbi, Amara

Khadairi fort

Kut Al Amara

Fort

Liquorice
factory

High wall

Shatt-al-Hai

Dujaila

reached the fortification. To his astonishment it was empty. He ran back to report his finding only to be told by the brigadier in command that they must adhere to the agreed plan. When Kemball's men attacked at ten o'clock next morning Khalil had sent in a well-armed force of more than 3,000 men from across the river. Aylmer's force was massacred. They had already suffered more than 7,000 casualties in the attempts to relieve Kut. Another 4,000 died or were seriously injured at Dujaila. Fighting went on through the day but it was hopeless. On the morning of 9 March Aylmer sent an aeroplane to drop a message into Kut. It had been written the night before. It told Townshend: 'Today's operations terminated in a gallant but unsuccessful attempt to storm Dujaila redoubt. Unless the enemy evacuates the Essin position tonight, we shall be obliged to withdraw to our previous position at Wadi. Casualties today have been very heavy.'

An even more bitter note arrived from the enemy camp. It was from Khalil, Commander of the Turkish Forces in Irak,[12] to Townshend:

Your Excellency:
 . . .General Aylmer, who was a month and a half making his preparations, yesterday, when he thought he was strong enough, resumed the offensive, as you saw. But he was again compelled to retreat, with 4,000 casualties, and I am left with adequate forces. For your part you have heroically fulfilled your military duty . . . According to your deserters, I believe that you are without food and that diseases are prevalent among your troops. You are free to continue your resistance at Kut, or to surrender to my forces, which are growing larger and larger.

Townshend refused to surrender. And dishonour was now to be piled on humiliation.

Gorringe, Aylmer's Chief of Staff, took over from him after the battle. 'He has the manners of a roadhog and the same breeding, but fairly efficient, which is the great thing after all,' wrote Leachman. And he added: 'I am getting to loathe this place with a deadly loathing.'

As the 6th Division at Kut faced its fifth month of siege and the emaciated, starving men who were trapped there saw the last hope of relief fade, a host of newcomers, political and military, descended on Mesopotamia. Gertrude Bell arrived at Basra on 3 March 1916. She was followed shortly after by Captains T. E. Lawrence and Aubrey Herbert of the second echelon of the intelligence branch, Cairo. Gertrude had been working alongside Lawrence and Herbert for Lt-Cdr. Hogarth, the Admiralty's man within Clayton's military intelligence organization at GHQ, which was accommodated in the Savoy Hotel, Cairo. From there they had prodded the negotiations which were to lead to an agreement between Husain the Sharif of Mecca and Britain's Resident, Sir Henry McMahon: an agreement which recognized the Sharif as 'King of the Arab Lands' and gave to him and his sons dominion over lands equivalent in extent to the sub-continent of India, including Syria, except for its metropolitan districts of Beirut and the Lebanon (but including Palestine), the Saudi provinces of central Arabia and Mesopotamia excluding the Basra vilayet.

The Cairo brigade was made up of a strange assortment of Oxbridge predators and hagglers who were a cut above the army (and most other institutions), boasted endlessly of their academic prowess, and who made no secret of their intention to storm the corridors of power and impose their own settlement on the peoples of the Middle East, whatever they or the politicians at home or the generals in the field, might be disposed to think. For the moment, however, the war had to be won and they descended on Mesopotamia at the bleakest hour, to a less than wholehearted welcome. Their aim was stated to be the setting up of a branch of the Arab Bureau, just established in Cairo, as an integral part of Col. Beach's intelligence department. They also proposed to bring with them two Arab nationalist leaders who had been prominent in *Al Ahad*, Aziz Ali al Masri and the Gallipoli deserter from the Ottoman army, Al Faruqi; the guests would join up with two nationalists already in Basra, Dr Shahbandar and Nuri as-Said, another Ottoman officer who had offered his services to the British.

Telegrams flew thick and fast. Cairo cabled Lawrence aboard the *Royal George* in the Red Sea: 'Nationalist leaders. General MacMunn on way. He knows all about you.'[13] Lake to War Office: 'Unable to concur in deputation of Faruqi and Masri.' War Office to Lake: 'Lord Kitchener doesn't approve of Al Masri.' FO telegram (sent from Cabinet meeting): 'Too late to stop him.' (It referred to Al Masri.) Lawrence to Cairo: 'I want to bring Gertrude Bell back with me, then our Arabian office will be complete.'

They hoped to persuade Cox to call back Sayyid Talib from India to be party to their schemes.

But there was more than met the eye, or was contained in their own avowals, in this unexpected invasion. Before leaving for Basra Lawrence had hurried from Cairo to Greece, calling at the Piraeus headquarters of Mediterranean intelligence, where he was given secret instructions for his mission. When he and Herbert eventually arrived at Basra, they brought with them instructions from Kitchener that would give a final twist to the events which had led to the deaths of tens of thousands of soldiers of the British and Indian armies – armies which so far, even in the most abject defeat, had behaved with courage and dignity.

Cox would have nothing to do with their schemes. Neither would Gen. Lake. The visitors were cold-shouldered. Lawrence, 'all teeth and claws', to use his own expression, never forgave them. Neither did Lawrence ever tell the truth of the matter, of their fawning in the presence of Khalil, of their attempt to obtain by bribes the liberation of the Kut garrison. But Herbert, ever willing to see good in friend and enemy, brought himself to tell half the truth, and in so doing he drew the last picture we have of Leachman at Kut.

Herbert had arrived at Bushire aboard HMS *Euryalus* and was taken up the Shatt al Arab in the Constantinople embassy yacht, now HMS *Imogen*. Lawrence had taken refuge with Gertrude Bell and the hospitable Van Ess family, but even they, the most charitable of missionaries, could find little to admire in the swaggering diminutive man whom Gertrude brought to their home. 'He was an unimpressive young man,' wrote Mrs Van Ess, whose husband was the outstanding Arabist among all the Europeans in Mesopotamia. Herbert sailed up to al Gharbi on 10 April, recently the scene of a visit by Cossacks who had galloped down after the taking of Erzurum by the Russians, a victory in which Lawrence was to claim a hand. Herbert and Lawrence met at field HQ, on Wednesday 19 April.

The day before, the Black Watch had made a desperate relief attempt but were driven back to their own positions. By Easter Sunday the generals were discussing peace terms. Khalil had asked Enver if Townshend's men could be paroled.

Sand-grouse flew overhead. Flies filled the eyes, ears and mouths of men and horses. Lawrence went down with fever. A young corporal went mad, wandering in the trenches, a hand-grenade in each hand, shouting 'For the —— Arabs.' He threw the grenades at the officers' mess and killed the colonel. As survivors fought to quell the demented corporal, the Black Watch attacked again at Sanniyat and the unit was wiped out. A second force swept forward and was annihilated.

Amid the pandemonium Aubrey Herbert, half-blind, went grouse shooting, perhaps as an act of political metaphor. On Monday the 24th he was summoned by the intelligence chief, Col. Beach, who was with Leachman aboard the staff launch at Fallahiya some twenty-five miles down the Hai river. Townshend had already decided to accept the Turks' surrender terms. But there would be one last attempt to get through to the stranded men. The Tigris river steamer *Julnar* on which Leachman had travelled in peacetime would make a last bid to reach the starving thousands. Admiral Wemyss who had come down from the Red Sea with Herbert aboard the *Euryalus* had said that he would raise a volunteer crew. When the naval ratings present were asked who would go on that suicidal mission every man present raised his hand.

The *Julnar* left Fallahiya with 270 tons of supplies on board at eight o'clock in the evening. Lieut Firman RN was in command. Lt-Cdr. Cowley, an older and more experienced officer, was made his deputy; he knew the river like the back of his hand and would act as navigator. But not even he knew where the mines had been laid by the Turks or where their shore guns were situated. Air reconnaisance was virtually impossible. The few British pilots on the scene were sick with overwork and their planes no match for the German craft.

No cheers were permitted as the ship raised anchor and steamed off. Only a farewell of bagpipes, a sound which would not alert the Turks for the Black Watch had played their mournful tunes for many a day by the riverside. Troops were ordered to set up a massive volley of fire as the ship proceeded along the river to drown the sound of its engines. The rest of the story is a legendary tale of war heroism. Firman was hit by a shell as he negotiated the twists and turns of the river beyond Essin, ten miles from Kut. Cowley, though seriously wounded, took over and guided the *Julnar* through shells and bullets ever nearer to

Kut. But the Turks had drawn a stretch-wire across the Hai and the ship was caught up in it. Cowley was forced to surrender, taken prisoner and shot in cold blood. The crew were taken prisoner and sent with the men of Kut to work and die in the saltmines of Turkey. Firman and Cowley were awarded posthumous VCs.

Herbert stood with Beach and Leachman on the river bank as the little ship made its way up river. There were tears in Leachman's eyes. He was not a man for tears, but he cried unashamedly that evening. His deeds were already known far and wide, in Cairo and London and India as well as Mesopotamia. 'A very good fellow whom everyone likes,' Herbert wrote in his diary.

Next day Leachman and Beach led Herbert and Lawrence through the enemy lines to Khalil's camp outside Kut. All else having failed the Cairo negotiators asked Khalil if he would parole the men for £1 million. Enver had already refused Khalil's own recommendation to parole Townshend if he left his ammunition and radio installation intact. Now the same answer was given. Herbert then offered £2 million. The same reply. Beach was present during the discussion. Leachman had left as soon as the delegation was safely delivered. He did not know Herbert or Lawrence from Brown or Smith and he had no desire to be associated with their plans. 'We cannot be bribed,' said Enver in a telegram which closed the matter once and for all. One of the most corrupt and venal men in the world had been given undeserved dignity by a maladroit plot foisted on a courageous army. There was vibrant irony in the fact that one of the perpetrators was to become the war-hero of the British people, his legend sponsored by the 'Easterners', the authors of the twin calamities of Gallipoli and Kut al Amara.

Gen. Lake came close to kicking the two men out of Mesopotamia when their work was done. He told the War Office:

The experiment made in attempting to handle affairs in Iraq through Cairo without previously consulting us can hardly be regarded as fortunate . . . the experience gained by one or two officers in Cairo who have paid us visits has I hope resulted in a considerable removal of wrong impressions.

12

Turn of the Tide

They shall not return to us, the resolute, the young,
   The eager and wholehearted whom we gave:
But the men who left them thriftily to die in their own dung,
   Shall they come with years and honour to the grave?
          Rudyard Kipling, *Mesopotamia 1917.*

As Leachman guided the myopic Herbert and the unkempt purposeful Lawrence through enemy lines for their meeting with Khalil, a Turk said to them, 'Why don't we stop killing each other and kill Arabs instead?' Herbert, the incurable Turcophile, thought it not a bad idea. Leachman was in no mood for alliances with Turk or Arab.

It was time for recrimination in high places, and for rebuilding the shattered army of Mesopotamia. The prisoners made their way along the course of the Tigris to Samarra and Baghdad, the men on foot, officers aboard launches, on to captivity in Turkey. They were escorted by Arab guards. Many of the men had exchanged their last stitch of clothing, even their boots, for a morsel of food before lying down by the wayside to wait for the comfort of death. Of those who reached their destinations few survived the ordeal of the work they were put to. Townshend was received as an honoured guest, entitled by order of the Sultan to the courtesies due to a corps commander.

For Leachman, the war was to start again. He had to return to his desert haunts to build up a new chain of information gathering, and to inflict due punishment on those men and their shaikhs who had pillaged his countrymen in their adversity and murdered sick and injured soldiers.

There was no time for writing. His parents heard little. For most of 1916 he disappeared, his uniform replaced by the abba and kaffiyeh of the Arab, his trusted disobedient 'boy' Hassan at his side, returning every now and again to HQ to keep the generals informed. He had to give up his launch which had carried him up and down the river in the last fateful weeks of the siege.

The wounds of Kut were hard to heal. If Leachman's parents heard little from their son, they learnt a good deal from officers and men who returned home on leave or who retired wounded from the war. One note arrived at Petersfield from an anonymous source, though its wording and unsteady, almost illegible hand suggested that it was written by a wounded officer from another front. It said simply:

From officers returning from Mespot I hear great things of Gerard Leachman. He is there attached to the staff as Political and Intelligence Officer. I am told that before our disastrous advance to Baghdad his intelligence was so good that he was able to inform Nixon of exactly the number of troops he had up against him, even to the names of battalions. Nixon did not believe him, hence the disaster. Gerard can go about among the Arabs quite freely and none of them will molest him.

After Kut one of Cox's clever young men from the Indian political and civil services came up to Amara as a revenue commissioner – H. St John Philby, Jack to his friends. It is through him that we glimpse the comings and goings of Leachman at this time.

'Such had been the repercussions of the fall of Kut that his old friend Ibn Rashid, now a young man of eighteen, came down to the very fringe of the Basra desert, though he appears to have decided that it would not be good for his health to come any nearer,' wrote Philby. As for Leachman he had been 'delicate for a few days but congratulated himself on his general immunity from the ills suffered by most of the force', and complained only of the 'fat people who live at the base and on the lines of communication and help themselves to the stuff coming up for the troops in the fighting line'.

The fighting line was quiescent now. Flushed with success the Turks had foolishly turned their attention to Persia and occupied Karind and Kermanshah, again threatening the vital Allied oil supply. But von der Goltz was no longer there to warn them of the classic mistake of over extending their lines of supply. Von der Goltz had died at Baghdad immediately before the surrender of Kut, officially of spotted fever, though foul play was suspected.

Leachman was enjoying a temporary and well-earned respite. The Russians who had come down from Kermanshah after the push into Armenia and Persia which the Turks were not effectively reversing, had made themselves at home at Al Gharbi and Leachman found them 'splendid fellows'. They found the heat too much for their Cossack blood and spent most of the day sitting in the river shallows with their uniforms on, 'very rough and untidy, they looked full of use', he said. He had now obtained a new boat for his river trips, a pleasure-boat from the Thames at Oxford which had been sent out to do war duty and which took the place of *Lewis Pelly*. Its deck was fitted out with deck-chairs, and Leachman took the Russians for excursions while Tommies shouted rude remarks about the 'idle rich' from the banks.

At the end of June there was an alarm. He had gone to Amara 'for a change' and suddenly became aware of heart flutter. 'The doctor discovered something wrong with my heart,' he wrote to his mother, adding, 'You know that my heart, like yours I think, is intermittent and I suppose that that particular day it was behaving badly.'

It was discovered that he had paratyphoid fever, and that he had endured the disease for three weeks before reporting sick. The doctors wanted to send him to India for treatment and rest but he adamantly refused, discharging himself from hospital at Amara as soon as he was able to walk.

By the end of July he was back with the tribes close to enemy lines, celebrating his thirty-sixth birthday with a bottle of Bollinger 1906 which he had put aside for the occasion. He shared it with Hassan; there was no one else in the desert to join in the festivity, 'except Arabs'. Generally, Leachman forbade Hassan alcohol. The little servant-boy was showing a dangerous liking for it and would go to any lengths to get his hands on the bottle which his master usually took with him for occasional

170

comfort and sometimes medicinal use. When Hassan was found the worse for wear the customary Punch and Judy show would start up again and Leachman would pursue his charge round the camp and give him a salutary cuff. On this occasion, though, he was allowed to enjoy his drink and the lonely wanderers supped like Osmin and Pedrillo, toasting Bacchus perhaps in their make-shift serai.

A few days after his birthday Leachman learnt that he had been made a Companion of the Order of the Indian Empire. 'Thank you very much for your telegram of congratulations on the CIE,' he wrote to his mother and sisters. 'I suppose that is it, though I have not heard of it from any other source.' His family had read about it in *The Times*. The recipient was not much impressed. 'Young men who sit in offices in Simla get it, and it is not given for service in the field, I think, but it is alright.'

A few days later he told them it had 'a beautiful blue ribbon'. He added: 'You will grieve to hear that I have hardly a hair on my head. It may come again but it does not look like it. It is so very dry and we are beyond the reach of hair-grease.'

By September the Turks were becoming active after the lassitude of summer. The now replenished British front-line force was holding a jumping competition when it was reminded that there was still a war to contend with. A visiting bishop had just arrived to proffer his blessing and join in the fun. 'The Turks thought it a good opportunity to plump some exceedingly big shells into the camp, not far from the entertainment: we were not disturbed.'

By September operations had begun in earnest. Fighting had broken out again along the Euphrates in the Nasiriya region, scene of British victory in July 1915. The War Office in London had assumed control of operations and Lt-Gen. Sir Stanley Maude had been sent out to take over command from Gen. Lake. The new GOC had a reputation for careful planning and steady, unhurried campaigning. The troops called him 'Systematic Joe' and he lived up to his nickname.

On 11 September the first action took place at Sahilan near Nasiriya. Leachman was called on to resume his work among the tribes and he was sent down to Muhammerah 'where they have the luxury of ice and electric fans'. In the course of his briefing there he again met Arnold Wilson, the work-glutton who impressed the most formidable of men by his assertive ways and abrupt telephone manner. Leachman thought he looked 'rather ill, from overwork', but 'very full of himself'. Wilson for his part thought that Leachman was in need of rest and begged him to go to India. But though the effects of ten years of privation and refusal to rest up when sick were beginning to tell, this was no moment for taking it easy. His new task was to impose a desert blockade on the Turks as Maude's army battled over familiar ground on its way up the Tigris to Baghdad. From now on he was 'OC Desert', but he had no army. He and his great adversary, Preusser, still doing his work of fomenting jihad along the Euphrates, would battle it out alone. Neither would have witnesses to his achievements and privations. Only occasionally would their comrades have glimpses of them, from the air, and thus report to base that Leachman's adventurous and silent saga was still in progress.

There would be a few minor skirmishes, another briefing, and promotion, before he left behind the makeshift trappings of civilization which the army managed to maintain even in the front line.

On 9 November he set off on what he called an 'Arab strafe' – only a minor affair and when it was over he thought it worth telling the family about it.

I have had a splendid adventure since I last wrote. A certain camp of hostile Arabs had been very annoying lately in raiding our camels and generally being violent. I collected a crowd of mounted Arabs, about 600 strong . . . I crossed them over the bridge at Shaikh Saad and, starting at dusk, reached the neighbourhood of the camp that we were going for by dawn. That was fifty miles. We successfully rounded up their sheep, about 10,000, and started to drive them back without any trouble. After we had got about 15 miles the enemy began to get troublesome, and they were assisted by some gendarmes (Arab police in Turkish service) who shot more or less straight, which is not the game among Arabs. Three hundred of my crowd had enough of it, and pushed off and waited for me twenty miles further on. We kept on dropping our sheep and finally reached home with only about 2,000. We had a few losses and so did they. But the people who really distinguished themselves were the sheep, who marched fifty miles in fifteen hours, and on a hot day too. We did about 100 miles in 24 hours, and I now consider myself fit.

It was a typical skirmish. Leachman's parish now extended from the front, where the two armies were entrenched on either side of the Tigris between Sanniyat and Kut, to the desert beyond Najaf, 100 miles to the south-west. He patrolled it alone, with a band of hand-picked Arabs and occasional help from the Tigris force. His deeds will never be recorded, except for a single account given by one of the pilots who came to Mesopotamia after the fall of Kut to command the miniature air force belatedly sent out from France to counter Turco-German superiority in the air. They left the Somme in June as 'hell let loose' and sailed for Mesopotamia, looking forward to 'sunny days ahead', until they struck the heat of the Red Sea and the ship's doctor died of sunstroke, and a sailor died on deck from heat exhaustion.

They had come to relieve the little group of men who contested the skies over southern Mesopotamia with the well-armed Germans who flew from the air park of Shumran, protected by a broad bend of the river. In July 1916, soon after their arrival, Lt-Col. J.E. Tennant and his deputy, Captain Geoffrey de Havilland, moved up to a makeshift strip at the western extremity of the British line, which they called the Sinn Abtar aerodrome. From there they began a daily (and sometimes nightly) assault on the Turks and engaged in a series of dog-fights with the dare-devil and accomplished German pilots from Shumran. Nobody would accuse Tennant and de Havilland of lack of courage. Already, in France, they had demonstrated that they and their fellow-fliers were men for whom the word fear had little meaning. Yet even they were reluctant to fly over the desert, for they knew that if they were forced down or compelled to land through engine failure, they would assuredly be torn to pieces by marauding Arabs.[14]

Sometimes Tennant and de Havilland and their colleagues were compelled to fly over Leachman's 'parish', and once or twice they witnessed their lone fellow-countryman in action, though at the time they were unaware of his identity since he wore Arab dress. As they came to know of his deeds they kept a look-out, and when they thought he might be below they dipped or rolled their craft in salute, and if they were right he would wave to them in acknowledgement.

Thus, Col. Tennant, whose actions won him the DSO, the MC

and innumerable commendations from the main battlefronts of the war, gave us the only record we have of Leachman in the months that led up to Maude's campaign and the march against Baghdad which began in late January 1917.

Looking back on the events of that time, he wrote:

It was my fortune once to witness from the air a battle of one tribe against another to the north of the Suwaikia Marsh, a sideshow quite apart from the Turks or British. But it was an Englishman who led one side, one Englishman alone leading a wild savage tribe into fierce battle against Turkish friendlies on our right flank. The career of this Englishman may never be written, yet in the history of the world there is probably no romance that can equal it.

As the months went by the airmen came to know Leachman and looked forward to his rare appearances from his desert lairs, where he had become an acknowledged tribal leader of whom the great chief of the Anaiza, Fahad Bey, was to say, 'He was one of us, just like one of our own shaikhs.'

When he did return to base, Leachman was called on to administer punishment to Arab rogue bands which marauded in his absence. 'All our camps had to be fortified,' said Tennant, 'wired in, and defended, for the marauders were out on a foray every night. The cunning and skill of the Pathan on the North-Western Frontier were nothing compared with that of the Bedouin. Somehow he would get through the wire and sentries and make away with a rifle from under a sleeper's pillow without awakening him.'

And of Leachman, he went on:

His prestige was amazing, and his name known to every Bedouin from Aden to Mosul. He lived in that desert from January to December dressed as an Arab, and with his boy Hassan wandered about amongst the tribes, perhaps even behind the Turks, organising, compelling, acquiring priceless information. There was a price on his head, and he lived with his life in his hands, but he could shoot a tribesman dead for misdeeds in front of the tribe and no hand would be lifted against him. Occasional visits to GHQ and he would be gone, riding out to the horizon on his little Arab pony with his long legs dangling nearly to the ground. Eventually he would return wizened and thin, with probably a severe dose of fever after months in the desert in the heat of summer, living on Arab food and water.

Tennant also said that throughout eastern Arabia people 'were under the impression that it was Leachman who commanded the British forces'. Special cards were printed for flying-officers which they could produce if forced to land in the desert. On them was written the name 'Lijman' in Arabic. 'Such,' said Tennant 'was the magic of his personality.' Tennant was not a man to exaggerate. In his account of the wartime adventures of his remarkable corps of flying-men, he never revealed his own part, and except for his friend Geoffrey de Havilland, whom he always referred to as 'DH', he never divulged the names of the RFC colleagues who won so much acclaim for their tireless and courageous work. To them, Leachman was the supreme hero. The soldier's soldier.

Christmas 1916 was spent in the desert. He hoped that one day he might 'enjoy the luxury of Christmas dinner at home'. And he looked to the future at that time: 'If this war ever ends and we remain in possession of this country, I shall be one of the mugs who will find a difficulty in getting away.'

As Maude's army marched back into Kut al Amara to avenge the past and set foot on the road to Baghdad, news came of promotion.

'Do you know I am a colonel?' he asked his mother on 16 January 1917. 'I got a brevet on January 1st for some unknown reason. You may have missed it among the mass of names.' He was obviously pleased with the reward for his labours, though he still wondered why he had been given a civilian decoration earlier, the CIE. 'All the same, doesn't it sound beautiful – Colonel Leachman?'

In February he went to Basra to receive his final instructions for the campaign which was coming to fruition. They were not at all what he expected.

When Lawrence and Herbert returned to Cairo in June 1916 after the fall of Kut they were just in time to greet their friend Ronald Storrs who had come hot-foot from Jidda with news that the Arab revolt for which they had laboured a year and a half was under way. They were also in time to learn that their founding father in London, Field-Marshal Lord Kitchener, was dead, drowned in the icy waters of Scapa Flow on the very day that the Sharif of Mecca turned on his Ottoman host and declared a state of rebellion. The 5th of June 1916 was a day of mixed jubilation and sorrow for the men of the Arab Bureau in Cairo. If they were deprived of the support of the man who had initiated their scheme, which was more political than military in its nature, they had at least realized their aim, and in the process had promised through their unsuspecting chief the High Commissioner, Sir Henry McMahon, that the Sharif and his sons would be amply rewarded. The Sharif would receive £125,000 a month in subsidy from Britain, and his family would inherit virtually the entire Arabian peninsula. The Sharif was good enough to agree that Britain could remain in Mesopotamia for the time being so long as compensation was paid.

The Indian Government was less than pleased, but in June 1916 it was in no position to influence events. It was in disgrace over the Mesopotamian campaign, and it licked its wounds quietly, merely protesting that it noted that the Arab Bureau in Cairo appeared to be dictating the war policy of HMG and that the loyalty of millions of Muslim subjects in India, who had no quarrel with their Caliph the Sultan of Turkey, was at grave risk. Secretary of State Chamberlain told the Viceroy in reply, 'HMG and not the Cairo Bureau will decide all questions of policy.'

Within days of the proclamation of rebellion, Cairo was telling London that the key city of Madina, the Prophet's city, was about to be taken by the Sharif's eldest son, Ali. It was to remain in Turkish hands until the end of the war, never seriously threatened.

By February 1917, however, the situation had changed dramatically. The battles in lower Mesopotamia for the Hai salient, for the Dahra bend and Sanniyat had all been successfully accomplished. By the time Leachman reached Basra to hear what Sir Percy Cox had on offer, Maude's army was on the road to Baghdad. The Turkish rearguard was being mopped up.

Cox wanted Leachman to go to Cairo. Sir Mark Sykes, the great amateur of the political and intelligence services, the intemperate liaison officer between the Foreign and War Offices who had been Kitchener's right-hand man in the Sharif negotiations, wanted someone from Mesopotamia to join him in

Cairo, to hear from the horse's mouth what was happening in the Hijaz and to see for himself the fruit of the Arab Bureau's labours. 'Cokkus', an adroit man if ever there was one, was taking no chances. The prestige of the Mesopotamian army stood high again, but he knew that his representative would be under considerable pressure to support the Sharifian adventure and perhaps join in the desert revolt as a political officer attached to Cairo. It was an adventure which the GOC-in-Chief of the Egyptian Expeditionary Force, Gen. Murray, had disowned, sacking the intelligence chief Clayton who had joined the Arab Bureau breakaway staff officers, and appointing his own man, Colonel Holdich, in his place. Cox knew his Lawrence too, who was by that time attached as Political Officer to the third son of the Sharif, Faisal, and was camped with him on the Hijaz coast. He knew that Lawrence would try to upstage the Mesopotamian army's man. Let him upstage Leachman if he could.

It was decided that Leachman should go to Cairo in April. On 11 March Maude's victorious army marched into Baghdad. The 'beloved city' of the Arabs had been liberated and Arab aspirations were raised to fever-pitch. The 'King of the Arab Lands' in Mecca sent his congratulations and looked forward to an Arab administration in the country, and renewed his demand for a 'rent' from Britain while her troops remained there.

Leachman returned to the desert after spending a few days with the HQ Staff in Basra, sharing the crowded offices of Beach and his men who worked sometimes three to a cubby-hole as they went about their business of winkling out Turkish and German agents and uncovering the plots of the Pan-Islamic movement which still preached holy war behind and before the army's lines. And he crossed swords, not for the first time, with the great lady of Cox's staff, Gertrude Bell, who was in charge of the Basra Office of the Arab Bureau.

'I am wandering about in the desert,' he wrote on 4 March. 'I seem to have left Kut side at a bad moment. It is the first stroke of bad luck I have had for a long time, so I ought not to grumble. It does, however, feel a bit hard sitting in front of the Turks for a year, to have to leave at the moment of success.'

Seven days later Maude entered Baghdad. Leachman came out of the desert between the dissident holy cities of Najaf and Karbala in the middle of March and wrote to his brother-in-law, Bernard Parham, before taking ship for Cairo:

It is my fate never to get into a house. Every other political officer lives in a comfortable house with every luxury, while I, the miserable one, wander about on horse, launch or camel. This last stint beats the lot for hard life, and though shells do not fall about me everyone has a shot at me.

He reckoned that he had been missed narrowly on eight occasions in three weeks by the time he left the Euphrates tribesmen. He had taught some of them a hard enough lesson to be confident of their passivity as he proceeded to Basra and on to Cairo.

He arrived in Cairo on 24 April, 'an absolutely new world of soldiering, full of Australians in smasher hats (I cannot love them)', and of officers all of whom 'have about ten medals apiece of every sort except war-medals'. He booked in at Shepheard's Hotel, whose manager and head waiter along with several other members of the staff had recently been arrested as German spies. He commented:

It is a great gathering place for MPs and sprigs of nobility, for, if you can go to war from Shepheard's Hotel there is no particular hardship. They are great sticklers for dress and the wearing of a pair of spurs is of much the same importance as beating the Turks. I am afraid we are very uncivilised in poor old Mesopotamia; however we do defeat the Turks.

Philby, still following in the wake of the army as it marched on from Baghdad to Samarra, observed in retrospect that Leachman was in for a shock: 'General Maude was already introducing a strict regime of spurs and Sam Brownes in a climate which made at any rate the latter definitely uncomfortable and even injurious to health!'

Not that Leachman was in favour of sloppiness. He was a noted disciplinarian. But neither was he much in favour of officers whose priorities were first and foremost their own prestige and comfort and only secondarily the duties and obligations of wartime leadership. That his own approach found favour with the troops who came to know him there can be little doubt. His one-time Mess Sergeant with the Royal Sussex in India, now serving in Mesopotamia, wrote to him: 'You will be sorry to hear that the new officers do not keep up the old customs. I wish you were back, Sir, and so does the Regiment.'

The privations of two years in the deserts and swamps of Mesopotamia, and of his testing life for many years before the war, began to catch up with him now that he was introduced to the soft world of Cairo. 'I am most miserably seedy and can hardly walk up stairs.' He thought he might have to heed the doctor's advice and go into hospital. But as always he put off the much-needed rest and check-up. As a doctor's son he was a poor patient. Fevers, jaundice, malaria and a dozen other ailments had racked his body, but there was never time for proper treatment or adequate attention.

Now he must go down to the Hijaz to meet the cronies of Gen. Wingate, the Sirdar of the Egyptian army who had taken over the conduct of the Arab Bureau's affairs from McMahon. Still he must put off a hospital visit. 'We cannot rest in war time.' He was taken to meet the Sultan at the Abdin Palace and had lunch with Wingate. 'I lunch with the High Commissioner Sir Reginald Wingate and thanks be to the gods that it is lunch, as his household has gone "dry" and though I do not drink at lunch it adds to the cheeriness of nations at dinner.'

He went to the Hijaz in late April. His servant, Hassan, was with him. Wingate's representative at the court of Husain the Sharif was Col. Wilson. The intelligence officers working with schizophrenic zeal for Wingate at one moment and for the new Commander-in-Chief, Gen. Allenby, the next were Col. Parker (who was Kitchener's nephew) and Capt. Bray. Leachman had little to say of his visit, except that he disliked the country and its inhabitants, and apparently found the Englishman he was taken to meet unworthy of comment. Bray recorded the gathering in some detail:

Leachman visited Rabegh and Wejh. At the latter place Faisal had his temporary headquarters and he invited Leachman and myself to a meal in his guest tent at which Lawrence was also present. It was an interesting experience, sitting there on the ground, partaking of Faisal's hospitality and listening to these three men who met in this arid, desolate spot for the first and last time.

That was not quite true of course. Leachman had taken Lawrence to Khali's camp at Kut. Bray continued:

Faisal, simple and charming, asking questions . . . Lawrence in full Arab robes, richly embroidered, a gold dagger at his waist, speaking as softly as Faisal, carefully choosing his words and then lapsing into long silences. Leachman, clothed in faded khaki, inscrutable, with that puzzling smile of his lurking at the corners of his mouth, but straightforward and decisive in speech. The contrast between the two Englishmen was patent: Lawrence acting the Arab and maintaining his prestige through the medium of his magnificent clothes. His servility to Faisal and his seeming unreality form a picture which still lingers in my mind. Leachman on the other hand was so obviously and unashamedly the Englishman, and a masterful one. His sufferings and hardships were mapped on his lean visage and pride showed behind the curtains of his eyes. He had endured five years of toil and danger, and three more still harsher years were in store for him.

Bray's words were written in 1935. 'All three are dead now,' he said, 'but while of the edifice the first two built not one vestige remains, the work the other accomplished endures today and will endure.'

Lawrence told a different story. In 1925 an ex-corporal in the Royal Tank Corps was writing a war adventure called *Singapore Patrol*, and he sought Lawrence's view of Leachman. 'Aurens' replied:

Leachman was a thin jumpy nervous long fellow, with a plucked face and neck. He was full of courage, and as hard as French nails. He had an abiding contempt for everything native (an attitude picked up in India). Now this contempt may be a conviction, an opinion, a point of view. It is inevitable perhaps, and therefore neither to be praised nor blamed. Leachman allowed it to be a rule of conduct. This made him inconsiderate, harsh, overbearing towards his servants and subjects: and there was, I stake my oath, no justification for the airs he took. Leachman was an ordinary mind, but a character of no ordinary hardness. I do not say a great character, for I think it made its impression more by its tough skin and unyielding texture than by any great spread of degree. I should call him a man too little sensitive to be aware of other points of view than his own: too little fine to see degrees of

180

greatness, degrees of rightness in others. He was blunt and outspoken to a degree. Such is a good point in a preacher, a bad point in a diplomat. It makes a bullying judge, too. I think he was first and foremost a bully: but not a fleshy bully. He had no meat or bulk on him: a sinewy wasted man, very yellow and dissatisfied in face. He was jealous of other people's being praised.

For his few days with us in Hijaz we were nor prepared. 'Leachman', it was a great name and repute in Mesopotamia (a land of fourth-raters) and we thought to find a colleague in him. After less than a week we had to return him on board ship, not for anything he said, though he spoke sourly always, but because he used to chase his servant so unmercifully that our camp took scandal at it. The servant was a worm, a long worm, who never turned or showed a spark of spirit. Any decent servant would have shot him.[1]

The rest of Lawrence's dissertation must await the events to which it refers. He was an obtuse man, practised at the half-truth, his colourful and articulate accounts of personalities and events in the 'Desert War' circumscribed by a ruthless streak, observed by his chief and benefactor in Cairo, Dr Hogarth, which was hostile to any opposition.[2] What, for example, did he mean by 'jealous of other people's being praised'? Lawrence was too astute a writer to mix his plurals and his possessives inadvertently. Allowing for the misplaced apostrophe, did he mean that he was jealous of people other than the British being praised, e.g. the Arabs, while conveying to the unwary the idea that he was jealous of his own fame and reputation and disliked hearing praise of others? As Lawrence demonstrated in *Seven Pillars of Wisdom* he was a master of denigration by inference and omission. The most important Britishers in the Hijaz, like Ross (whose Arabic was so good he was the only man among them who needed no interpreter), Dawnay, Newcombe, Parker, Vickery and Chauvel were spotlighted only as asides to his own thunderous achievements. One man who worked alongside him before going to Mesopotamia, Capt. Hubert Young, later an under-secretary at the Colonial Office, was so appalled by Lawrence's boasting that he could never afterwards be civil to him. And Young was himself no stranger to self aggrandizement.

As for the references to Leachman's appearance, none of the

hundreds of men who knew him at close quarters in the awful conditions in which the 'fourth-raters' worked, and often died, in wartime Mesopotamia had anything but admiration for the tenacity with which he had overcome disease and exhaustion, and expended his strength and health so extravagantly in the service of his country. Lawrence's verdict was not only unjust. It was malicious.

It may be instructive to compare Lawrence's assessment with an observation from the pen of Arnold Wilson, for 'AT' was never known to praise men who were unworthy of approbation.[3]

His unfailing cheerfulness, his gift of sarcasm, his mordant wit and his outspokenness (he was no respecter of persons) – were each in their turn invaluable. The last-named quality was, however, not so much the product of a hasty temper as of a burning hatred of shams, of injustice and of inefficiency in whatever quarter displayed . . . Hospitable and generous to a fault, he would share his last ration and even his scanty kit with others in need, and in private life he was liberality itself.

As for Lawrence's suggestion that Leachman had to be bundled aboard ship and sent away after less than a week, as though he had somehow come to stay and had been given marching orders, it can only be observed that T.E.L. made the same kind of observations a year later when he wound up in Damascus and, so he would have us believe, had Gen. Chauvel the Australian commander of cavalry following his lead, 'his hesitations ruled by my certainty'. Even the insubordinate Lawrence, still a lieutenant in rank though calling himself 'Captain', did not order colonels and generals about with impunity, though he was not above trying. It is most unlikely that he would have been so rash as to try any such thing with Leachman.

Leachman was back in Cairo on 9 May: ' . . . commend me to the Arabian coast of the Red Sea for absolute hopelessness. Not a blade of grass or bush but miles of volcanic desert and stones. Most vile form of Arab, worse than the worst Mesopotamian specimen.' He had nothing to say of Lawrence or Faisal.

He rejoiced to be in Cairo this time, having recovered his vigour. 'I am enjoying myself and the good food,' he wrote, though he wasn't impressed by Shepheard's or its waiters. 'I travel round with Sir Mark Sykes, who you probably know of,' he told his mother on 10 May. 'He is about my age and most amusing and astoundingly clever. I have learnt many things about the world . . . ' It is a pity he did not say more, for it is not hard to imagine the fraternity of the two men, the impatient and brilliant aristocrat of Sledmere in Yorkshire who kicked open the door of the Cabinet room when it was in session if he thought the national interest demanded his intervention and who could imitate an entire orchestra and almost every member of the House of Commons, and the equally intemperate soldier whose deeds went before him. But Leachman was not a man of words. He left few worthwhile descriptions of the men of all nationalities whom he met over the years.

He caught the P&O to Bombay and paid a flying visit to the Regiment at Peshawar. From Aden he wrote: 'I shall be a week in India as I have some things to do, and then I shall go back to Mespot and very pleased I shall be to get there. I wish I had never left it . . . '

GHQ was installed at Baghdad by the time Leachman arrived back from Egypt and India. The Chief Political Officer and the civil administration had moved up too, all accommodated in the palaces and offices which had until recently been occupied by the Turks and their German allies.

Women walked the streets in safety for the first time in their lives. The penalty for refusing the advances of Turk and German occupiers had been hospitalization with the label 'diseased' strung round their necks. Now many had thrown away their yashmaks and in the excitement of liberation wore stockings, imported by astute merchants within weeks of the army's entrance, multicoloured and hanging round their ankles. The merchants had forgotten to order garters or suspenders.

But the euphoria was not to last. Already the guns being handed out by Allenby's army to Lawrence's friends in the Hijaz were finding their way to the nationalist committees and to the tribes of the Euphrates, and were being used to pick off the Political Officers left in the rear of the advancing army to maintain law and order.

Among the events which occurred in Leachman's absence and which made topics for mealtime conversation at the Baghdad mess, one could be described as tragi-comedy, another as farce.

Early in May while he was in Cairo, Ronald Storrs arrived in Baghdad. His fellow Carthusian had long nursed an ambition to try his hand at desert travel. Like many men who lead sedentary and bookish lives, the idea of facing physical hardship had a persistent appeal for Storrs. He had made brief and not very testing sorties into Sinai and Syria in the past. By the summer of 1917 a chance of real adventure came to him. The Government wanted a mission to go from the Sharif of Mecca to Ibn Saud in an attempt to bring the two Arab leaders together. Storrs had called on the Sharif to tell him of the scheme and obtain his views before going on to Baghdad, whence he would go to Kuwait and across the Dahana sands to Riyadh. He turned up in Baghdad in mid May with praise for his 'little genius', T.E. Lawrence, on the tip of his tongue, and spent a jocular few days visiting the *suqs* and Arab notables of the city. He took lessons in Najdi Arabic from Gertrude Bell and proceeded to Kuwait laden with good books, a portable gramophone and a supply of classical records. His caravan was led by Shakespear's little camel-jemader Abdal Aziz, who could hardly believe his eyes when he met the immaculate Englishman he was supposed to take into the desert. To every question he replied *salamtak* – 'Don't know'. They set off on 9 June, with Storrs cursing his camel in Latin. Three days later they were back at their starting-point. They had been approached by Bedouin friends of Abdal Aziz and Storrs, thinking it was a raiding-party, had a sudden attack of sunstroke. It was his first and last venture in exploration. It was vital that someone should go to Ibn Saud, however, and the India Office cabled Cox telling him to send Leachman. But Cairo, party to the scheme of bringing about an *entente* between the Arab chiefs, preferred Philby.

More tragic than comic perhaps was the episode known as the 'Diwaniya Affair'. The Ottoman army at the last fled in the face of the British advance on Baghdad, rushing north to escape capture. Only one soldier stood his ground, a Circassian *bimbashi* who proudly claimed that he was an Arab, Muhammad Hakim Farukh. With almost unimaginable heroism he set up a post at Samawah on the road from Hillah to Diwaniya and defied the entire strength of the British army in its attempts to remove him. He court-martialled three Turks who were with him for refusing to fight and executed them. With thirty-three men he held out from March to September, despite daily bombing and assaults by vastly superior land forces. And by the time Leachman arrived on the scene he had successfully prevented any attempt to deal with the fermenting tribes at his rear. Not even Leachman could remove him until he gave himself up after six months of unceasing attack. He made only one request when he was taken prisoner, that he should be allowed to take with him to India the Arab girl he had married at Samawah. His request was granted.

Two of Leachman's regimental friends had died in his absence. Captain Mitchell was killed on his second day at the front in the advance on Baghdad. Thorne, an officer who had recently pestered him about telegrams when his wife was having a baby had gone too. Already the politicians were trafficking the territories won by blood and toil, and battle still raged in the north. The armies of Syria and Iraq were joined under the command of the victor of Gallipoli, Liman von Sanders, and given the boastful name 'Yilderim' (Thunderbolt). The men who battled on along the Tigris towards Mosul read in their newspapers of devastating losses on the Western Front, of squabbles between the Allies as to the future division of territories won in battle, of promises made to Arab and Jew, Armenian and Greek. The Indian troops who were promised nothing and the Tommies who fought with them might themselves have composed Kipling's Mesopotamian valediction of 1917.

13

The Shadow of Death

'At last you see me in the beloved city,' he wrote on 5 July. And he observed with obvious relief that his only nephew, his sister's son, Hetman Jack Parham, was carrying on the army tradition and was safe and well in Egypt where he had arrived just too late to meet his uncle Gerard.

He had met old friends and enemies on his way up river, most of whom 'were good enough to say that they had missed Lijman'. One Arab who was not so pleased to see him was the gentleman who appropriated his horse after the battle of Ctesiphon. 'He nearly had a fit, and when I suggested that he had come in especially to return my horse he swore he had no idea where it was and that surely I had punished him enough by killing seventy of his Arabs.' In fact, it was a detachment of Townshend's men who pursued the thieving Arabs after the battle and exacted payment for various crimes in 'deaduns'. In a day or two Leachman's horse appeared miraculously, over a year after it was stolen, 'almost unmanageable after his stay with the Arabs'. Unfortunately its owner had 'stuck' the Government for £50 compensation and now had to pay it back. Leachman was still averse to parting with money, especially to the Government which had cut his pay for the period of his stay in Cairo, presumably under the impression that 'Shepheard's Hotel is cheaper living than the desert'.

Baghdad was not to his liking. The new administration was already beginning to strangle itself with red tape under the military governorship of Gen. Hawker. The men of the Indian Civil and Political Services had arrived in force – good, bad and indifferent, and mostly exceedingly clever. In fact it was a woman who came in the vanguard, Gertrude Bell. A state of open war already existed between Leachman and her and they carried on where they had left off at Basra from the moment they met at No. 1 mess, where Wilson, the forthright arrogant non-university man among them, kept an uneasy peace by the force of his personality, and by his habit of taking the 'politicals' for walks before dinner, arm-in-arm, and lecturing them like a mobile *Encyclopaedia Britannica.*

Since his visit to Basra at the beginning of the year, Leachman had been transferred from the army staff to Cox's regime. He was a 'political' now, white tabs distinguishing him from his army brothers. It was not a role that he relished, but someone had to administer the conquered territories and keep order in them, and nobody doubted that he was just the man for the most difficult regions.

He was rescued from the tedium of No. 1 mess shortly after his introduction. He found himself briefly in the erudite company of Gertrude Bell and her friend Reader Bullard, the Magdalen fellow Lionel Smith who had been tutor to the Prince of Wales, the opinionated Philby, and the charming monocled Balfour. He got on with them well enough but he wasn't a man for the chatter of elite societies when there was work to be done. And Baghdad's British administrators were a remarkably élite band, though reduced to an ultimate equality not so much by the inconveniences of war as by that uniquely British device the travelling commode, the rooftop 'thunder box'.

Leachman soon returned to more congenial company. There was increasing unrest around the Euphrates city of Karbala. A wild Irishman by the name of O'Flanagan was detailed to accompany him to the holy city of the Shi'a. They were a well-matched pair who fell easily into the company of Karbala's rogue element, from which they learnt that two brothers who had been Pan-Islamic agents in the pay of Preusser, still at large in the desert, were behind the latest call to jihad against the *Ingleez*. They devised an ingenious plan of action but thought that they had better return to Baghdad and put Sir Percy Cox in the picture before carrying it into effect. The idea was to park a motor-van at the rear of one of the brothers' houses (by late 1917 the motor-car was a familiar sight in Mesopotamia, and Leachman himself had been equipped with a large American Dodge saloon), while the two men called to pay their respects. In the course of conversation they would suggest to their host that his brother should be invited to take part in the discussion as they had an important message from 'Cokkus'. When the brother appeared they would leap on the unsuspecting ringleaders, gag and bind them, and carry them off to the waiting van. They would be well on the road to Baghdad before the alarm was raised.

Cox was horrified. The scheme offended against all the Arab laws of chivalry and hospitality, he said, and if it was unsuccessful the consequences could be disastrous. The Chief Political Officer was a man for the velvet glove, and he suggested a polite invitation to the men to call on him (Sir Percy) if they happened to be in Baghdad. Leachman thought it an anaemic solution, and no less dangerous in its Machiavellian artfulness than their own plan. But he and O'Flanagan went back to Karbala and tamely delivered the message. The brothers appeared at Cox's office in their Friday best and were promptly arrested.

'I am getting tired of the Political Department,' he wrote after a month or so in its service.

It is not at all like old times when one did exactly what one liked and never referred to anyone. Now we have a lot of specimens of young Oxford, who never get out of an office chair and bother unfortunate people like myself who lead a strenuous life but, thank goodness, have neither the time nor the inclination to do much office work.

He began to pine for the regiment. 'I would be much happier with them', he wrote with reference to his old friends and India's still turbulent North-West Frontier.

But he returned to Karbala where he set up his HQ with another 'character', Radwell, who kept him greatly amused. 'I never saw anyone so lethargic. He looked at me as if I was mad and could not understand the frantic state of bustle one has to be in to keep things moving.'

And so he went in to the familiar desert beyond Karbala where he had first met up with the Anaiza of Fahad Bey ten years before, while Radwell kept house at his HQ in the city. The occasional discomfort of a resumed life in the saddle – he complained of a sore rump and the misery of sleeping out in freezing nights after a day's hard riding – was compounded by his having to ' do' for himself. His boy, Hassan, had disappeared. 'I am afraid he discovered a charmer in Baghdad and, being of an impressionable age, could not tear himself away. He will return in time but I don't know if I shall keep him as, when they get these fits on them, Arabs are a nuisance and are not really responsible for their actions.'

He was to remain at Karbala for much of 1918, in sole charge of a vast stretch of the Euphrates desert from south of Najaf to Ramadi in the north. There were only seven letters to his family from September 1917 until the armistice, and they told only of his occasional and reluctant visits to Baghdad. But there were witnesses to his work and adventures at this time. One of them, Capt. Chalmers, was stationed at the walled city of Kufa just a few miles north-east of Najaf, and he was to bring Leachman's work as 'OC Desert' to vivid life in *Blackwood's Magazine*, long after the war and its sequel.

That sequel had its sinister beginnings along the Euphrates from the early months of 1918 when Leachman was in full stride, pursuing the gun-runners and agents who began to spread seditious thoughts among the Shi'a Arabs who seldom needed much persuasion when it came to hot-headed opposition to authority. Chalmers's anecdotes kindled a public awareness of a war which was never reported, for even in the period of the rout of the Turkish army in Mesopotamia censorship was strict and the public was told as little of victory as it knew, at the time, of defeat.

In March 1918 Capt. Marshall the young Political Officer at Najaf was murdered. At daybreak on 21 March a volley of rifle fire was heard outside his house and he opened the door to see what was going on. He was shot at close range, and another officer was badly wounded as he came to Marshall's aid. He was a pleasant young man with genuine sympathy for the Arabs. Leachman was given the responsibility of tracking down his killers by Wilson who had taken over the civil administration from Cox, the latter having been sent by Curzon to Tehran to help establish order in that other Shi'a centre. Najaf, like its neighbour city of Kufa, was surrounded by a high wall to protect it from the hostile Sunni tribes and raiders who more than once had sacked the place and terrorized its inhabitants. Leachman used the wall to blockade the city while he roamed the desert in Arab disguise as a shaikh of the Anaiza, keeping eyes and ears open for Marshall's murderers.

One day Chalmers sat in his room in Kufa worrying about local reaction to a story that his men had killed some pigeons – birds sacred to the Shi'a – for their evening meal. Chalmers's chief, Capt. Balfour, had gone off to meet Miss Bell who was on her way from Baghdad. Chalmers would have to face the consequences of his men's action. He wandered out into the garden to consider the matter when the tall figure of Leachman emerged from the direction of the river, his cap in his hand and his 'carroty head bent in profound study'.

'I say, Colonel, I'm afraid my men have been killing these infernal pigeons,' said Chalmers by way of greeting. 'Fellows on eternal corn-beef and hard biscuits can't stand that sort of temptation.'

Leachman drew him aside and told him:

'The Arabs have a story they firmly believe; it is said that those birds convey their own punishment to the infidel who slays and eats them; their flesh is deadly poison.'

Chalmers believed the story and stopped worrying. They went to a local coffee-house, the *Gahwa*, and Leachman stretched his legs along the length of a wooden bench.

'Have you found the shaikhs responsible for Marshall's murder?' asked Chalmers.

'Yes.'

'It must have been pretty tough going out in the blue, hunting for them.'

'So, so.'

'A story was wafted here the other day that you had been fired on by an Arab rascal hiding among pomegranate trees near Musaiyib and that you rode at him while he was having another pot at you, and after cuffing his ears you gave him a brotherly scolding,' said Chalmers by way of making conversation.

Leachman smiled.

'If you had brought that fellow in he would have faced a firing-squad.'

'Yes. Poor devil. I expect he has reformed now. Good God I've got some cider!'

The two men sat propped up against a wall, Leachman's legs stretched along the bench, celebrating their meeting with the beverage the 'OC' carried with him for nightly comfort. He left a bottle behind which Chalmers shared with Gertrude Bell and Balfour. Leachman changed into his Arab garb and was gone.[1]

Gertrude Bell and Balfour stayed at Kufa and one day as they were crossing the Euphrates bridge they caught a glimpse of Naj'm as the Arabs of Fahad Bey's tribe called him; the 'star' of the night sky. Gertrude wrote:

> To us, from the sandy hillocks, emerged a strange company, half in uniform, half in Arab robes, Colonel Leachman in the midst of it and, except for the white tabs of the political officer . . . indistinguishable from the rest. All were armed, one carrying a hawk on his wrist, the Arab greyhounds at the horses' heels – Naj'm travelled like any of his brother magnates of the desert.

The British party stayed at the same house that evening. At midnight Gertrude tactfully retired to bed and the men talked and drank, and were all the worse for wear next morning – except Leachman. 'Naj'm's countenance was inscrutable, and after a hearty breakfast he mounted his horse, collected his rapscallion escort and set out on his way to God knows where.'

There were inevitable journeys to Baghdad, where he enjoyed talking to Wilson over endless coffee and immense piles of work, for Wilson was no great delegator, preferring to shoulder the detail as well as the decision-making himself. Otherwise Leachman hated the routine and the unreality of it all. 'I have been having a bad attack of Baghdad . . . I have just come in from the desert, and am still simmering from the effects of living in a sort of furnace for the last ten days . . . I have just come back from a several days' journey, most of it in the rain . . .' And so the seasons passed by. 'I have just had another visit to Baghdad. I received a hoarse order to go in and when I got there after a journey of 75 miles, they said they were sorry but did not want me. As I am no lover of Baghdad I was somewhat annoyed.' It was not a lost journey, however; Hassan learned that he was in town and decided to forgo the joys of the city and rejoin his master among the black tents of the desert. Gertrude Bell, back in her office in the civil headquarters where she argued constantly with Wilson and found Leachman an abrasive defender of her chief's causes, nevertheless wrote another testament to Naj'm's splendour in his chosen setting:

His duties did not lead him often to headquarters, though when they did, there was no one who more enjoyed a good dinner with selected friends and no one who could make the hours pass more gaily with caustic tales of the ways and sayings of the folk who lived in his native lands, the wilds, but the stories were not all from his quarter. A Badawin shaikh would drop into your office and relate how Naj'm had arrived in his *trambail* (motor-car, which Leachman used as well as his horse, often in impossible motoring conditions) at some remote grazing ground: 'And wallah! that *trambail* is like a steed under him. It leaps the wadis and it rushes over the Spring grass, wallah; like a horse bred among the tribes. And then we offered the slaughtering (Qadanna al dhabibah – the narrator alluded to the sheep which had been seethed for supper) and Naj'm sat by the fire and we talked through the night.' But he would add ruefully: 'He has a strong hand, wallah!' from which it might be gathered that the talk was not wholly unrelated to tribal misdemeanours.

There was another witness: an official 'Eye-Witness' as they called the man who travelled as a kind of erstwhile public relations offcer with the army in those days. He was the distinguished writer Edmund Candler who made notes as he went and sent them to his publisher in London so that a book could be produced immediately the war was over when the censor was no longer able to impose his blue pencil on the story of the army in Mespot.

I often envied the Political Officer, [wrote Candler in *The Long Road to Baghdad*, published in 1919,] whose life was passed in intimate relation with these mysteries (spies, hun-agents, gun-runners, holy men from Persia and Afghanistan); many of them are very young, with just a smattering of Arabic . . . There are one or two men, notably Colonel Leachman the OC of the desert, who could pass as Arabs and read what was on their minds, as one turns over the pages of a book. Leachman gained an extraordinary ascendancy over the Arab tribes; he had a rough and ready way with them, a sense of humour which they understood, and when displeased a very angry eye, which they feared. Very rarely would he talk of his adventures, but they covered a very wide field. He knew the desert from Mesopotamia to Syria and the Hijaz.

And he added: 'Leachman was generally to be found in some unorthodox zone, preferably hostile.'

Keen though they were to follow Leachman's adventures at this time, fellow Britishers knew next to nothing of his movements. He melted into the Bedouin life of the desert, a vast unknown wilderness now became his parish, 20,000 square miles in area, 500 miles along the Euphrates, 400 miles from east to west as far as the frontier between Ibn Saud's Najd and the mountainous homeland of the Rashids, Jabal Shammar. When he was wanted urgently at Baghdad a special messenger attached to the Anaiza tribe was sent to contact him. Only the chiefs of the Anaiza knew his exact movements, and only the chief of them all, Fahad Bey, knew his English friend's mission in all its valour and demi-madness.

When Leachman returned to the Euphrates at the end of 1917, bent on alliance with Fahad's tribes and the pacification of the Euphrates deserts, he took the old chief aside and told him that his former indifference to Britain's cause would not do. He had not actively supported the Turks, but he had not opposed them either, and he had once or twice shown Leachman himself discourtesy. Fahad apologized for past defects and swore eternal loyalty to Britain. He was then given a subsidy of £1,000 a month from the coffers of the Indian Government and he was as good as his word until his death in his late eighties in 1928.

It is Fahad Bey who tells us what happened in the spring of 1918 when Capt. Marshall was killed, and British intelligence became aware of a conspiracy among the shaikhs of Baghdad and the Euphrates who were being incited to insurrection by Faisal's Syrian agents and their masters of the old *Ahad* and *Fattah* in Egypt, financed with British gold given to the Sharif of Mecca and his sons in vast amounts to help them fight the Turks and Germans. Fahad's pension was small enough by comparison.

In February 1918, when Leachman returned to Najaf from Baghdad, he took 120 Anaiza horsemen led by Fahad Bey's son Mutib to the wells of Al Latif, two days' journey from Najaf.

Fahad Bey wrote:[2] 'There they encountered a caravan of *ageyl* carrying goods from Samawa to the Turks. He attacked them at the head of our horsemen and succeeded in capturing them with their goods. And then he went to Baghdad pleased.'

No sooner had Leachman returned to the tribes than news came to him of Marshall's cowardly murder. It took little time to discover that the raiding party at the Political Officer's gate had been led by Atiyah abu Gulal, the Arab headman of Najaf. Immediately after the murder he and his accomplices went off to the Shamiya desert in the south where they received the protection of Ajaimi ibn Sadun's Muntafiq.

Fahad Bey takes up the story again:

> The Colonel ordered my son Mutib to attack them (Atiyah and his protectors, some 12,000 strong). Our son at the head of ten thousand men, accompanied by Colonel Leachman, attacked and defeated them and killed six hundred of their men – thanks to Colonel Leachman's personal leadership. Atiyah, seeing that the fight was going against him, fled away on horseback and sought the protection of the Political Officer of Shinafiya. After the raid the Colonel proceeded to Baghdad.

In fact, the Shamiya desert in which the Muntafiq wandered was the parish of another exceptional Political Officer of the time, Maj. Harold Dickson, whose method of dealing with recalcitrant tribes differed a good deal from Leachman's. He was based at Suq ash-Shuyukh on the Lower Euphrates, and he was the unique expert on the Muntafiq tribes. In the shambles which preceded the march on Baghdad, however, Dickson was ordered to leave the territory of the Muntafiq and to go and buy grain and sheep, of which he knew nothing. Hubert Young who had come down from the Hijaz disillusioned with Lawrence and company and the caprices of the Arab Bureau, was appointed to the Muntafiq *liwa* as they called it. Eventually a monster deputation of shaikhs from the region went down to Basra to plead for Dickson's reinstatement, and the major returned.[3]

When Leachman came back after a conference with Wilson at Baghdad he ordered a further attack on Ajaimi who had proved the most loyal of Arab chiefs to the Turks and their German allies and had been well paid by their agents. Now he gave succour to Britain's enemies among the Arabs. Fahad's story goes on:

> He (Ajaimi) was a continual cause of serious trouble. An expedition of thousands of our fighting men was mustered and led by Colonel Leachman and my son Mutib, set out to attack and capture Ajaimi, who had fled away and entered the Jabal Sinjar. Heat and fatigue played havoc with our camels and horses. The expedition pursued Ajaimi for over a month. He had a long start, unfortunately, and Leachman, although at one time close on his heels, never got within actual striking distance of him. Finally exhaustion forced the abandonment of the chase and Ajaimi crossed the river and joined the Turks. He was prevented however from returning while the war lasted.

The notes scribbled by Fahad Bey before he died were the only testimony we have to Leachman's activities in his private war in the early months of 1918. But they are enough.

The war had entered its final phase, and there had been dramatic changes in the Mesopotamian command. The world picture had changed too. In November 1917 Gen. Maude had been taken to hospital in Baghdad suffering, it was said, from cholera. He died a few days after admission, amid rumours spread by German propaganda that there had been foul play. Doubtless the German Eastern Bureau recalled similar rumours spread by Britain when Field-Marshal von der Goltz died in the same hospital a year earlier as the surrender of Kut was being negotiated.

The Foreign Office treatment of the affair was not without an element of mystery. The Sultan of Egypt, fearing for his own life, had asked Wingate, the new High Commissioner, what the 'mystery of Maude's death was all about'. Wingate replied that he was 'unable to enlighten him'. Philby who was on the spot in Baghdad commented that his death was due 'to the combination of the sun and the heat and his own cure for both'. The Foreign Office file was put away with a note from Under-Secretary Sir Ronald Graham: 'Room 16. Not to be copied. Sir R. Graham does not want to have this back.' Conspiracy lurked throughout the eastern war sphere as Allenby made slow, careful progress in

Palestine, as the Bolsheviks overthrew the Provisional Government in Russia, as America came to play an active part in the war, as the Balfour Declaration reverberated across the world and the Sykes–Picot agreement which divided the Arab lands between the Allies was divulged by Lenin in the first few days of the Red regime; and most specially as the allied civil administration in occupied territories came into conflict with the military authorities.

The Turco-German army in north-west Persia began to move towards Georgia and Armenia at the end of the year, hoping in the chaos of revolution and the fight between Reds and Whites to occupy the oil centre of Baku. 'Stalky' himself, Maj.-Gen. Dunsterville, of Leachman's own regiment, arrived in Baghdad in January 1918 and in February set out with a party of officers in forty motor-cars to head off the enemy, following the route Leachman had taken into Armenia and Kurdistan. In the War Office in London the intelligence department was at work on Shakespear's 1914 route trying to find a way for a motorized army from the Euphrates along the pilgrim road and then by the wells of Hayaniya to Jauf, so that it could link with Allenby's advancing army. Had that scheme come to anything, Leachman would undoubtedly have played a vital part in its realization. But it was considered too risky in the end, and the army in Mesopotamia was ordered to push the Turks from their last strongholds on the Euphrates, from Hit northward.

In March 1918 General Brooking advanced on Hit, took the town on the 9th, and began the pursuit of the Turks to Khan Baghdadi in the north. Leachman was called from Karbala to help deal with the tribes. But he could not be away from the lower region for too long. The Turks had pockets along the river and at Shithatha, forty miles west of Karbala, they were still in control, using that oasis as a depot for the supply of arms to the Muntafiq and to friendly tribes higher up in the Dulaim division where Brooking's army was taking over. The 'OC desert' was called on to make superhuman efforts as his parish extended by another 200 miles or so and he had to make frantic journeys back and forth whenever tribal difficulties arose. The affairs of the outside world were far removed from Leachman's mind at that critical time. As Brooking advanced northward, GHQ decided that Leachman should tackle the Turkish menace at its rear in Shithatha. Chalmers had taken over at Karbala while his 'OC' carried out his wandering mission and he accompanied Leachman in the last bid to clear the Turks from the regions of the Shi'a holy cities. It is Chalmers's story.

Shithatha lay isolated in the desert, across a rolling plain, a place of three hundred thousand palm trees. The number was known in the round for they had been counted for taxation purposes by the Turks. The township itself was a collection of mud-brick huts in the midst of the palm forest.

Leachman drove up with Hassan in a Ford van loaded with Mills bombs. He left his companion in the car concealed in the trees and went alone to the village square where the caravan to Damascus always rested to feed and water its animals. He carried Mills Bombs in his pockets and an automatic rifle. As he approached he was fired at from several angles and he was forced to retreat and take cover. An Arab youth on a roof-top came closest to hitting him. The rest of the fire was erratic. He zig-zagged towards the houses again and the youth on the roof-top kept up his fire, bullets hitting the ground near him and whistling past his head. He took the pin from one of his bombs as he came close enough and tossed it on to the roof. The house and the sniper were blown to pieces, and the male population appeared warily from the cover of the houses, hands above thier heads. They had never heard or seen an explosion like it.

Leachman then ordered the men to sit in the square while he held *majlis*. He sacked the existing council and appointed two men whom he knew to be reliable as *rais al balad* (mayor or minister of the land) and assistant. They formed a new council and were told in no uncertain terms that any help given to Britain's enemies would bring dire punishment on their heads.

A few days later Leachman returned to the scene with Chalmers. As the two men walked through the town an old woman appeared raising her skinny arms to heaven and scream-ing at the top of her voice.

'What is she on about?' asked Chalmers.

'Oh she's mad and is cursing me,' said Leachman.

Later Chalmers went alone to Shithatha which formed part of the territory he controlled from Karbala. He found that the old woman was the mother of the boy Leachman had blown up when he first approached the town. And she spoke kindly of the Englishman though she continued to lament the death of her son. Chalmers discovered that Leachman was paying her a regular

197

sum of money from his own pocket and whenever he returned to the district he brought her gifts and took tea with her.

At the end of March when Brooking's force took the village of Khan Baghdadi a party of Turks and Germans escaped and made off northward towards Ana. They were pursued by a unit of armoured vehicles led by Capt. Tod of intelligence, a member of the Basra family who had shown Leachman such generous hospitality before the war. Leachman had been recalled from an excursion with the Anaiza to help deal with the tribesmen of the Dulaim region which now came within his purview. He arrived at Khan Baghdadi early in April, in time to greet Tod and the enemy party which he had intercepted seventy-five miles to the north. A German in the ranks of the PoWs clicked his heels and stepped forward with outstretched hand. 'I have always wanted to meet you, though circumstances made us enemies,' he said. It was Conrad Preusser, the remarkable agent with whom Leachman had played Cox–and–Box throughout the war.

Tod confiscated Preusser's diary which was taken with other documents to Staff HQ. When it was studied it was seen to contain the note: 'Not all the blandishments of the Turks, nor all the gold they have distributed, nor any German effort can undermine the influence among the tribes of one man, Leachman.'

In July Leachman was back at Karbala, sorting out a disturbance which arose from the ever-present antipathy of the fellahin towards the townsmen. A crowd of the former had entered the town and engaged in an orgy of looting, led by one of the desert shaikhs. He and Hassan singled out the ringleader, brought him down with a two-man rugby tackle, and Leachman gave him a salutary thrashing. The firing ceased and the culprits handed over their loot with reluctance.

On 4 July Leachman wrote one of his few letters of the period to the family. 'We have had somewhat stirring times lately, and I have been rushing around the country in a wild way. It has been raining violently, so a car has been of no use.' He had saddle soreness, and was finding it increasingly hard to sleep. There were bouts, too, of sickness and stomach pains but he said nothing of that to his mother and sisters. Only of insomnia did he complain. 'Another of my sufferings is my inability to sleep. I don't think I am ever really asleep . . . I think it must be from being perpetually on the move at earliest dawn, as I have been for the last three years. We await news from home with great anxiety, but thank the gods it seems to be going well.'

Now Leachman was responsible for the Karbala district and the Dulaim tribal region higher up the Euphrates. Other Political Officers looked after the towns, but he remained in sole command of the desert regions covering 150,000 square miles, with only Hassan to accompany him on his lone vigil, and occasionally a small muster of troops when exceptional trouble brewed. It is to be doubted whether a like task was ever undertaken by a single officer in the entire history of warfare. In October, as the enemy sued for peace in Europe and the East, Gen. Marshall, the new C-in-C returned from leave in England to Mesopotamia with orders to advance as far north as possible from the Baghdad line. Lloyd George and his ministers were determined to go to the peace table with as many trump cards as possible. Leachman was ordered to join Gen. Cobbe's army in the advance on Mosul and Kurdistan. But he was not relieved of his other tasks. An aircraft was placed at his disposal so that he could keep in touch with the Anaiza shaikhs and with those of the potentially dangerous Dulaim territory whose tribes had collaborated with the Turks.

Cobbe's army consisted of two divisions, the 17th under Maj.-Gen. Leslie on the right bank of the Tigris above Baghdad and the 18th under Maj.-Gen. Fanshawe on the left bank of the river. Two cavalry divisions, the 7th and 11th, commanded by Gen. Cassels were assigned to Fanshawe's division, while a Light Armoured Motor Brigade was attached to Leslie's force. Leachman was posted to the LAMBs. It was, he said, 'the one job of all others I would have chosen'. They were a specially chosen body of men, most of whom had already proved themselves in the Euphrates campaign – men of mixed nationality and incomparable courage. Two of the most prodigal were the Americans, Captain Kermit Roosevelt, son of President 'Teddy' who was to return to the East as a big-game hunter when the war was over, and Lance-Corporal Jack Summers, who became Leachman's driver. There was also the Swiss dispatch rider, Corporal Milson, who spoke little English but could ride a motorcycle as few others, and was the coolest of men under fire. They were a close and adventurous band.

The offensive was launched on 23 October with the advance on the Lesser Zab river position of Kalat Shergat. The task of the LAMBs was to cut off the Turkish retreat and within two days they were astride the river just north of Shergat which was defended by a thousand men. Meanwhile Gen. Cassels, supported by the 11th Cavalry, forced a crossing of the Tigris and began an encircling movement. It was essential that the LAMBs should hold up the retreating Turkish army and prevent its escape. The superior enemy force could easily have broken through the position held by Leachman's small force to the north of them, but they failed to seize the chance. On the night of the 28th, the 7th Cavalry Brigade crossed the Tigris and joined up with Gen. Cassels's army. His line stretched some forty-five miles from the Tigris practically to the Zab, just above the LAMB's position. But Turkish infantry do not easily succumb to encirclement. They are among the fiercest of fighters when trapped. They made repeated attempts to break through Cassels's line and there were heavy casualties on both sides.

As the battle raged, Leachman and Summers decided to make an excursion by armoured car behind the Turkish lines to see if they could find the aerodrome from which enemy planes were taking off to strafe the British positions. They found the aerodrome easily enough, drove in at daybreak, fired about ten rounds at the Turkish mechanics and others who were foolish enough to be around, hoisted the tail of a German Halberstadt fighter on to their armoured car, and dragged it back to the British position. Summers calmly took a photograph as Leachman hauled it across the sandy plain in no-man's-land.

The entire Turkish force surrendered on 30 October. Over 11,000 Turks were taken prisoner and fifty-one field-guns were captured. There were 1,800 casualties on the British side. On 31 October the LAMBs and the cavalry advanced to Qaiyara just south of Mosul.

The armistice with Turkey had been signed on the previous day at Port Mudros on the island of Lemnos. But news of it did not reach Gen. Marshall from the War Office until 1 November. The C-in-C decided none the less to order Cassels to push on to Mosul from his position at Hammam Ali. The order reached Cassels just before midnight on the day that the armistice announcement was telegraphed to Baghdad. Cassels had taken matters into his own hands in the interval. The afternoon before on 31 October Leachman was sent to meet the commander of the Turkish 5th Division outside Mosul, Ali Ihsan Pasha, to ask for the surrender of the enemy force. Ali Ihsan gave Leachman a note asking Cassels to withdraw his army to Qaiyara, the point it had reached at noon on that day, where Gen. Fanshawe had established his headquarters. On receipt of the Turkish commander's letter, Cassels went forward to meet him at a position some five miles south of Mosul. He returned at six o'clock in the evening to Hammam Ali. Fanshawe, when he received the news that Ali Ihsan refused to budge, ordered Cassels to stay put while Leachman proceeded to Mosul to interview the enemy commander.

Leachman set off at 6.30 a.m. on 2 November for another interview with the Turks, and obtained a promise that they would withdraw from the hills commanding the city on its southern side, but no more. The Turks claimed that the armistice agreement bound the British to accept the status quo. Gen. Marshall argued that it clearly laid down the obligation of Turkish units to surrender to the nearest allied commander. And so Leachman was sent in again next day to bring back Ali Ihsan to Cassels's camp. Not until 7 November did the Pasha agree to evacuate his army. Next day the British army moved in and the Turks began their withdrawal. Leachman was appointed military governor of the vilayet. He had returned as war-lord to the stamping ground of earlier days.

Leachman and Kermit Roosevelt among the LAMBs were awarded the DSO for their bravery in the campaign. Jack Summers received the DCM. After he left the scene of his sterling deeds to become a rancher in New Mexico, Summers wrote of 'The Skipper, a swell guy and a grand soldier', whom he drove in the last campaign of the war in Mesopotamia.

Six months earlier Maj. Bray came to Karbala to take over from Chalmers. At the end of 1917 he had left the Hijaz, where he was intelligence officer to Wilson Pasha, Wingate's senior representative at the court of the Sharif, and volunteered for duty in France, to find peace at Ypres and on the Somme after a year of interminable squabbling and intrigue between the old man of Mecca, his sons and the Arab Bureau men. But he was sent to Mesopotamia and there he found his hero. They sat one evening on the steps of the Political Officer's house at Karbala and Leachman told him: 'I can't be as strenuous with the Arabs as I need be and if I cannot impress them enough they will get me; but I would like to get the DSO before they do it.'

Even then he knew that time was running out for him. 'Now I

can die happy,' he wrote when he received the decoration for valour at the battle of Shargat.

He wasn't happy for long as the governor of Mosul. Turkish agents swarmed down from Anatolia and the district of Van, and officials of the old regime soon resumed their time-honoured practices of extortion and bullying, and in response the inhabitants, Arab, Assyrian, Kurd and Jew, began to squabble and pillage. Leachman imposed martial law and went off in his aeroplane to outlying districts to impose order on the tribes. A touching tribute was paid to him by the chief of the Yezidi tribes of Jabal Sinjar in the mountains of Kurdistan:

> He shone upon us as the full moon on a cloudy night and dispersed the Turkish tyrants with one gallant stroke . . . He sent me word to join him in Mosul, and in spite of my old age I welcomed the call and went to him with my following . . . On seeing him I could not control myself from bending to kiss his hands. Within a week he entrusted to me the governorship of the Jabal so we all started back. I performed the duty he entrusted to me to his and everybody's satisfaction. Justice and tranquillity hitherto unknown to the people on account of the oppression of the Turks brought back confidence and things moved quickly to brighten the Jabal and help in its progress . . . His dear memory will forever live in our minds and the Jabal Sinjar cannot forget him for generations to come, God have mercy upon him. *Hamo Sharro*, chief of the Jabal Sinjar Yezidis.

Able men were sent by Arnold Wilson to help him. Men such as Maj. Reader Bullard whom he had found tiresome at administrative headquarters, and Lt-Col. Nalder and Capt. Bradshawe.

But already Wilson was at odds with the military authorities in Baghdad. As a mere captain in rank – though he was given a knighthood on his appointment as Civil Commissioner – he received scant respect at GHQ. Neither he nor Leachman could stem the tide of sedition which was being let loose by Mustafa Kemal's Turks, by Faisal's agents in Syria, and by forces as yet unknown to them and to the intelligence department.

Leachman's resources of strength and energy were being stretched beyond endurance. He was still keeping an eye on the Euphrates trouble-spots as well as governing the most unruly of all the areas of the old Ottoman Empire. Just before joining the Tigris army on its march to Mosul, he had made a hurried visit by plane to the Dulaim region where he had ordered Fahad's son, Mutib, to attack the Shammar. Soon afterwards Mutib died from wounds he received in battle. In 1919 Leachman flew over from Mosul to order Fahad's other son, Mahrut, to attack the same tribe, which was being harassed by Ibn Saud's men and was causing trouble along the Euphrates. 'When Mahrut was in pursuit Colonel Leachman reconnoitred in an aeroplane and finding that the Shammar were in full flight and that they had entered Turkish territory, he ordered Mahrut to return,' wrote Fahad Bey.

At the end of December 1918 he told his mother,

> I have been doing a lot of flying lately, not that I like it, but from necessity . . . Wilson has gone to Paris and I dare say you will see him in England . . . he is the most amazing man . . . I have just got out the whole of my possessions from India; about half are ruined by moth. I caused some joy in our mess by trying on my red Sandhurst tunic. I am pretty thin now . . . I flew up to the snows recently to correct a contrary Kurdish tribe; it was very wonderful but very unpleasant.

In May he wrote: 'I am not at all sure that I am cut out as the ideal political officer; my methods are too abrupt, but I have a splendid lot of fellows under me.'

Through the year 1919 dissent grew into open rebellion. The first months of the year were quiet, as the peacemakers went about their work in Paris and national groups argued mainly among themselves about the future. But as the mandates over Syria and Mesopotamia were handed to France and Britain, and Britain was given the unenviable charge of Palestine, open revolt came to the streets, and sinister agents of the defeated powers and of the Pan-Islamites and Pan-Arabs caused tempers to rise and bombs to be thrown.

During the summer months three young political officers in Kurdistan were murdered, Captains Pearson, Willey and Macdonald. Wilson, who felt keenly the loss of any one of his men and who never failed to go immediately to the source of trouble when it arose, keeping an aircraft at the ready so that he could be there within hours and sometimes minutes, decided that

Leachman should go home on leave. An Indian civil servant of considerable experience took his place in October 1919, Mr J. H. H. Bill. But he was no more successful in quelling the calls to jihad and murder, and he himself died at the hand of a Kurdish insurgent within a month of his appointment.

Leachman left for home in June. He took Hassan with him for his faithful servant could not endure the thought of being parted from his master. He arrived at his home in Petersfield for the first visit in five years, ill and intermittently doubled up with pain. He was taken into a nursing home almost straight away and operated on for appendicitis. He had just about recovered his strength by Christmas time when he received an urgent cable from Wilson in Baghdad asking him to return. The country was in turmoil. Publishers had sent representatives to him at home and in hospital pleading with him to publish his war story. But he decided that he could not face the publicity.

He and Hassan had their Christmas dinner with the family – the first time he had done so since joining the army nearly twenty years earlier – and then packed their bags for Mespot. He and the world had changed out of recognition in the years of his exile. His father had died in his absence, his mother old and frail had grown apart from him. Only sister Mabel and her family in Wiltshire gave him cause to want to stay in England. But he was too weak to take part in riding and hunting and the pastimes of the countryside. His years of uninterrupted army service had sapped his strength. He was not yet forty when he spent his leave in England, but he felt and looked an old man. The real Gerard Leachman could only exist in the wilds and wastelands of the world. The only life he knew or savoured now was that of the desert, where he could share a knife-edge existence and an enveloping asperity with the nomad.

14

Farewell, Iraq!

Five days before Christmas in 1919 the India Office called Leachman to London to offer him the Kuwait political agency. To fill the post which his arch-rival Shakespear had once held with such distinction was a tempting thought. But he had received Wilson's urgent call to help him in Baghdad and he would not let his chief down. He refused the offer and announced that he would go back to his wartime haunts. Mesopotamia might be on the verge of conflagration; the journey back would be leisurely for Leachman. He had bought a motor-car of his own while on leave and he took it with him on the ship from Southampton to Le Havre, crossing with Winston Churchill, Sir Henry Wilson (the military intelligence chief whom Asquith had kept at arms length in the war, and now Chief of the Imperial General Staff) and Admiral Lord Beatty, on their way to the Peace Conference. It was a cold January day and already the newspapers carried harbingers of things to come: 'Mustafa Kemal at Damascus', 'Unrest in Mesopotamia – War Office details of raid on Dair az-Zor', 'Faisal orders surrender of tribesmen'.

Leachman motored across southern Europe to Naples, Hassan at his side, and making good progress, the car behaving 'beautifully'. By the end of the month he was at Naples where he took ship to Alexandria. From there he motored to Baghdad, though he gave no details of his route, arriving in the first few days of March, just as the balloon went up.

Never had Wilson been so pleased to welcome an old friend

and ally – the man on whom, above all others, he could rely for resolute action in time of trouble.

Wilson had not wanted the job of Civil Commissioner. Cox's departure for Tehran at the end of the war had forced it on him, a reluctant act of patriotism, for he was expected from the outset to promote and implement policies with which he was in total disagreement. In what he described as a 'rash moment' he asked Whitehall for a clarification of its attitude in the light of the 'Twelfth Commandment', President Wilson's assertion of the rights of liberated peoples to an unmolested opportunity of autonomous development. The India Office referred him to instructions given in August 1917 after the taking of Baghdad that 'no large or controversial questions were to be raised'. There were few subsequent policy guide-lines. 'The Oracles were dumb,' said Wilson. 'Our duty as *men on the spot* seemed clear – to go ahead and, to the best of our ability, to re-create out of the wreckage of war a system of civil administration adequate to the needs of the people . . . so that when peace should come they might seek, not vainly, to trace the pathway to a fitting destiny.'

Wilson believed, and Leachman was his first supporter and comforter, that Britain had taken on no obligations to the Arabs in winning the war. On the contrary, Arabs had constituted the mass of the Turkish army, and those who were left in the rear of the battle did everything in their power to obstruct the allied effort. Having won the war, the allied powers should govern or get out.[1] The pervasive Anglo-Saxon view that all subject peoples should be granted a short-cut to democratic government and the rule of law, even when they actively opposed any such regime, and that British blood should be spilled if necessary in the process of conferring it, was not a philosophy which appealed either to Wilson or Leachman. But it had powerful supporters in London. Not for nothing had the 'Easterners' in Lloyd George's Cabinet come triumphantly out of the war. Not for nothing were they scheming, as Lord Milner admitted in Cabinet, to 'diddle France out of Syria', despite the solemn agreements of the war.

While Leachman had rested quietly at home in England, Lawrence and Gertrude Bell had met at Paris and formulated plans for the succession of the Sharif's sons to the Arab lands. Bringing their considerable gifts of persuasion to bear on the questions of the moment, they began to bombard the press and the men of government with their views, which amounted to the implementation of those promises about which Sir Edward Grey admitted he hadn't 'a clear head', but which gave the Sharifians hegemony over Syria, Mesopotamia and even over Ibn Saud's lands. While Leachman had refused the advances of publishers and newspaper proprietors, terrified of publicity, the American professor Lowell Thomas, who had met Lawrence briefly in Cairo, began a series of lectures in London which would enthrall millions as the years went by with their tales of desert adventure. 'Lawrence of Arabia' was born, the English embraced the war myth for which they yearned in the lean years of peace, while T.E.L. himself flitted back and forth between London and Paris at the side of Faisal.

Three days before Lowell Thomas began his sensational lecture tour, Leachman's successor at Mosul, Mr Bill, was murdered. A few days later Leachman's friend Capt. Walker was shot dead. Gertrude Bell, officially Wilson's Oriental Secretary, returned to Baghdad by way of Syria and prepared a brilliant report 'Syria in 1919' in which she proclaimed the virtues of Arab nationalism. Wilson forwarded it to Whitehall with a personal note, praising its diligence and disassociating himself from its conclusions. Gertrude began a campaign to undermine Wilson's policy of tough control, writing over his head to the friends of her youth who now walked the corridors of power: Edwin Montagu, Winston Churchill, Arthur Hirtzel at the India Office, Hardinge at the Foreign Office, Chirol her closest friend who had been Foreign Editor of *The Times* and a Foreign Office intelligence agent. Wilson's involuntary task was impossible from the beginning, and the Political and Secret files of the India Office and the newspaper reports of the day plot with chilling precision the road to disaster.

On 3 March 1920 Leachman went at Wilson's request to Ramadi. 'At the front!' he told his family with the brevity which characterized most of his pronouncements. As he arrived at his new station the Arab nationalists of Damascus and Cairo proclaimed Faisal 'King of Syria', and his brother Abdullah 'King of Mesopotamia', and a group of notables met secretly in Baghdad to formulate a demand for Arab independence. Gertrude Bell met a representative of the group afterwards and noted their 'friendly feelings' which she passed on to the army commander, Marshall's successor, Gen. Aylmer Haldane. The GOC believed her and kept the troops in barracks.

Philby, another of Wilson's lieutenants who wore his loyalty lightly, followed Leachman's excursion into the cut-throat territory of the Dulaim tribes with fascination, and meanwhile flirted with the conspirator-in-chief of Mesopotamian Arabs, Sayyid Talib Naqib of Basra who had returned from wartime exile to resume his role as the vagabond prince of Basra's underworld.

'Sharifian propaganda was raging furiously all down the Euphrates,' wrote Philby, 'and Leachman was in the thick of it.' Leachman delayed at Ramadi only long enough to deposit his baggage before proceeding with Hassan by plane to Abu Kamal which was, Philby said, 'Wilson's advanced front in his private war against the Arabs'. Six officers had been killed in ten days before his arrival. The Arab culprits were 'doing the peaceful cultivator stunt' when he arrived. They, the 'cultivators', were not pleased to see him. He quickly put them to the sword. With a party of troops and loyal Arabs he burnt ten miles of huts, drove in the cattle, destroyed everything in sight and wiped out the few Arabs who were courageous enough to resist. 'The lowest of the low,' he called them, 'but quite dangerous.'

It was the tail-end of an exceptionally cold winter in which the north-east of the country had been covered by snow a foot deep. He was glad to go back to Baghdad, to warm up in a house, after he had taught the semi-nomads of Abu Kamal a lesson. 'We are beginning to learn them,' he said before leaving. 'I shall have to stay up here until we have got them in hand, and shall then go back to Ramadi. Carver is there, and a nice lot of officers though not one of them is over 25.' Reinforcements were beginning to arrive from Britain and India, young men inexperienced in battle to take the place of troops who had been demobbed after the war. His old staff, horses and dogs were sent over from Mosul to join him and keep him company in the parish he had re-inherited. He wrote home at the end of March.

> We are not in for a very easy time out here. Why we should want to keep this particular part of Mesopotamia I am in at present quite defeats me. The country is an absolute waste except for a very narrow strip along the Euphrates and there are no big towns except Dair az-Zor a little further up the river, in which the Arab Government (i.e. Faisal's Syrian government) are sitting.

By 30 March he was at Salahiya, twenty-five miles upstream from Abu Kamal: 'I have the honour of being the most advanced post on the Euphrates.'

There was trouble with Hassan as he returned to the battle-ground. Back in Baghdad the little man had found a supply of liquor and guessing what had happened Leachman went in search of him at two o'clock in the morning. He found him in a lock-up, unconscious, with empty bottles by his side. One of the reasons for taking him to England was to keep an eye on him in the hope that he would 'dry out' and lose his dependence on alcohol. But it was not to be. Leachman and his lad resumed their circus act as they pursued the warring tribes along the Euphrates.

Early in April he had to go off on a 150-mile car journey to the familiar desert post-road from Hit to Damascus to rescue a party of British officers:

> A party of our heaven-born political officers were making their way across the desert . . . a way I have been many times. They had tents and lumber with them of all sorts, and a raiding party came down on them and stripped them to the skin, wounding one of them . . . I brought them back here . . . I have two of Wilson's particular blue-eyed boys under me here. They are both perfectly useless and look at me as though I were a strange beast . . . all our planes are rotten and crash all over the country . . . I went to the camp of my own special Bedouin tribe (the Anaiza Amarat) the other day and had a great reception, as they had heard that I had been killed. They were very disgusted to hear that I had not bought a wife while I was at home and say that I must make the best of it with an Arab damsel.

At the end of April Wilson asked Leachman to take on a three-year contract of service, and he agreed to sign it, subject to a three months' notice clause. 'It is not bad as things go.' But his mind was on other matters: the collection of fines imposed on the Abu Kamal tribesmen which they were refusing to pay despite regular bombing 'which they don't seem to mind much', and on Hassan, who had been sick for some time. Leachman attributed his bouts of pain to his drinking, and his pining for drink when he was denied access to it. In the end Leachman sent him to the army hospital that had been set up at Ramadi, and a stomach operation was performed. Leachman, the father-figure, worried constantly about the young man who had been his single companion in the harsh world he had inhabited for five years.

He was concerned, too, at the quality of the new staff officers at Baghdad, neither 'gentlemen nor soldiers' and 'loathed by the military'.

As an outcome of the peace talks in Paris and of Arab nationality claims, the country which had been called Mesopotamia since the days of ancient Greece became *Iraq*.

'Raids on Upper Euphrates – Sheikhs fined' read the headlines back home. 'San Remo – Palestine Mandate confirmed', 'San Remo – Britain's Iraq Mandate', 'Riots in Jerusalem', 'Bolsheviks invade Persia', 'Greece invades Turkey' were others. Herbert Samuel was in Jerusalem setting up his 'regime of sweet reason' and Meinertzhagen, Allenby's intelligence chief in Palestine, declared that Faisal sought a federation of the Arab states including Palestine under one crown – Faisal's – whereupon Allenby sacked him and he joined the Colonial Office under Churchill, the new Colonial Secretary, as the protagonist of the Zionist cause. Iraq was seen to be but part of a wider more complex conspiracy than anyone had imagined.

No sooner had Leachman collected the last of the fines from the Abu Kamal shaikhs than the Government ordered Wilson to hand over the whole of the territory from Dair az-Zor to Abu Kamal to Faisal's Arabs as part of the new Sharifian Syria.

We have a detailed record of Leachman's activities at this time. One of his desert comrades was Corporal Frank Wing of the 6th LAMBs, and he kept a diary which recorded each day from their first encounter in March 1920. It contained a short essay on the Colonel.

Colonel Leachman was wonderfully well informed – no information was too trivial for him . . . He used to employ a lot of children to whom he paid a small fee. He had a man whom he used chiefly to train his army of mounted Arabs which he employed principally in patrolling the desert and in helping to collect taxes . . . He inaugurated an irrigation scheme at Ramadi by having trenches dug from the river bank inland to a distance of a mile or even two. These were filled by a water-wheel or by ponies continually pulling skin buckets up from the river . . . He had an office in Ramadi and the wall of

210

the room in which he worked was at one period riddled from bullets which had been fired by his enemies at night on the off chance of getting him.

That was a brief sketch of a half-fit Leachman at work in an office nearly a hundred miles from the nearest compatriots.

There was also an account of Leachman the traditionalist officer, seldom neglectful of his own responsibility or of the welfare of his men:

'Look here you chaps, I don't know you, but you'll do for me. Are there any of you who drive a car?'

'No sir.'

'Right then, we'll teach you sharp – because these men you have come to relieve haven't got home from the war yet.'

Leachman promised them they would be on their way home in three weeks. He kept his word and the new men were trained in that time. Corporal Wing became Leachman's driver in the armoured cars *Avenger, Impregnable* and *Chatham* with which he swept the desert and put the fear of God into the rebels.

A typical diary entry was that of 5 May 1920:

'We thought he was joking when he said with a grin "If you were wanted for action how long would it take you to get on the road?"

'"Two minutes, sir."

'"Right, have the *Avenger* on the road in two minutes."'

They went out along the Damascus road in pursuit of a raiding party that had cut the telegraph wires.

They caught up with the culprits and Leachman told the men that he was going to dash into the middle of the raiders' party and if he shouted they were to fire at the group. 'What about you?' the men asked. 'Never you mind about me, do as I tell you. I will stand as much chance as they will!'

'We saw a sight I shall never forget as long as I live,' wrote Wing. 'There were thirty armed Bedouin and he had nothing but a stick, but he dashed in among them. Hell was let loose – we stood spellbound . . . while he fought [them] single handed. Believe me there were some cracked skulls when he had finished. Every Arab, with the exception of five who ran away, were down and out . . . yelling for mercy, but he showed none . . . he picked two of them up and dragged them back to the car.

'If ever there was an action better worthy of a VC I should like

211

to know of it,' wrote the Corporal.

His diary for 30 May records: 'Colonel Leachman took three armoured cars to put down trouble which had broken out with two tribes near an old fort two miles east of al Qaim . . . There was fighting going on, but it ceased the moment they recognised Colonel Leachman.'

Wing's last sight of Leachman was on 12 July 1919. His diary for that day notes:

> Colonel Leachman came to the camp at Ramadi with secret orders. Hostile Arabs had taken two of his political officers prisoner as hostages to Ana and wanted a big price for them. Six of us and two officers were selected . . . he preferred to have unmarried men as there was not much chance of getting back, as there were thousands of hostile Arabs in Ana, and he advised us to make our wills if we had anything to leave . . . He intended to make a *smash and grab* business of it . . . We set off in the dead of night. No lights were allowed. We reached Hit well before dawn . . . Here we had to wait for one of his spies. He came and informed us that the Arabs had dug up the road to Adetha. Our way was therefore barred. Colonel Leachman decided to wait concealed till the following nightfall and then to make a detour through the desert to Ana. At four o'clock in the afternoon another informer came in and reported that the officers had been murdered. So we regretfully returned to Ramadi.

Such was the daily round of the man who had dominated the Euphrates deserts and even enemy-held territory for five long and searing years. Never once did he divulge the true nature of his work, even to his family.

> When we left Abu Kamal the whole country seemed to rise and go for us and we had a very stiff fight all the way back to Ana, 70 miles. There are raiders all over the place at the present time, but we are now in a position to deal with them. I spend hours in the air bombing camps . . . The brightest spot we have had for many a long day was when early one morning we jumped across twenty-five Arabs asleep in a hole in the ground . . . I can see no end to this turmoil and, though it is strenuous, uncomfortable and dangerous, it is better than

sitting in an office.

He complained of the young 'gentlemen' sipping drinks in the Baghdad club and giving no assistance whatever to the old hands like himself and Carver, and Dickson in the far south, who bore the brunt of the mounting insurrection, or to the astonishing Maj. Noel over in Kurdistan where his Arab irregulars held down the fiercest and most ruthless of all the tribes until, with the backing of foreign money and the fervour of the nationalist call to arms, the dam burst, with the murder of more British officers and a massive uprising.

Leachman saw red, and he turned on his chief and closest confidant, Wilson. He must be held to blame for the lack of military support, for the failure to take decisive action at a time when the troubles could so easily have been nipped in the bud. He did not know, and could not have known, that the 'Chief' was powerless in Baghdad, that the army would not listen to him, that London suspected him of all kinds of schemes, and was intending to replace him at any moment. It was Gertrude Bell and Philby among the civil administrators who had the ear of Gen. Haldane, and especially the former, 'Al Khatun', who – as Wilson was to write at a later date – 'expressed the belief that the bottom had dropped out of the agitation' at a critical moment. Haldane believed her. It was, said Wilson, 'imprudent of him to prefer her private miscalculations to the measured misgivings of her official superior'.

But Leachman knew nothing then of the disputes in Baghdad. He was making his way through a hail of bullets by armoured car from Ana to Ramadi, and then back by air when another disturbance was reported. He found time to write home, despairingly, 'They have just given Wilson a knighthood. It might have been the boot with more advantage.'

In another letter he said: 'It is rather a desperate state of affairs, but I thrive on it, though I would be happier if they would give us a little more help from Baghdad.'

Philby, viewing the matter from inside but with the dispassion of one above and outside it all, wrote:

He [Wilson] was doomed and his country round him lay in ruins and revolt; and, too late, the Government behind him woke up. Those who had slept in Whitehall, and not for want of would-be wakers, were responsible, if responsibility can ever be fixed for anything, for the lives that were laid down for the repairing of their negligence.

Military intelligence in London was undergoing a shake-up in May 1920, with Iraq being lumped together with Armenia, Georgia, Turkey, Azerbaijan, Persia and the Arabian peninsula under MI2 (b), while Syria and Palestine came under a different department, 2(c). It was in for a shock when its new personnel came to examine the telegrams from Baghdad in June. Mirza Muhammad Riza, a leading Arab of Karbala, had been arrested on a tip-off from Leachman. It was a friendly arrest, and the Arab divulged the source of much of the money being paid to the tribes of the lower Euphrates – the Standard Oil Company of America.

Wilson told intelligence, under the heading 'financial aid to extremists', that he had 'the wolf by the ears'. But it was the Foreign Office that was caught by the ears. It had already had representations from the State Department demanding 'equal opportunities for American citizens in oil concession negotiations', approaches which reached the sensitive hearing of Fleet Street by July.

A few weeks later Lawrence was writing in the *Observer* newspaper: 'It would be child's play for a decent man to run Mesopotamia, so long as he ran it like Cromer's Egypt, not like the Egypt of the Protectorate.'

'Mesopotamia – Tribes being bribed' said a *Times* headline on 19 June. On the 24th the same newspaper reported 'Mesopotamia – British mandate renewed. Mosul to be included'. A refinery was being built north of Baghdad and the concession for the Mosul fields was under review. Oil imperialism had become another bargaining counter in the vicious cycle of events which was to explode at any moment into a violent rebellion, and to drive Wilson from political office and into the welcoming arms of the Anglo-Persian Oil Company.

On 2 June 1920 Wilson had seen a self-appointed committee of fifteen Baghdadis who demanded a Constituent Assembly in place of the existing Provisional Government, to be guaranteed by the League of Nations. Wilson said that he would obtain the views of his Government. On the 12th Wilson reported the death of another four officers at Tel Afar near Mosul, and he told the

Government that he could not give effect to the mandate without a large well-armed army. The War Office replied through the GOC that he 'should not interfere in military matters'.

Press and public in Britain began to demand the withdrawal of the army, and in a House of Lords debate the wartime Secretary of State for India, Lord Crewe, said that Britain was trying to play 'fairy godmother to all the underdeveloped countries of the world . . . We simply cannot afford it.' Wilson warned again: 'Our military strength is insufficient.' But it was too late for warnings. Percy Cox arrived in London on 22 July to take instructions from Curzon for his new job, High Commissioner in Baghdad. Rebellion broke out in Ireland and the GOC there asked for two of India's senior secret service men, Denham and Tegart, who were working in Iraq. Lloyd George insisted on the transfer despite the resistance of Montagu, the India Office Secretary. Faisal's Government in Syria was kicked out by the French, and so the Sharif's son needed a new home. He had paid well for the favour of the nationalists in Iraq.

'My division are still good boys and the rest of Mespot is in appalling disorder,' wrote Leachman in early July. He had been asked to leave his parishioners for the moment, incredibly, to carry out a railway survey between the Euphrates and Damascus. Lawrence had been asked to carry out the task by London and had agreed, but after the discovery by Whitehall that a dubious French agent, M. Maimon, was involved in a plot to obtain a concession, it was decided on Lawrence's recommendation that Leachman should be given the task. It is tempting to seek a deep-laid plot in so frivolous a scheme to be rid of Leachman, who had become a positive embarrassment to the Sharifite lobby in London.

Still, Leachman was delighted to have a pleasant diversion put in his lap. 'It's rather wonderful doing a trip in four days by car over trackless desert, which before would have taken a fortnight on a camel.' The desert was full of raiding parties, but they were of no great concern: 'I expect the next move will be a reconnaissance right across to Jerusalem, in which case I shall get a few days at Cairo.'

He reported that the only way of dealing with the tribes now was 'wholesale slaughter' in the disaffected areas. 'It is the only way.'

His fortieth birthday approached and he looked forward to a

cake from home, and he was bucked by the presence of a very good officer who had been sent to join him, Maj. Eadie. 'He has a temper almost worse than my own.' The Arabs had their own name for James Inglis Eadie, *Abu al hurrat wa felfel*, 'Father of Cats and Peppers'.

On 1 August the second battalion of the Manchester Regiment and a battery of the Royal Field Artillery were attacked by a vast mob of tribesmen and Shi'a fanatics at Hillah, the rail terminus south-west of Baghdad, near the site of Babylon. Most of the Manchester Regiment men were new recruits who had been sent to their Euphrates station unprepared for the terrors of a wild Moslem mob on the rampage. Over 300 young men who went unsuspectingly to maintain the rule of law were killed or mutilated that day. Fighting went on for several weeks on the plain of Babylon as hundreds of tribesmen came in from the desert to join the slaughter and pillage.[2]

In the country trains were held up and passengers dragged from carriages and killed. A coach full of passengers was burnt after its inmates had been robbed. Chanting mobs marched through towns and cities shouting the name of *Allah* and declaring jihad. Parts of Kurdistan were in revolt and Noel's Arab levies were ordered to withdraw in order to help on the Lower Euphrates where they did magnificent work. Only Leachman's Dulaim district was quiet. Its shaikhs had learnt hard lessons and were reluctant to risk more.

Leachman wrote home on 6 August:

> We are still in the throes of internal strife. The whole of Mespot seems to be fighting. I am thankful to say that my people have behaved excellently so far. I have no troops and am holding the 150 miles between here [Ramadi] and the frontier with tribesmen. Carver is alone with 400 cut-throats at Ana, 130 miles up, and I have officers dotted about.

He told his mother and sisters of another adventure at Shithatha where he was set upon by gunmen: 'they gave it to me very hot indeed getting away'.

Cox was on his way from London to take over from Wilson. Faisal of Mecca, who had stirred the tribes and financed them, had been moved on by the French from Deraa to Haifa where Herbert Samuel invited him to Jerusalem and gave him a civic reception, 'the least that Britain could do'. It was intimated to Faisal that he might be offered the throne of Iraq if he was interested. And the Sunday *Observer*, egged on by Lawrence, proclaimed that the French in Syria 'merely followed the tyrannical ways of the British'.[3]

Leachman gave his family news of his servant. 'I regret he has fallen from grace. He drinks heavily and is a general nuisance. He is at present absent and, I believe, has gone to Baghdad.

'I understand that I am to go across to Palestine with a railway survey almost at once. It is madness to leave my district at such a time, but Wilson is mad. The surveyor is arranging today to discuss matters. It will be a change. I have very nearly had as much of this as I can stand.'

They were the last words he ever committed to paper.

He motored to Baghdad on 11 August, to find Hassan in one or other of his drinking lairs, and to receive instructions for his survey of the proposed rail route to Palestine. A car following behind his was fired on.

Wilson tells us:

He [Leachman] seemed fairly confident that so long as Ali Sulaiman could retain his hold over the Dulaim there would be no serious trouble between Baghdad and Falluja, or further north. He left my office at about eleven o'clock next morning, saying that he would be in Falluja by three o'clock and would telegraph to me. He added that he had told Shaikh Dhari to meet him at Khan Nuqta, midway betwen Baghdad and Falluja, and asked for authority to waive the repayment by Shaikh Dhari of certain advances made to him for the purpose of seed grain during the previous year.

Ali Sulaiman was a senior shaikh of the Dulaim tribes and a staunch ally of Leachman. He had remained constant in the face of calls to jihad and attempts at bribery. Dhari al Mahmud, chief of the Zoba tribe, was sullen and unreliable, but had taken no active part in the rebellion. Like other shaikhs of the region he had thought discretion the better part of valour. But why had Leachman arranged to meet Dhari on the road? And when was the arrangement made? There is no clue in any of the various statements made by Wilson, or in intelligence reports. He had come straight from Ramadi to Baghdad and there was no suggestion of having met any of the Dulaim shaikhs on the way.

Early on the morning of the 12th he went in search of Hassan but was unable to find him. He left not at 11 a.m. as Wilson suggested, but at 9 a.m., and at 11 was at the meeting-place of Khan Nuqta. The rest of the story is confused. Philby states:

> Dhari was at the trysting-place at about 11 a.m. with his son Khamis, another son Sulaiman, another member of his tribe and a slave. Leaving the driver outside with the car (in which was also his revolver as usual), Leachman with the rest of the party entered the Khan and there immediately ensued a discussion on the matter which had brought them all together. In the course of the discussion it was arranged (and Dhari had doubtless worked the matter round to this point in pursuance of a prearranged plot) that the *shabanas* (local levies) should go off at once with Khamis to arrest some miscreant whom Dhari professed himself unable to deal with without government help. Their immediate departure left Leachman and another Hassan [Leachman's driver who was also, coincidentally, of that name] with Dhari and his younger son, and a slave and kinsman. The conversation dragged on for a few moments and then Leachman rose to go. As he reached the door he was shot in the back and fell dead. Hassan the driver was also killed and the tragedy was complete.

Philby was in Baghdad at the time and inside the government. He must have heard a fairly authentic account of what happened. Yet his story is most unsatisfactory. It was Khamis, the son he said was sent away, who actually shot Leachman.

The intelligence department account filed two days later, on the 14th, was very different and just as unsatisfactory:

> With regard to Colonel Leachman's death, the following story is circulated at Kadhimain: He told an Iraqi to mend certain culverts. The Iraqi told his men that Leachman was strong and might do them harm if they did not obey. Leachman left to show them the way and Dhari's men fired and killed him.

There was a brief telegram from Baghdad to the India Office on 13 August: 'It is reported that Lt.Colonel Leachman was ambushed and killed on 12 August near Falluja.' Haldane the

GOC was to give an equally unsatisfactory account of the murder two years later.[4]

Not until seven years after the event was a plausibly detailed story told, when Capt. Williams, the police chief of Leachman's district, gave his account to the *Daily Mail*:

> On August 11, I slept the night in Shaikh Dhari's tent. Dhari was absent, settling a tribal dispute, so they said, but actually, I found out later, in conference with hostile shaikhs. Next day I returned to Ramadi to report to Colonel Leachman that the country was up in arms. Colonel Leachman set out for Baghdad by car to confer with headquarters, and on the way sent a message to Shaikh Dhari that he would like to see him on his return that evening at the Arab police post of Khan Nuqta. Dhari, his two sons, and a strong escort of Arab horsemen were waiting when he returned. They were engaged in conversation when Arab merchants arrived with a report that their caravan had been looted. Colonel Leachman immediately sent the twelve mounted Arab police of the post to arrest the robbers, and Dhari sent his youngest son and 30 horsemen to reinforce them. This left Khan Nuqta guarded by one sentry. Colonel Leachman suggested that he should go with Dhari to the latter's tent, and Dhari, stating that he would fetch horses as the land was too soft for the car, left the post, returning with his son Khamis and some of his men. At his order, Colonel Leachman was shot as he sat inside the police post. The raided caravan may or may not have been genuine, but Dhari's horsemen overpowered the police two miles along the road, and Dhari and his sons set off with 200 tribesmen . . . Dhari later escaped to Turkish territory.[5]

On the 17th, five days after the event, Wilson wired the Secretary of State for India:

> Deeply regret to report Lt. Colonel Gerard Leachman killed Khan Nuqta 12 August and buried by brother officers 15 August. He was shot dead by Khamis, elder son of Shaikh Dhari ibn Mahmud, chief of the Zoba tribe, at order of Dhari.

He also wired the statement issued to the press and published in the Baghdad and Basra *Times*:

Distinguished alike by his soldierly qualities and his strong sense of duty and discipline, his courage, enterprise and ability had earned him both amongst his countrymen and amongst Arabs a reputation enjoyed by no other political officer and his death is a serious blow to our position on the Upper Euphrates.

On the day of the assassination news spread to the Euphrates. The tribes rose. There were enough troops in Falluja to hold the town itself, but the rest of the country was in the hands of the insurgents. Leachman lay for two days where he had fallen. Then, on the 14th, Lieut Charles Goring of the 6th LAMBs ventured out in his armoured car *Harvester* and found his body. He took it to Falluja where it was buried with the others that had fallen in the rebellion. His fortieth birthday had passed unnoticed three weeks before as he patrolled his 'parish' – living, as he died, by the sword.

15

Postscript

For a month after Leachman's death the tribes responded to the signal and anarchy reigned. The call to holy war went out again. The Muntafiq rose in the south, the Dulaim tribes invested the troops at Falluja. Kifri was occupied and another officer, Capt. Salmon, was brutally murdered at Kufa. At Istabulat, Hilla, Nasiriya and Samarra Arabs attacked the British and their own villagers, trains were derailed, and the dead were counted in thousands. But the British forces were roused too. Early in September the RAF bombed the Zoba encampment. Troops gathered at Ramadi in force. The fort of a hostile shaikh near Khan Nuqta was bombed. And then the army took severe retribution. Led by Leachman's men at Ramadi and by the LAMBs they burnt the villages and the encampments of the Zoba tribe and of their allies. The Dulaim district was razed, its tribes put to the sword. Shaikh Dhari and his sons had gone. They sought refuge first with friendly tribes and then with the Turks.

Hassan, Leachman's faithful but errant servant, was never heard of again.

Two days after the assassination a young servant of a notable of Karbala, Shaikh Fakhrud al Din Khomaini, was taken into custody and questioned. His name was Awaad and he told the police a story which seemed to implicate a prominent Baghdadi, Yusef al Suwaidi.

I was coming from Karbala to Baghdad with a letter from Hamid Khan to the Civil Commissioner when I was detained . . . by the followers of Alwan Shallal and taken to the latter. They wanted to kill me on the way but it was decided . . . that they should take me to their shaikh . . . he sent me to Faisal the Shaikh of the Juhaish . . . I spent the night at his house. At the dead hours of the night a messenger came to Faisal from Dhari with an urgent letter and demanded that Faisal should be wakened. This was done and Faisal read the letter. The letter informed Faisal that Leachman had been staying the night with Dhari and that the latter, or some ignorant persons, had killed him. I do not remember well whether Dhari stated that he himself had killed Leachman or whether ignorant persons had done so. When I was with Faisal at Yusafiyeh, a man whom people called Chalabi and who appears to have been a man of Baghdad, came to the place and told the Arabs in the name of Yusef al Suwaidi that while it had been arranged for them to meet at a certain place, Yusef al Suwaidi has now decided that the meeting should not be held and that he would let them know later on. Faisal permitted me to come to Baghdad.

That interview does not seem to have been followed up. There is no official record of an interview with Yusef al Suwaidi, or with Faisal the Shaikh of Juhaish. Perhaps a CID file long since shredded told the definitive story of a murder that was almost certainly planned.

As letters of sympathy flooded in to the Leachman home at Petersfield some interesting facts came to light. Capt. G.D. Pitcairn told Leachman's mother that only a few days before the tragedy Capt. Williams, Leachman's commandant of gendarmerie at Ramadi, had stayed overnight in Shaikh Dhari's tent. 'None of us,' said Pitcairn, 'had the slightest idea that anything was being contemplated . . . I am certain too that Colonel Leachman himself, although not happy in his mind regarding the situation, suspected nothing.'

His friend Capt. Carver wrote:

The country at the time was everywhere fermenting and few save your son would have had the gallantry to carry on just as though nothing was happening . . . They would never have dared to raise a rifle to his face; his presence was too great among them . . . nothing can dim the memory of a man whom all who served under him loved and whose justice every Arab knew and sought.

A few days after the murder Gertrude Bell wrote: 'He always used extremely unmeasured language to the Arabs and Shaikh Dhari had many grudges against him. He was a wild soldier of fortune but a very gallant officer and his name was known all over Arabia.' And she admitted to Philby after the event, 'Colonel Leachman told me the other day that my unbounded conceit was the talk of Iraq.'

Lawrence wrote to his friend Alex Dixon: 'Then Leachman wasn't quite what you call a decent fellow, and the shaikh (whom I met a year later) was febrile. As L. died tragically we must hide his fault. Don't make him a hero in your book. He was too shrill, too hot-tempered, too little generous.'

Why, it may be asked, did not Lawrence tell the British security forces where Dhari was if he met him a year later, since they were scouring the East for him?

One of the distinguished missionaries of the East, Dr W. A. Wigram, who was then at St Albans, wrote to Mrs Leachman on 23 August 1920:

I knew him originally when I was residing (in what is known as the Archbishop's Mission) in Kurdistan, and met him again at Mosul when sent there after the war. He was almost the ideal English officer among the Arabs, standing among them as the embodiment of straightness, disinterestedness, and utter fearlessness. There was not an English officer or soldier in Mesopotamia who did not know of him and admire him though he was one of those men who do not get all the recognition they deserve from authority, because their finest things are done where there is nobody to see; and they face all the risks knowing that there is nobody to blame them if they shirk. I know of at least one case (the Dujaila redoubt by Kut) where your son took all the risks, did all his share of the work, and would have received a well-earned VC and the credit for a big success if only his advice had been taken.[1]

One of the new officers who arrived in Iraq just after

Leachman's death was John Glubb, later to lead the Arab Legion as Glubb Pasha. He wrote to a friend:

Unfortunately he [Leachman] was completely a man of action and scarcely ever put pen to paper. Even the government he was serving could never extract any reports or office returns from him. This has undoubtedly militated against his fame. Lawrence is famous because he wrote a book describing his own exploits![2]

Iraq gained its nationhood, and the Hashemite King Faisal came in 1921 to garner the harvest which Lawrence and Gertrude Bell and their friends of the Arab Bureau had sown. A new dispensation came to replace the Provisional regime, with British advisers at the helm. At the moment of the Manchester Regiment's baptism of fire in Hillah, as the Political Agent there Maj. Tyler was snatched from the hands of the insurgents, Gertrude Bell wrote: 'we have sketched out a scheme for a joint Sunni and Shi'a commission to go to Karbala and Najaf, and I took it to AT . . .' As disaster struck and Leachman made his final journey to Baghdad she told her father: 'Captain Clayton, Major Bullard and I, Major Bowman and others went to a patriotic play which was got up by ardent young nationalists . . . Whenever the word independence occurred – which it did often – they clapped to the echo.' And when it was all over she discovered among the staff officers of Baghdad a young man, Capt. Thomas, who was an up-and-coming concert pianist, and sent him out with a grand piano to entertain the shaikhs of Shatra. The bearded nobles gathered round to hear him play Beethoven's Sonata Pathètique, and when Capt. Thomas finished and took his bow, one shaikh turned to another and exclaimed *Wallahi. Khosh daqqar*, 'By Allah! A good thumping.'[3]

And so mad dogs and Englishmen played out the revolution, until peace came under the monarchy of Faisal ibn Husain, until the edifice that Britain built collapsed in a new wave of terror and the Kingdom became a republic, and one republic gave rise to another in successive exhibitions of fanaticism and bloodshed.

Wilson in his *Memoir* of Leachman for the Royal Sussex Regiment magazine wrote the final obituary:

224

Yet perhaps he was happy in the moment of his death: he did not live to see the destruction of his work by ignorant Arabs in a moment of infatuation; he did not live to hear them curse, vainly, the city-bred priests who had misled them; he did not live to witness the downfall of the high hopes that he, like others, had cherished for the future of these ancient lands. The reputation of his country was in his hands, and he added lustre to it. He met his death as he had faced life, for he lived and gloried in strife and died undefeated. His memory will live in Mesopotamia so long as a single Arab chief of the generation that knew him survives, and perhaps longer, for the ideals of which we are all proud, and which inspired his public life, remain.

On 5 June 1926 the Treaty of Ankara was signed, confirming the peace of Lausanne and the independent status of Iraq. It was ratified by the Iraq Parliament nine days later. Its signature marked a general amnesty for prisoners within the old Ottoman Empire, even for murderers. But it made a single exception, insisted upon by Sir Percy Cox. It excluded the murderers of Leachman.

And so Shaikh Dhari and his sons wandered in the wilderness for a few more months. But in November 1927 the name Leachman once more occupied the headlines of the world press. A cab driver in Mosul was taking his fare, an Arab shaikh, to his destination when a face on a wall poster came to his mind, with its promise of reward. He recognized the old man in the back of his vehicle and drove him to the offices of the Governor of Mosul. Dhari was taken to Baghdad where he stood trial under the old Turkish law which still prevailed in the country. On 30 January 1928 he was found guilty of complicity in Leachman's murder and sentenced to death, but in view of his age and infirmity and the suffering of his exile (which had been spent mostly in the Jezirah desert) the court recommended that he suffer penal servitude for life. Next day he was found dead in his prison cell. Dr Sinderson, who had visited him the night before, testified that he died from a heart attack.

The old Shaikh's son, Khamis, who fired the fatal shot, was never found.

Notes

Chapter 3   *What Ho!*

1. Bray and others were apparently unaware that his name was correctly Gerard.

Chapter 5   *Playing the Game*

1. Anglo-Tibet Treaty, 7 Sept. 1904; modified 27 April 1906. (*India Office Records*).

2. In 1905 Indian Army Intelligence, hitherto under the control of the Quartermaster-General, was reorganized along the lines of the General Staff organization established at the War Office, London, in 1904. From this time the 'Near East' (including the Ottoman Empire) was controlled by MO2(b), while India, Tibet, Afghanistan and Persia were the provinces of MO2(h). In the new arrangement, which came into effect in 1906, a line was drawn across Arabia from Aqaba to Basra, and the peninsula south of that line (but excluding the Red Sea provinces of Hijaz, Asir and Yemen) became the responsibility of the DMO Simla, Brig.-Gen. Mullaly and his Intelligence chief, Lt-Col. Malleson. Excluded areas together with Syria, Mesopotamia and Egypt came directly under Col. 'Wully' Robertson (the head of MO2 London), later Field-Marshal Sir William Robertson, Chief of the Imperial General Staff. From this, the misuse of the term 'Middle East', properly referring to India, Persia and the Gulf, arose, embracing the area from Egypt to India and central Asia. In 1907 most of the areas known collectively as the 'Middle East' came under the control of a new department, MO3, directed by Col. Haldane, and the old MO3 became MO5 (counter-intelligence). Col. Count Gleichen took over from Robertson at MO2, with responsibility for Ottoman territories in Europe and peripheral Arab zones.

Chapter 6 The Long, Long Trail

1. Berlin–Baghdad Railway. Concession for line from Konia in Asia Minor to the Persian Gulf, via Baghdad, 'definitely secured by Germans in 1899', Lorimer, *Gazetteer of the Persian Gulf*, p. 346.

2. By 1905 Germany had secured 'practical monopoly for excavation of ancient sites'. Work at Babylon begun by Deutsche Orient Gesellshaft in 1898, Lorimer, *Gazetteer of the Persian Gulf*, p. 347.

3. *Candia*, arrived in Gulf 26 Aug. 1906, Lorimer, ibid. See also Murphy, *Soldiers of the Prophet*, p. 47.

4. Ovseenko took charge of Russian Consulate at Bandar Abbas 14 February 1906, Lorimer, *Gazetteer*. The Russians described their Intelligence officers in consular service as 'officers of special ability', rather than as 'on special duty', the term employed by Britain. Details of differences with Shakespear in author's *Captain Shakespear*, p. 39.

5. The activities of Fitzmaurice the embassy dragoman at Constantinople deserve a biographical study. They are amusingly portrayed, in brief, in Aubrey Herbert's *Ben Kendim* (Hutchinson, 1924). Admiral Fisher also gives details of his secret service work in the Mediterranean in his letters, *Fear God and Dread Nought*, (ed.) Marder (Cape, 1959). But the Admiral always got his name wrong, calling him repeatedly Maurice Fitzgerald. Not surprisingly perhaps, since the Director of Naval Intelligence when Fisher was at the Admiralty was Maurice Fitzmaurice.

6. Both Leachman and Shakespear kept in regular touch with MO2 in the War Office through Maunsell from 1909 when the new chief of that department, Col. Count Gleichen, called Maunsell back to London. Generally they dealt with him through the Royal Geographical Society and its honorary map-room official Douglas Carruthers (correspondence between Maunsell and Leachman, Shakespear and Carruthers in possession of author).

Chapter 7 Special Duty

1. Lt-Col. F. Fraser Hunter, 'Reminiscences of the Map of Arabia and the Persian Gulf', *Geographical Journal*, vol LIV, no. 5 (Nov. 1919). Hunter worked closely with Shakespear and Leachman in compiling his map of Arabia, which he took over from Col. W. Coote Hedley (appointed head of MO4 at War Office) in 1905. Hunter's men were working on the Gulf and Qatar in particular when the dispute broke out.

2. Abdal Aziz ibn Rashid killed in battle of Raudhat Muhanna, April 1906.

3. Morley's tenure of the India Office (1905–10) was marked by violent disagreement with the Government of India over the 'Arabian' question. His favourite retort to both the Viceroy and the C-in-C when they sought to establish contact with central Arabian chiefs or to obtain permission for officers to travel in the Arabia pensinsula, was a statement from Ambassador O'Conor in Constantinople to the Foreign Office, 'No entanglement with the Wahhabees'. (India Office, *Home*

Correspondence, vol. 250). Correspondence between the General Staff and the Secretary of State regarding prospective travellers is contained in the India Office (Persian Gulf) file R/15/5/55.

4. Maj.-Gen. Hetman Jack Parham, d. 1974.

5. Mackie was a director of Frank Strick and Co. connected through a Basra lawyer Mirza Muhammad with the Anglo-Persian Oil Co., and the Hamburg firm Traun, Stürken & Co. for whom Herr Wönckhaus established agencies throughout the Gulf from 1899.

6. The fanaticism of the Shi'a derives, of course, from the conflict between the followers of Ali, the Prophet's cousin, and the Sunnites who accepted the Caliphates of Abu Bakr and his nominated successor Omar in the first century of the Muslim era, 7th century AD.

Chapter 8   Desert Encounters

1. Douglas Carruthers, naturalist, explorer and intelligence officer. Spent most of the year 1909 in the Syrian desert, following two years in Russian Turkistan (1907–8). See lecture by Professor Owen Lattimore in *Geographical Journal,* vol. 144, Part 2 (July 1978). He arrived in Damascus in December 1909, but gave no details of dates of his wanderings in his own account, *Arabian Adventure.*

2. Jauf, taken by Ibn Rashid sixty years before, captured by Ibn Shalan's son Nawwaf 8 Jan. 1909, Musil, *Northern Negd.*

3. March 1911, see Bibliography.

4. *Geographical Journal*, May 1909, see Bibliography.

5. The Rashids under the indomitable Amir Muhammad ibn Rashid occupied Riyadh in 1891 and installed their own governor. The titular Saudi Amir Abdurrahman ibn Faisal and his sons were exiled to Al Hasa, where the Turks were in control, and then to Kuwait where they were protected by Mubarak who ever after referred to the young Abdal Aziz, the heir apparent, as 'My son'. Muhammad ibn Rashid left no issue. He committed, according to Charles Doughty, crimes such as 'the world had not known'.

6. The word 'araif' derives from the name given to camels of uncertain ownership among the tribes, and was used in a jocular sense by Najdis to denote the 'lost ones', the sons and grandsons of Saud ibn Faisal, Ibn Saud's uncle (his father's brother).

7. Ibn Saud's favourite sister, Nura, subsequently married one of the guilty cousins Saud ibn Abdal Aziz (or Saud Kabeer). If Shakespear's version of events in the family is accurate, this must have been the most bloodless of all Arab domestic revolutions.

8. Until recently the Mutair had been in temporary alliance with Ibn Rashid, but they had changed sides under the duress of Mubarak.

9. Muhammad ibn Abdal Wahhab, b. 1703, converted Shaikh Muhammad ibn Saud of Dariyah around the year 1744. Enthused by his puritanical version of the faith, the Sauds had conquered almost the entire Arabian peninsula by the first decade of the nineteenth century, including the holy cities of Mecca and Madina; but the Egyptian army of

Muhammad Ali intervened in 1818–19, and destroyed the first Saudi Empire. 'Even the disorders of the desert were repressed by the sword of the Wahhaby religion.' (Doughty, *Arabia Deserta*).

10. Doughty, *Arabia Deserta*: Abdullah ibn Rashid 'sent home by Ibn Saud' to be 'his constable of the west marches of Nejd'.

11. This story, familiar in the lore of the Bedouin, is told in Palgrave's *Personal Narrative of a Year's Journey Through Central and Eastern Arabia*.

12. The Naqibs of Basra claim descent from the Sunni saint Sayid Ahmad ar-Rifai. Large tracts of land were assigned to the Naqibs by the faithful and many possessions were taken by *force majeur*. The Naqib Rajjab, father of Sayyid Talib, was appointed in 1890. In 1899 the Naqib and Shaikh Mubarak of Kuwait, both heavily involved in gun-running, persuaded the Porte to dismiss the moderate Wali of Basra, Hamdi Pasha. After his removal, father and son, with Mubarak and Shaikh Khazal of Muhammerah, dominated the region by bullying, blackmail and extortion. (*A report on the family of Sayyid Talib* by Sir Henry Dobbs in India Office file L/P&S/10/586).

13. Early in 1911 the Muntafiq rebelled against Talib's regime of terror. Talib destroyed their leader Sadun by decoying him into power of the Wali, and earned the undying enmity of his son Ajaimi. Sadun died 25 Nov. 1911. 'Poison suspected.' (Secret report in L/P&S/10/617).

Chapter 9 Through Kurdistan and Syria

1. Attack took place 4 Dec. 1910 (Murphy, *Soldiers of the Prophet*).

Chapter 10 Mission to Ibn Saud

1. Vol. xxxvii, No. 3, Mar. 1911.

2. For discovery of the Wadi al Khur, west of Darb Zobaida. Chesney (1837) and Wallin (1848) had come close to it but neither identified it as a major feature.

3. Talks proposed by Turks in March 1911. Britain agreed in July. (India Office file R/15/5/59, and Public Record Office, CAB 37/107.)

4. Strictly speaking, *al Ahad* was the military wing of the clandestine movement. The civil wing was known as *al Fattah*.

5. 1911 was also the year of the Agadir crisis between Britain and Germany, of the Italian invasion of Ottoman Tripoli, the massacre of Armenians in the Adana region, and the outbreak of rebellion against the Turks in the Balkans.

6. The stones of 'Ayun' have been the subject of controversy from Palgrave's visit to Kasim in 1862 to the present day. Philby insisted that Palgrave's description of his own journey through Arabia was a fabrication, 'wild and fanciful', and he added: 'Leachman, who alone, I believe, of Europeans since Palgrave's time has visited the spot, failed to notice that monument.' Leachman's would-be biographer had, it seems, not read Leachman's report of his journey in the *Geographical Journal*. Had he done so, he would have known that the stones were not, as

Palgrave asserted, at Ayun, but at Kusaiba some twenty-five miles to the north-west. Philby insisted to the end that the stones were not there. Modern Saudi authorities believe that they were, but that they were lost by human and natural erosion. See 'Palgrave', in *Explorers of Arabia* by Freeth and Winstone, p. 174.

7. Mubarak's dates were slightly awry. Leachman was on his way from Riyadh to Ujair in al Hasa on Christmas Day. He spent several days in the Saudi capital and probably arrived there about 20 Dec.

Chapter 11   War by the Waters of Babylon

1. Calcutta, officially army GHQ, but the staff moved to Simla in the hot months. Permanent offices were established in both places.

2. Kitchener still prized the Viceroyalty of India, but denied that office by Morley he agreed to take over in Cairo after the Coronation of King George V in 1911, which he was called home from India to supervise. He arrived in Cairo on 28 Sept. 1911.

3. Consul F. E. Crow of Basra, quoted in Longrigg, *Iraq*, p. 47.

4. Technically the day that Russia declared war following a Turkish naval attack on Odessa. On the same day the Royal Navy bombarded the Dardanelles forts on the order of Churchill, the First Lord, despite the opposition of the First Sea Lord. Britain and France officially declared a state of war on 4 November.

5. Shakespear was cut down by the slave of the Minister Saud – the same man who murdered Zamil, according to Musil who was at camp near by.

6. Lord Crewe, commenting on events which led to death of Shakespear and alienation of Ibn Saud wrote: 'Not for the first time the FO put its money on the wrong horse.'

7. T. E. Lawrence, *Seven Pillars of Wisdom*.

8. Correspondence between Shakespear and Money, 11 September 1910 to 10 May 1922. (Royal Geographical Society archive.)

9. Early in 1912 the Ottoman Grand Vizier Kiamil advised Talib to sell his services to Britain, and in February of that year he visited Kitchener in Cairo. In the following month he went to the Viceroy at Simla. Both decided that his price was too high. On his return to Basra he allied himself to Abudllah al-Faleh, enemy of Ajaimi and a claimant to the leadership of the Muntafiq. On 19 June 1913 Talib's men murdered the Turkish military commandant of Basra. Enver, the new leader of the Young Turks, ordered his arrest, but the Wali was too afraid of his thugs to carry out the order. In May 1914 the Ottoman Government promised Talib the governorship of Basra and, at the same time, sent a military detachment from Baghdad to arrest him. The fugitive fled to Kuwait with his private army and then to Ibn Saud. Neither Mubarak nor Ibn Saud would treat with him by then. Shakespear described him as 'strong, wilful and utterly unscrupulous'.

10. Gribbon took over from Gibbon at General Staff Office Simla in 1914, when the latter went to France. A confusing nomenclature.

11. Almost all writers and commentators on this question, and on the subsequent campaign, have relied on the Parliamentary White Paper of 1917 (Cmd 8610), which was not so much a White Paper as a whitewash of the politicians involved, and an outrageously biased condemnation of the Generals. There is not the least doubt from the India Office records, the War Office telegrams, and Cabinet records (suspiciously incomplete) that the Indian administration and the GOC Mesopotamia opposed the advance on Baghdad at this time. Cox, the Chief Political Officer, had suggested in a private telegram to the Viceroy (23 Nov. 1914) that an advance could succeed at the beginning of 1915, when in fact the Turks were in retreat in Mesopotamia and were defeated in the Caucasus and at Suez; but by the summer of 1915 nobody outside the Cabinet doubted that it would be suicidal.

12. Irak used correctly by the Turks and Germans to denote the region between the two rivers from Baghdad to Qurna the reputed Garden of Eden at the junction of the rivers; the name derives from Uruk of ancient Babylonia.

13. MacMunn sent by Cairo, with Kitchener's approval, as Inspector-General of Communications, a powerful staff role. He succeeded Gen. Maude as GOC at the end of 1917.

14. In fact, Tennant was shot down in March 1917 and captured by the Turks. He was rescued soon after by a British 'commando' unit.

Chapter 12   Turn of the Tide

1. *The Letters of T.E. Lawrence*, no. 126 to Alec Dixon, 29 Dec. 1925.

2. 'It is better to be his partner than his opponent, for when he is not bluffing, he has a way of holding all the aces: and he can be ruthless, caring little what eggs he breaks to make his omelettes.' D.G. Hogarth, quoted in William Rothenstein's *Twenty-Four Portraits* (Allen & Unwin, 1920.)

3. Wilson to Royal Sussex Regimental Magazine, undated.

Chapter 13   The Shadow of Death

1. I have taken slight liberties with Captain Chalmers's text for the sake of brevity. (Author.)

2. Notes written by Fahad Bey ibn Hadhal before his death in 1928. Cited in Bray, *Paladin of Arabia*.

3. Deputation led by Ajaimi's son Thamir. (Philby, unpublished manuscript.)

Chapter 14   Farewell, Iraq!

1. On 30 July 1920 Wilson wired Cox in London: 'Have expressed opinion since 16 Nov. 1918, that lines on which they (HMG) are working would not lead to anything but disaster and have latterly told them that they must govern or go.'

2. It is an interesting reflection on Britain's much criticized regime that when the new Political Officer, Maj. Dickson, arrived at Hillah from India with his wife in 1921, he expressed surprise at finding so many of the town's notables in prison. He arranged for an amnesty for all of them, except the thirteen condemned to death. He even pleaded with 'Cokkus' to reprieve them. When Faisal came to occupy the throne in July 1921 he reprieved them all, with no protest from the High Commissioner or the British Government. (Dame Violet Dickson, *Forty Years in Kuwait*.)

3. *Observer*, 8 Aug. 1920.

4. General Haldane in his account of the murder in *The Insurrection in Mesopotamia, 1920*, published 1922, told yet another story (p. 170). He asserted that Leachman was shot and injured by one of Dhari's followers and then cut down by the Shaikh. But his story is contrary to the evidence of witnesses and of police investigations.

5. *Daily Mail*, 18 Nov. 1927.

Chapter 15   Postscript

1. Rev W. A. Wigram, Watling House, St Albans to Mrs Leachman, 23 Aug. 1920.

2. Sir John Glubb to Mr C. H. Imray, 30 June 1976.

3. *Letters* of Gertrude Bell, 26 July–8 Aug. 1920, and 25 April 1921.

Bibliography

General

Adelson, R., *Mark Sykes: Portrait of an Amateur* (Cape, 1975).
Aldington, Richard, *Lawrence of Arabia* (Collins, 1955).
Amana, Muhammad, *Arabia Unified* (Hutchinson, Benham, 1980).
Asquith, Lord Oxford and, *Memories and Reflections* (Cassell, 1928).
Balfour, Lord, *Speeches on Zionism* (Arrowsmith, 1928).
Barber, C.H., *Besieged in Kut and After* (Blackwood, 1917).
Bell, Gertrude L., *The Desert and the Sown* (Heinemann, 1907).
——*Amurath to Amurath* (Heineman, 1911).
——'Postroad through the Syrian Desert', *Blackwood's Magazine*, vol. 190 (1911).
——*Letters*, (ed.) Lady Bell (Benn, 1927).
Braddon, Russell, *The Siege* (Cape, 1969).
Bray, N.N.E., *A Paladin of Arabia* (Unicorn Press, 1936).
——*Shifting Sands* (Unicorn Press, 1934).
Burgoyne, Elizabeth, *Gertrude Bell from her Personal Papers*, 2 vols. (Benn, 1958–61).
Busch, Briton Cooper, *Britain, India and the Arabs* (California University Press, 1971).
Candler, Edmund, *The Long Road to Baghdad*, 2 vols. (Cassell, 1919).
Carruthers, A.D.M., *Arabian Adventure to the Great Nafud* (Witherby, 1935).
Cassar, George H., *Kitchener – Architect of Victory* (Kimber, 1977).
Chalmers, I., 'O.C. Desert', *Blackwood's Magazine*, Feb. 1932.
Churchill, Sir Winston, *The World Crisis*, 4 vols. (Thornton Butterworth, 1923–26).
Cunliffe Owen, F., 'The Assyrian Adventure of 1920', *Journal of the Central Asiatic Society*, 1922.

233

Dane, E., *British Campaigns in the Near East,* 2 vols. (London, 1918).

De Gaury, Gerald, *Three Kings in Baghdad* (Hutchinson, 1961).

Dickson, H.R.P., *Kuwait and Her Neighbours* (Allen & Unwin, 1926).

Dickson, Violet, *Forty Years in Kuwait* (Allen & Unwin, 1971).

Doughty, Charles, *Travels in Arabia Deserta* (Cape 1921/1964).

Dunsterville, Maj.-Gen. A.C., *The Adventures of Dunsterforce,* (Edward Arnold, 1920).

Fraser, Lovat, *India under Lord Curzon and After* (London, 1921).

Freeth, Zahra, *Kuwait was My Home* (Allen & Unwin, 1956).

——*A New Look at Kuwait* (Allen & Unwin, 1972).

——and Winstone, H.V.F., *Kuwait: Prospect & Reality* (Allen & Unwin, 1972).

Glubb, Sir John, *A Soldier with the Arabs* (Hodder & Stoughton, 1957).

——*Britain and the Arabs* (Hodder & Stoughton, 1959).

Graves, Philip, *The Life of Sir Percy Cox* (Hutchinson, 1941).

——*The Land of Three Faiths* (Cape, 1923).

Graves, R.W., *Storm Centres of the Middle East, 1879–1929* (London, 1933).

Haldane, Lt-Gen. Sir Aylmer, *The Insurrection in Mesopotamia, 1920* (Blackwood, 1922).

——*A Soldier's Saga* (Blackwood, 1948).

Herbert, Aubrey, *Mons, Anzac and Kut* (Hutchinson, 1919).

Hogarth, David, *The Penetration of Arabia* (Clarendon Press, 1922).

Howarth, David, *Desert King* (Collins, 1964).

Hunter, F. Fraser, 'Mapping Arabia', *Geographical Journal,* vol. 54 (1919).

Ireland, P.W., *Iraq: A Study in Political Development* (Cape, 1937).

Kearsey, A., *Notes on the Mesopotamian Campaign* (London, 1927).

Keeling, E.H., *Adventures in Turkey and Russia* (Murray, 1924).

Kedourie, Elie, *England and The Middle East* (Bowes and Bowes, 1956).

——*In the Anglo-Arab Labyrinth* (Cambridge University Press, 1976).

Kelly, J.B., *Britain and The Persian Gulf, 1788–1880* (Oxford University Press, 1968).

Khadduri, Majid, *Independent Iraq, 1832–1958* (Oxford University Press, 1960).

Kiesling, Hans von, *Mit Feldmarschall Von der Goltz Pasha in Mesopotamia und Persia* (Berlin, 1926).

Kingsmill, A.G., *The Silver Badge* (Stockwell, 1966).

Knightley, Philip, and Simpson, Colin, *The Secret Lives of Lawrence of Arabia* (Nelson, 1969).

Lawrence, T.E., *The Seven Pillars of Wisdom* (Penguin/Cape, 1962).

——*T.E. Lawrence by his Friends* (ed.) A.W. Lawrence (London, 1937).

——*The Letters of TEL* (ed.) Garnett (Cape, 1938).

——*The Home Letters of TEL to his Brothers* (Blackwell, 1954).

——*Secret Despatches from Arabia* (ed.) A.W. Lawrence (Golden

Cockerel Press, 1939).

Lee, D. Fitzgerald, *'D' Force Mesopotamia in the Great War* (London, 1927).

Leslie, Sir Shane, *Mark Sykes: His Life and Letters* (London, 1929).

Liddell Hart, B. H. and Graves, R. T., *T. E. Lawrence to his Biographer* (Faber, 1939).

Loder, J. de V., *The Truth about Mesopotamia, Palestine and Syria* (London, 1923).

Long, P. W., *Other Ranks of Kut* (Williams & Norgate, 1938).

Longrigg, S. H., *Four Centuries of Modern Iraq* (Clarendon Press, 1925).

——*Iraq 1900–1950* (Royal Institute of International Affairs, Oxford University Press, 1953).

Lorimer, J. G., *Gazetteer of the Persian Gulf* (Government Press, Bombay, 1913).

Mack, John E., *A Prince of our Disorder* (Weidenfeld & Nicolson, 1976).

MacMunn, Lt-Gen. Sir G. F., 'Gertrude Bell and T. E. Lawrence: the other side of their stories', *The World Today*, Nov./Dec. 1927.

Marlowe, John, 'Anglo-Persian Rivalry in the Persian Gulf', *Journal of the Central Asia Society*, vol. LI, no. 1 (1963).

——*Late Victorian: The Life of Sir Arnold Wilson* (Cresset Press, 1967).

Marshall, Gen. Sir William, *Memories of Four Fronts* (Benn, 1929).

Meinertzhagen, R. M., *Middle East Diary, 1917–56* (Cresset Press, 1959).

Monroe, Elizabeth, *Britain's Moment in the Middle East, 1914–1956* (Chatto & Windus, 1963).

——*Philby of Arabia* (Faber, 1973).

Mouseley, E. O., *Secrets of a Kuttite* (John Lane, 1922).

Murphy, C. C. R., *Soldiers of the Prophet* (John Hogg, 1921).

Musil, Alois, *Arabia Petraea* (New York, 1927).

——*Northern Negd* (New York, 1927).

Neave, Dorina, *Remembering Kut* (Arthur Barker, 1937).

Nutting, Anthony, *The Arabs* (Hollis, 1964).

Oppenheim, Max von, *Von Mittelmeer zum Persischen Golf, durch den Hauran, die Syrische Wueste und Mesopotamien* (Berlin, 1900).

Ormsby-Gore, W., 'Great Britain, Mesopotamia and the Arabs', *Nineteenth Century and After*, Aug. 1920.

Palgrave, W. G., *Personal Narrative of a Year's Journey Through Central and Eastern Arabia* (Gregg, 1969).

Parfit, Canon, J. T., *Twenty Years in Baghdad and Syria* (London, 1916).

Philby, H. St J. Unpublished manuscript (1928), *The Legend of Lijman* (MEC, St Anthony's College, Oxford).

——*The Heart of Arabia* (Constable, 1922).

——*Arabia of the Wahhabis* (Constable, 1928).

——*Arabia* (Benn, 1930).

——*Arabian Days* (Hale, 1948).

——*Arabian Jubilee* (Hale 1952).

Raswan, Carl R., *The Black Tents of Arabia* (Hutchinson, 1939).

Raunkiaer, Barclay, *Through Wahhabiland on Camel-Back*, (ed.) de Gaury (Routledge & Kegan Paul, 1969).

Ronaldshay, Earl of, *The Life of Lord Curzon*, 3 vols. (London, 1928).

Sachar, Howard M., *The Emergence of the Middle East* (Penguin, 1969).

Sandes, E. W. C., *In Kut and Captivity* (Murray, 1919).

Sharp, Martin D.H., *An Outline of de Havilland History* (London, 1961).

Sherson, E., *Townshend of Chitral and Kut* (London, 1928).

Soane, E. B., *To Mesopotamia and Kurdistan in Disguise* (London, 1912).

Storrs, Sir Ronald, *Orientations* (Nicolson & Watson, 1937).

Sykes, Christopher, *Wassmuss* (Longmans, 1936).

Sykes, Sir Percy, *A History of Persia* (Macmillan, 1930).

Tennant, J. E., *In the Clouds Above Baghdad* (Palmer, 1920).

Townshend, Maj.-Gen. Sir Charles, *My Campaign in Mesopotamia* (Butterworth, 1920).

Trumpener, Ulrich, *Germany and the Ottoman Empire* (Princeton University Press, 1968).

Van Ess, Dorothy, *Pioneers in the Arab World; 3 (Gertrude Bell)* (Dutch Reformed Church of America, Michigan, USA, 1974).

Van Ess, John, *Meet the Arab* (Museum Press, 1947).

Vogel, Renate, *Die Persien und Afghanistanexpedition Oskar Ritter von Niedermayers* (Osnabrüch, 1976).

Wavell, Field-Marshal Viscount, *Allenby: Soldier and Statesman* (Harrap, 1946).

Wigram, W. A., *The Assyrian Settlement* (London, 1922).

——and E. T. A. Wigram, *The Cradle of Mankind* (London, 1914).

Wilson, Sir Arnold, *Loyalties, Mesopotamia 1914–21*, 2 vols. (Oxford University Press, 1930–1)

Wingate, Sir Ronald, *Not in the Limelight* (Hutchinson, 1959).

Winstone, H. V. F., *Captain Shakespear* (Cape, 1976/Quartet, 1978).

——*Gertrude Bell* (Cape, 1978/Quartet, 1980).

Woolley, Sir C. L. (ed.), *From Kastumani to Keddos* (Blackwell, 1921).

Wright, Denis, *The English Among the Persians* (Heinemann, 1977).

Younghusband, Lt-Gen. Sir G. J., *Forty Years a Soldier* (London, 1923).

Zeine, Z., *The Struggle for Arab Independence* (Beirut, 1960).

Zwemer, Rev. S. M., *Arabia: the Cradle of Islam* (New York, 1900).

Official Publications

Official History of the War 1914–18.
Committee of Imperial Defence, Historical Division, 1920–33.
Military Operations Gallipoli, C. F. Aspinall-Oglander.
The Campaign in Mesopotamia, F. T. Moberly.
Australian Contingent BEF, 1914–18, C. E. W. Bean.
Military Operations in Egypt and Palestine, to June 1917, G. MacMunn

and Cyril Falls.
Military Operations in Egypt and Palestine June 1917 to end of war, Cyril Falls.
Naval Operations, vol. 3, *Mesopotamia*, Sir Julian Corbett.
Naval Operations, Sir Henry Newbolt.
Mesopotamian Commission Report, 1917 (Cmd 8610).

Cabinet Records

CAB 37/86, Army reorganization, Jan. 1907.
CAB 42/6, Meeting of War Committee, 1 Dec. 1915; Mesopotamia; Gallipoli; the Arab Question.
CAB 27/22, Meeting of Mesopotamian Committee, Baghdad Declaration, 16 March 1917).

Foreign Office Records

FO371/3062, Report on Ibn Saud; affairs of Kuwait, 1918.

House of Lords Records

Lloyd George Papers, F/40/3/11. Secret Service officers.

India Office Records

Records consulted in the India Office files (India Office Library and Records, Foreign and Commonwealth Office) are in the Political and Secret series (L/P&S) and Persian Gulf (R).

L/P&S/10/69, *Lewis Pelly*, Kuwait Agency yacht; later HM Steam yacht.
L/P&S/10/135, Travellers in Arabia, including Leachman.
L/P&S/10/158–9, Arms traffic in Gulf, 1909–10.
L/P&S/10/162, Turkish aggression in Gulf, 1909–11.
L/P&S/10/259, Arabian travellers, 1909–20: Leachman; Shakespear; Raunkiaer. South Persian trade; German documents; Wönckhaus activities.
L/P&S/10/325–7, Persian telegraphs.
L/P&S/10/334–5, Perso-German affairs; Kerman; Sir Percy Sykes.
L/P&S/10/366, Gulf: German competitors.
L/P&S/10/369–70, North-West Frontier.
L/P&S/10/384–9, Shakespear; Ibn Saud; Al Hasa.
L/P&S/10/397, Rebellion in Muscat.
L/P&S/10/415, Baghdad Rail: negotiations with Germany.
L/P&S/10/425–7, Muscat and Oman rebellion.
L/P&S/10/437, Bushire Residency diaries, 1913–31.
L/P&S/10/513–19, Mesopotamia; Personnel; Moslem feeling.
L/P&S/10/523–7, Negotiations with Sharif of Mecca, 1915–17; the Caliphate.
L/P&S/10/532–5, War; Turkish prisoners; Sayyid Talib.
L/P&S/10/576, Arab Bureau.
L/P&S/10/586, Arabian Reports, (ed.) Hogarth.

L/P&S/10/597–9, Arab Revolt.
L/P&S/10/657–8, Arab Bulletin.
L/P&S/10/827, Kuwait 1912–20.
L/P&S/10/617, Reports by Political Officers, April 1919, including Leachman and Capt. C.F. Macpherson, on tribes of Tigris and Euphrates.
L/P&S/11/73–9, Pan-Arabs; German agents.
L/P&S/11/85, Persia; Sir Percy Sykes and Sir Arthur Hirtzel (Under-Secretary of State, India Office, and head of Political and Secret Department); Leachman's employment.
L/P&S/11/112, Railway survey, Euphrates–Damascus, 1920.
L/P&S/11/175, Death of Leachman; tribal risings.
L/P&S/18/A27, The Muntafiq.
L/P&S/18/A37, Ibn Saud.
L/P&S/18/B160, Baghdad Rail.
L/P&S/18/B164, Wahhabis.
L/P&S/18/166–166A, Persian Gulf.
L/P&S/18/B172, Baghdad Rail, 1909.
L/P&S/18/181, Relations with Turkey in Persian Gulf.
L/P&S/18/196, Arms traffic.
L/P&S/18/200, Non-interference in Najd; memo by Mr Parkes, Foreign Office.
L/P&S/18/B220, British advance on Baghdad.
L/P&S/18/B222, Arab Movement; Sharif's revolt.
L/P&S/18/B286, Ibn Saud and Philby.
L/P&S/18/B308–9, Sharif and Najd: report by Gertrude Bell.
L/P&S/18/B337, Gertrude Bell: Syria in 1919.
L/P&S/18/B437, Relations between Wahhabi Amirs and Eastern Arabia, and HMG.
L/P&S/18/B446, Jauf.
L/P&S/18/C138, General Staff: Handbook of Mesopotamia.
L/P&S/18/C152–3, Tribes of Mesopotamia, prepared for Arab Bureau.
L/P&S/18/C176, Oil in Kuwait.
L/P&S/18/C190, Mesopotamian Handbook, FO 1919.
L/P&S/20/128, Admiralty War Staff; Arab personalities.
L/P&S/20/132, Turkish personalities.
L/P&S/20/E84, Admiralty War Staff, *Handbook of Arabia*. Pictures of Central Arabia by Leachman and others.
R/15/5/8, Persian Gulf; Secret newsletters.
R/15/5/14–15, Maps.
R/15/5/16, Kuwait's ruling family, Al Sabah.
R/15/5/27, Kuwait–Najd affairs.
R/15/5/28–31, Ibn Saud.
R/15/5/55, Naval and Military Intelligence.
R/15/5/59, Kuwait, 1904.
R/15/5/63, Baghdad Rail.
R/15/5/64, Germany: Wönckhaus Company.

R/15/5/88, Shakespear.

War Office Documents

WO 33/820, Secret telegrams: Arab Revolt 1916.

WO 33/905, Intercepted enemy messages; Arab Revolt; campaign in Mesopotamia, 1917.

WO 33/969, Summary prepared by Sir Henry Wilson, CIGS from (1920) Military Intelligence Records: Sharif's Revolt, the tribal rebellion in Mesopotamia.

WO 106/729, Cabinet instructions to General Staff, Jan. 1918.

Institutional and Demi-Official Publications

Geographical Journal, (Royal Geographical Society).

'Description of journey in Euphrates desert, *Badiat Shamiyah*, in spring of 1910', vol. XXXVII, no. 3 (March 1911), pp. 265–74.

Award of Gill Memorial Medal to Leachman for journey of 1910. 'Survey of a difficult region not visited by a European for some twenty years', with map, vol. XXXVII, no. 3 (March 1911).

'Brief description of journey across Arabia from 31 Novemebr 1912', vol. XLI (1913), p. 147.

Leachman makes presentation of 32 photographs to Society of trans-Arabian journey, including first photos ever taken of Riyadh, vol. XLIII (Apr. 1914), p. 480.

'A Journey Through Central Arabia', by Capt. G. Leachman, the Royal Sussex Regiment, undertaken in the latter months of 1912, vol. XLIII (May 1914), p. 500–20; map of route, p. 604.

'Baghdad to Damascus via El Jauf', by Capt. S. S. Butler, vol. XXXIII (May 1909).

Leachman's maps in Society's Map Room:

Saudi Arabia (1919), S3.

NE Arabia (1910), Asia S/S 62.

Journey through Central Arabia, *Geographical Journal*, (May 1914), Asia S/S G3.

Journey 1912, detailed map of northern districts, received from War Office, 8 June 1923, Asia S161.

Army Lists, 1900–21.

Indian Army Lists, 1900–21.

Thacker's Indian Directory, 1903–14.

Bengal Directory, 1903–14.

History of the Royal Sussex Regiment, by G. D. Martineau.

The Rousillon Gazette (Journal of the Royal Sussex Regiment).

Private correspondence

Leachman's movements and map work, subject of letters between General Staffs London and India, and Mr Douglas Carruthers (Royal

239

Geographical Society, London).

Col. F. R. Maunsell, MI2, to Col. Hedley, MI4 (27 September 1916).

Col. Maunsell to Mr D. Carruthers (8 January 1917).

Col. C. C. R. Murphy, General Staff, Delhi, to Carruthers (8 February 1917).

Letters, which also refer to Shakespear and other travellers in Arabia, in possession of author.

Sir John Glubb: Reference to Leachman and Lawrence, letter to Mr C. H. Imray, 30 June 1976.

Newspaper reference

Leachman's murder, *The Times, Daily Mail, Morning Post*, 20 Aug. 1920.

Burial of Leachman, *Baghdad Times*, 4 March 1921.

Apprehension and trial of Shaikh Dhari ibn Mahmud, *Daily Express, The Times*, 15 Nov. 1927.

Capt. Leslie Williams's account of murder, *Daily Mail*, 16 Nov. 1927.

Trial and sentence of Shaikh Dhari, *The Times*, 31 Jan. 1928.

Rebellion in Iraq, *The Times*, June 1919–Dec. 1920.

Index

242

Fort William, Indian Army GHQ, Calcutta, 35, 118.
Franz Josef, Emperor of Austro-Hungary, 122.
Freemasonry, 37, 43.
Fry, General, 149.

Ganges river, 48.
Gaselee, Maj-Gen. Sir A., 42.
Gazetteer of the Persian Gulf, 103.
Geographical Journal, quoted, 83ff, 120.
George V, King Emperor, 101.
Germany, see also Nachrichtdienst, 5, 13, 47, 59, 60, 102, 145.
Ghadhaban al-Bunaiya, 147.
Gibbon, Capt., C.M., 71, 93.
Gilbert, Major, 27.
Giliyak, Russian warship, 59.
Gill, Capt. William J., 7ff.
Gill Memorial Medal, 120.
Gladstone, W.E., 5, 6, 35, 59.
Gleichen, Colonel the Count, 74.
Gloucester Regiment, 36.
Glubb, Sir John, 224.
Goltz, Field Marshal von der, 110, 146, 150ff, 195.
Goring, Lt. Charles, 2, 220.
Gorringe, General Sir George, 151, 163.
Grace, Dr W.G., 9.
Graham, Sir Ronald, 195.
Granville, 2nd Earl, 6.
Graves, Philip, 102, 141.
Gregson, Col. E.C., 148.
Grey, Lt-Col. W.G., 58, 61, 144.
Grey, Sir Edward, 69, 101ff, 112, 126, 141ff.
Gribbon, Captain, 148, 150.
Gulf Ports, 61.
Gun running in Gulf, 101.

Habibullah, Amir of Afghanistan, 72.
Haig Brown, Dr William, 10.
Hajara desert, 97.
Hakki Pasha, 141ff.
Haldane, Col. J.A., 71.
Haldane, Lt-Gen., Sir Aylmer, 2, 207, 218ff.
Hales, Rev. J.T., 3.
Halim Bey, 153.
Hall, Vice-Admiral Sir Reginald, 152.
Hamilton, Gen. Sir Ian, 19.
Hammam Ali, 200.
Hamo Sharro, Yezidi chief, 202.
Hardinge, Baron of Penshurst, 102, 112, 118, 142, 145, 158.
Hardinge, RIMS, 2.
Harling, Herr, 147, 166ff.
Hassan, Indian servant, 160, and *passim*.
Hauran desert, 66, 110ff, Bishop of,

111.
Hawker, General, 187.
Hedley, Colonel W. Coote, 121, 125.
Herbert, Capt. Hon. Aubrey, 74, 102, 164ff, 175.
Hijaz, campaign, 178ff.
Hijaz railway, 66, 113.
Hirtzel, Sir Arthur, 146, 207.
Hochwächter, Maj. von, 110ff.
Hogarth, Dr. D.G., 148, 164, 181.
Holdich, Col. G.W.V., 177
Home Rule policy, 6, 35, 59.
Horne, Maj. George, x.
Huber, Charles, 121.
Hunter, Gen. Sir Archibald, 20.
Hunter, Lt-Col. F. Fraser, 103.
Husain ibn Ali, Sharif of Mecca, 78, 123, 143, 164, 176, 184, 193.

Ikhwan, 98.
Imogen, Embassy yacht, 68, 165.
Imperial Military Geographical Institute, Vienna, 121.
Imray, Colin, x.
India, 32, and *passim*.
Indian Mutiny, 73.
India Office, x, and *passim*.
Indus river, 55.
Ireland and Home Rule, 5.
Ironside, Maj-Gen. Sir Edmund, 2.
Istiqlal, 2.

Jabir ibn Mubarak al-Sabah, 98.
Jafar Pasha al-Askari, 2.
Jamal Pasha, Ahmad, 142.
Jask, Gulf Intelligence HQ, 61, 101.
Jeffcoat, Lt-Col. A.C., 4.
Jelal Bey, 77.
Jihad, holy war, 1.
Joubert, General Piet J., 14.
Julna, HMS, 166.

Kabul, massacre at, 6.
Kasr Marid, al Jauf, 90.
Kemball, Lt-Col. C.A., 161.
Khadam ibn Faid, 97.
Khalifa, river boat, 63.
Khalil Pasha, General, 146, 158, 163ff, 179.
Khamis ibn Dhari, 218ff.
Khan Nuqta, 217ff.
Khazal, Shaikh of Muhammerah, 62, 75, 146.
Khidr ibn Abbas, guide, 79, 159.
Kiamil Pasha, Grand Vizier, 141.
Kildonian Castle, SS, 21.
Kipling, Rudyard, quoted, 15, 31, 48, 117, 168.
Kitchener, Field Marshal Earl, 12ff, 34ff, 43, 58, 143, 154, 164, 176.
Knott, Capt. G.P., 111.
Kola, RIMS, 62, 118.

Intelligence, 65, and *passim*.
Nafud desert, 81.
Naini Tal, 36ff, 52, 76.
Nain Singh, Pandit, 47.
Nalder, Lt-Colonel, 202.
Napier, General Sir Charles, 9.
Naqib of Basra, Sayyid Rajab, 100.
Nazim Pasha, 104.
Nelson, Lieutenant, 14.
Newcombe, Lt-Col. S.F., 74, 110, 181.
Niedermeyer, Oskar Ritter von, 145, 156.
Nixon, Gen. Sir John, 150ff.
Noel, Maj. Edward, 217.
Northbrook, Earl, 7.
Northcote, Lord, 37.
North-West Frontier, 41, 101, 119, 137.
Nureddin Pasha, 152.

Obaidallah (Obaid) ibn Ali al-Rashid, 97.
O'Conor, Sir Nicholas, 68, 118.
Oil, Kuwait, 142.
Oil, Persia, 145.
Oman, 58, 101.
Omdurman, 13, 15.
Oppenheim, Baron Max von, 66, 74.
Ottoman Empire; see Turkey, 8, 60, 74.
Ovseenko, M. (Russian Consul), 68.

Packe, Maj. F.E., 74, 110.
Palace Hotel, Aleppo, 110.
Palestine Exploration Fund, 74.
Palmer, Gen. Sir Arthur Power, 35.
Palmer, Prof E.H., 8.
Parham, Bernard, 25, 32, 177.
Parham, Brigadier John, x.
Parham, Gen. Hetman Jack, 71, 186.
Parham, Miss Belinda, x.
Parham, Mrs H.J., x.
Parham family, viii, x.
Parker, Col. Alfred Chevalier, 179, 181.
Pathans, 139.
Pavonia, SS, 13, 15ff.
Peace Conference, (1919), 2.
Pearson, Captain, 203.
Persia, 46, 145.
Persian Navy, 61.
Petersfield, Hampshire, *passim*.
Philby, H.St.J., vii, viii, ix, 44, and *passim*.
Picot, F. Georges, 141.
Pitcairn, Capt. G.D., 4, 222.
Pre-Raphaelite Movement, 9.
Prescott, Colonel, 2.
Preusser, Dr Conrad, 76, 102, 151, 172, 198.
Prideaux, Capt. F.B., 61.
Primrose League, 5.

Prince Abbas, ship, 66.
Pusht-i-Kuh mountains, 63.

Quay d'Orsay, 141.

Radwell, Captain, 188.
Ramsay, Col. J., 76.
Rashids of Hail, 67, 78, 118, 169.
Raunkiaer, Barclay, 102, 118, 122ff, 126.
Rawlinson, Sir H. Creswicke, 76.
Rees, Brian, x.
Rimington, Maj–Gen. L.M.F., 17.
Riyadh, 102, 125ff, 133ff, 184.
Roberts, Field Marshal Earl, 6, 15ff, 34.
Robinson, Captain, 14.
Rochefort, Colonel, 29.
Roosevelt, Capt. Kermit, 199ff.
Ross, Major, 181.
Rothwell, Frederica, 36ff, 45ff, 51, 55.
Rothwell, Harry, 45.
Royal Field Artillery, 216.
Royal Flying Corps, 154.
Royal Geographical Society, 7ff, 112, 121.
Royal George, HMS, 164.
Royal Sussex Regiment, vii, ix, 13, and *passim*.
Russo-Persian rail scheme, 61.
Ruwalla tribe, 83ff, 128.

Saad ibn Abdurrahman al-Saud, 123.
Sabaeans, 63.
Sadlier, Capt. George, 132.
Sadun Pasha, chief of Muntafiq, 80ff, 97ff.
Salaiba (Salubba), 82, 128.
Salisbury, Marquess of, 34.
Salmon, Captain, 221.
Sami Pasha, General, 111, 116.
Samuel, Sir Herbert, 210.
Sanders, General Liman von, 152, 185.
Sandhurst, Lord, 37.
Sandhurst, Royal Military College, 10, and *passim*.
Sasun Effendi Haskail, 2.
Saud, Ibn, King of Saudi Arabia, 67, 70, 75, 80ff, 94ff, 118, 123, 133ff, 137, 142ff, 184.
Saud ibn Abdal Aziz al-Rashid, 78, 89ff, 169.
Saud ibn Hamud al-Rashid, 90ff.
Saud ibn Subhan of Hail, 141ff.
Savoy Hotel, GHQ Cairo, 164.
Seaforth Highlanders, 14.
Shakespear, Capt. W.H.I., ix, 60ff, 80ff, 93ff, 102, 118, 26, 137ff, 196.
Shalan, Nawwaf ibn Nuri, 94, 128, 130.
Shalan, Nuri ibn (Amir of Anaiza tribes), 82ff, 130.

245